Grammatical Relations

OXFORD SURVEYS IN SYNTAX AND MORPHOLOGY

GENERAL EDITOR: Robert D Van Valin, Jr, *State University of New York*, Buffalo

ADVISORY EDITORS: Guglielmo Cinque, *University of Venice*; Daniel Everett, *University of Manchester*; Adele Goldberg, *Princeton University*; Kees Hengeveld, *University of Amsterdam*; Caroline Heycock, *University of Edinburgh*; David Pesetsky, *MIT*; Ian Roberts, *University of Cambridge*; Masayoshi Shibatani, *Rice University*; Andrew Spencer, *University of Essex*; Tom Wasow, *Stanford University*

PUBLISHED

Grammatical Relations
by Patrick Farrell

IN PREPARATION

The Acquisition of Syntax and Morphology
by Shanley Allen and Heike Behrens

The Processing of Syntax and Morphology
by Ina Bornkessel and Matthias Schlesewesky

Phrase Structure
by Andrew Carnie

Information Structure: the Syntax–Discourse Interface
by Nomi Erteschik-Shir

Morphology and the Lexicon
by Daniel Everett

Syntactic Change
by Olga Fischer

The Phonology–Morphology Interface
by Sharon Inkelas

The Syntax–Semantics Interface
by Jean-Pierre Koenig

Complex Sentences
by Toshio Ohori

Extraction Phenomena
by David Pesetsky and Norvin Richards

Syntactic Categories
by Gisa Rauh

Computational Approaches to Syntax and Morphology
by Brian Roark and Richard Sproat

Language Universals and Universal Grammar
by Anna Siewierska

Argument Structure: The Syntax–Lexicon Interface
by Stephen Weschler

Grammatical Relations

PATRICK FARRELL

OXFORD
UNIVERSITY PRESS

OXFORD
UNIVERSITY PRESS

Great Clarendon Street, Oxford OX2 6DP

Oxford University Press is a department of the University of Oxford.
It furthers the University's objective of excellence in research, scholarship,
and education by publishing worldwide in

Oxford New York

Auckland Cape Town Dar es Salaam Hong Kong Karachi
Kuala Lumpur Madrid Melbourne Mexico City Nairobi
New Delhi Shanghai Taipei Toronto

With offices in

Argentina Austria Brazil Chile Czech Republic France Greece
Guatemala Hungary Italy Japan Poland Portugal Singapore
South Korea Switzerland Thailand Turkey Ukraine Vietnam

Oxford is a registered trade mark of Oxford University Press
in the UK and in certain other countries

Published in the United States
by Oxford University Press Inc., New York

British Library Cataloguing in Publication Data
Data available

Library of Congress Cataloguing in Publication Data
Data available

Typeset by SPI Publisher Services, Pondicherry, India
Printed in Great Britain
on acid-free paper by
Biddles Ltd., King's Lynn, Norfolk

ISBN 0-19-926401-5   978-0-19-926401-8
ISBN 0-19-926402-3 (Pbk.)   978-0-19-926402-5 (Pbk.)

1 3 5 7 9 10 8 6 4 2

Contents

Abbreviations

1	1st person
2	2nd person
3	3rd person
A	Subject of transitive
Abl	Ablative
Abs	Absolutive
Acc	Accusative
Antipass	Antipassive
Appl	Applicative
APG	Arc Pair Grammar
Arb	Arbitrary (or unspecified) reference
Asp	Aspect
Aux	Auxiliary
Ben	Benefactive
C	Complementizer
CG	Cognitive Grammar
Cont	Continuative
CP	Complementizer phrase (= clause)
Dat	Dative
Decl	Declarative
Det	Determiner
DCA	Direct core argument
Dist	Distal realis mood
DS	Different subject
EPP	Extended projection principle (= clausal subject requirement)
Erg	Ergative
Excl	Exclusive
Fem	Feminine
FG	Functional Grammar
Fut	Future

Gen	Genitive
GB	Government-Binding Theory
I	Inflection
Imperf	Imperfective
Iness	Inessive
Ind	Indicative
Inf	Infinitive
Instr	Instrumental
Intr	Intransitive
Inv	Inverse voice
IP	Inflection phrase (= clause)
Irr	Irrealis mood
Lcontr	Limited control
LF	Logical form
LFG	Lexical-Functional Grammar
Neut	Neuter
Nom	Nominative
Nominal	Nominalization
Nonfut	Nonfuture
NP	Noun phrase
Masc	Masculine
M-transitive	Macrorole transitive
MR	Macrorole
Neg	Negative
NSg	Non-Singular
O	Object
Obj	Objective
Obl	Oblique
O1	Primary object
O2	Secondary object
P	Preposition
Part	Partitive
Pass	Passive
Perf	Perfective
Pl	Plural
Pos	Possessive
PP	Prepositional phrase

Pred	Predicative
Pres	Pesent tense
pro	null pronoun
PSA	Privileged syntactic argument
Purp	Purposive
Pst	Past tense
Real	Realis mood
Rec	Reciprocal
Recip	Recipient
Refl	Reflexive
Rel	Relational affix
Relat	Relative clause
RG	Relational Grammar
RRG	Role and Reference Grammar
S	Subject of intransitive
S_a	A-marked S
S_o	O-marked S
Sg	Singular
Subj	Subject
Sjunct	Subjunctive
Stim	Stimulus
TG	(Generative)-Transformational Grammar
Tns	Tense
Tr	Transitive
V	Verb
VP	Verb phrase

1

Introduction

Language is used to say things about things that happen in the world. We conceive of what happens in the world as involving people and other entities doing things, often to each other. In order to say something about things that happen, it is critical to identify the participants and the precise process in which they are involved. Noun phrases (NPs) such as *the boy, a dog,* and *the branches* are used to identify event participants, by virtue of the fact that they are built on nouns, which (typically) name kinds of things. Verbs, such as *touch, hit, sneeze,* and *shout,* are used to identify types of processes. Knowing the syntactic and semantic conventions for constructing NPs, how the world is generally considered to operate, and the meanings of the words *the, boy, touched,* and *branches* is not enough to tell me everything I need to know about the meaning of a sentence such as (1.1) in a hypothetical language like English—but with no conventions governing the relative order of verbs and noun phrases.

(1.1) Touched the branches the boy.
       Hypothetical free word-order English

I would know that contact was made between the participant named by *the branches* and the participant named by *the boy.* However, I wouldn't know whether the branches, affected perhaps by the wind, made contact with the boy who was stationary or whether, instead, the boy reached out and made contact with the branches. The participants in the touching event play different roles: one is conceived of as the entity that does something and one as the entity to which something is done. Languages use different mechanisms to indicate which entity plays which role. For example, the NPs themselves may be marked by a morpheme that indicates something crucial about the role they play. Thus, the *-t* and *-ick* suffixes in the following version of (1.1) in a hypothetical English might indicate that the boy is the acting participant and the branches are the target of his action.

(1.2) Touched the branches-ick the boy-t.
       Hypothetical free word-order English with dependent marking

I would simply need to know that by convention the NP marked with -*t* is to be interpreted as the toucher and that the NP marked with -*ick* is to be interpreted as the touched entity. Languages that mark role relationships in this way are said to be DEPENDENT-MARKING languages (Nichols 1986), because the morphological indicators of the roles played by the participants in the process designated by the verbal elements in the clause (i.e. the verb and/or any auxiliary verbs) occur on or within the phrases designating the participants themselves, that is the dependents of the verb or verbal complex. English actually uses dependent marking—but only in certain circumstances. For example, if a third person singular masculine pronoun were used in place of the NP *the boy*, the form *he* would be used rather than *him*. By convention the pronoun *he* is necessarily interpreted as identifying the toucher when used as a dependent of the active verb *touched*. For more peripheral roles, such as that of an instrument used in an action, English uses prepositions to mark dependents. In *The boy touched the branches with a stick*, the preposition *with* marks the NP *a stick* as the referent of an instrumental participant in the touching event.

Another kind of role-identifying mechanism that languages use is known as HEAD MARKING (Nichols 1986). In a head-marking language the verb of a clause and/or the auxiliary verb(s) bear morphological indications of the features of one or more of the participants in the designated process. In a hypothetical head-marking English, the suffix -*ish* on the verb *touch*, in a sentence such as (1.3), might indicate that the touched entity is designated by a third person plural NP and the suffix -*ant* might indicate that the toucher is designated by a 3rd person singular NP.

(1.3)   Touch-ish-ed-ant the branches the boy.
        Hypothetical free word-order English with head marking

The fact that *the branches* is plural and *the boy* is not would provide a sufficient clue for me to ascertain that the boy is to be interpreted as the toucher. Actual contemporary English also uses head marking to a limited extent, since present tense verbs with a 3rd person subject, for example, have a special morphological form that registers agreement with one of the participants (*The boy touches the branches* vs. *The branches touch the boy*).

A third common kind of role-identifying mechanism—the one that is most important in actual English—is constituent order. By convention the NP that precedes the active verb form *touch* is interpreted as designating the touching participant and the NP immediately following it is interpreted as designating the touched participant. Thus, in the following example, the fact that *the boy* comes first provides sufficient role information for me to know that the boy did the touching.

(1.4)   The boy touched the branches.
        Actual English

This book is devoted to the domain of grammar having to do with the ways in which languages identify these kinds of roles—broadly known as GRAM-MATICAL RELATIONS—and the function these roles play in the grammars of languages. Among the issues of concern are what kinds of roles are recognized in languages, how they should be categorized, how languages differ in their use and characterization of such roles, and how different theories of grammar approach these matters. The remainder of this chapter lays out the key issues surrounding grammatical relations. Chapter 2 surveys important phenomena in languages in which grammatical relations play a critical role and identifies different kinds of grammatical-relation systems employed in languages. The remaining chapters examine the varying approaches to grammatical relations and related phenomena of several different prominent theories.

1.1 Different kinds of grammatical relations

It is possible to imagine a dependent-marking language in which a particular suffix is devoted to identifying NPs whose referent plays the role of toucher with the verb *touch*, another is devoted to identifying NPs whose referent plays the role of thrower with the verb *throw*, yet another is devoted to identifying NPs whose referent plays the role of killer with the verb *kill*, and so forth. At one extreme of logical possibilities, for every verb there would be an idiosyncratic morphological mechanism for identifying the particular roles involved in the specific kind of process that verb designates. This kind of a system would obviously be very inefficient; and languages do not employ such a system. Instead, their marking systems are organized around relatively general role categories of various kinds. If one takes, for example, the set of English verbs shown in Figure 1.1, it is clear that, for each of the verbs, the roles of the dependents are essentially the same and could be given descriptive labels of some kind, as indicated.

A key question for a theory of grammar is what type of role categories play an integral role in the grammars of languages. For the set of verbs shown in Figure 1.1, at least two generalizations could be made: (a) recipients are indicated by the preposition *to* and (b) sources are in preverbal position. However, if more verbs are taken into account it becomes clear that, although it may be a relevant factor, designating what is commonly thought of as a recipient—that is someone who is conceived of as getting something—is not in fact requisite for an NP to co-occur with the preposition *to*, and designating

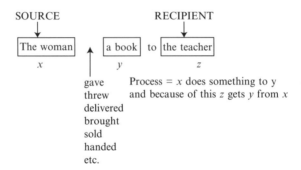

FIGURE 1.1 Potential role categories for one class of English verbs

what is commonly thought of as a source is not requisite for an NP to occupy the preverbal slot in sentence structure. One can see this from the four classes of verbs shown in Figure 1.2.

Sentences with verbs of communication, such as *promise* and *explain*, and sentences with certain verbs of perception, such as *seem* and *look*, show that the preposition *to* can go with dependents whose roles might better be described as addressee and perceiver. Now, although it might well be that *to* is simply a multifunctional word that is used to indicate diverse kinds of roles, because these roles are often indicated in the same way in many languages, it seems plausible that there is a single very general role category of some kind that encompasses these (and other) highly specific roles. However, although there may be enough similarity between the roles of addressee, perceiver, and recipient as to allow some kind of an abstract semantic characterization, perhaps something like 'participant that actively participates in a process in some kind of receptive way', there is no general purpose English word that names such a concept. One tack that has often been taken is to use a label with no independent meaning at all, such as 'indirect object'.

Along similar lines, sentences such as *The woman stole/took the book from the teacher* make it clear that the role of the preverbal NP can be described as that of recipient rather than source.[1] In both cases, however, there is an alternative way of looking at the role of the referent of the preverbal NP, since it can usually be interpreted as the participant that initiates the action that the verb designates. The descriptive label 'agent' is typically used for this more schematic and more encompassing role category. The acting participant in a communicative act can also be characterized as an agent. However, the preverbal NP in a sentence such as *The woman looks strange to me* doesn't seem to refer to an initiator of an action, at least not in anything like the same way. The question *What did the woman do?* can have *She promised me something* or

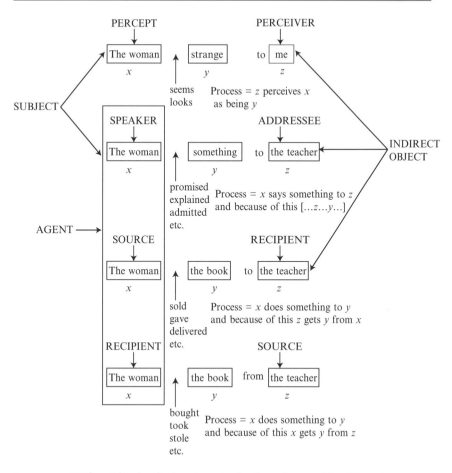

FIGURE 1.2 Different kinds of role categories for four classes of English verbs

She took something from me as an answer, but not *She seemed/looked strange to me*. Although there is clearly some kind of correlation between preverbal position and the role of agent, being an initiator of an action is not criterial. Even if one were to define the agent role in such a way as to have it encompass what might be characterized as a causing percept role,[2] there are other more problematic preverbal NPs, such as in *The books were stolen from the library*. Thus, if it is assumed that there is a single role category for the preverbal NP, there does not seem to be an obvious descriptive label that elucidates its conceptual character. The label that is generally used is 'subject'.

Just considering a few sets of verbs in English, it is clear that there are potentially various ways of categorizing the roles played by the dependents of verbs. One can use quite specific role categories with descriptive labels that emerge from a consideration of the detailed meanings of semantic verb classes (e.g. source, recipient, addressee, agent) as well as categories that conflate or encompass various specific roles and whose labels make little or no claim about their conceptual character (e.g. subject and indirect object). But which of these role categories are useful for describing the grammar of English and other languages? Considering, for example, the phenomenon of verb agreement in English (manifested, for example, in the use of the -*s* suffix on present tense verbs and the varying forms of the verb *be*), roles such as recipient, source, and agent are not directly relevant in any obvious way. The verb agrees with the preverbal NP (or subject), whatever more specific role it happens to play (*The woman steals books from people, The woman seems strange to us, The books were stolen from the library*). Although there do not appear to be any morphosyntactic phenomena in English whose characterization depends on such specific roles as percept or addressee, roles of this general kind can have grammatical ramifications in English and other languages. For example, there is a rule of English with the effect of ensuring that an NP with a source referent that is not realized as a subject is, at least by default, marked with the preposition *from*, as in *The woman stole the book from the library* or *I removed the label from the box* and another rule (Foley and Van Valin 1984: ch. 3) that ensures that if the source is encoded as the direct object (= immediately postverbal NP), the NP with the role of affected thing is necessarily marked with the preposition *of*, as in the case of *They robbed him of his cash* or *We'll have to rid the room of insects*. By contrast, if a goal, that is a location to which something is moved, is encoded as the direct object, the preposition *with* is used for the affected thing, as in *We filled the glass with water* or *They loaded the wagon with hay*.

The use of such role categories as agent and source in linguistic theorizing has its ultimate roots in Pāṇini's grammar of Sanskrit from the 5th century BC (Kiparsky and Staal 1969, Singh 2001, Kiparsky 2002), which includes a procedure for specifying the *kārakas* or roles of the dependents of verbs, on the basis of verb meanings, and various kinds of grammatical rules that depend on these. In the Sanskrit sentence corresponding to *The man came from the forest*, for example, a grammatical analysis would assign the role of *kartṛ* 'agent' to *the man*, because it refers to the participant that is 'independent', and the role of *apādpāna* 'source' to *the forest*, because it refers to the participant that is fixed in an act of separation. It is important to note that although these roles are recognized as having a bearing on choice of the inflectional affixes on nouns (i.e. the intricate system of dependent marking), they are not conceived of as the same thing at all. For example, even though *odana* 'rice' has the accusative ending in the active sentence (1.5a) and the nominative ending in the passive sentence (1.5b), it bears the *kāraka* of *kar-*

man 'patient/goal', because it refers to the participant in the action that is the agent's main target.

(1.5) a. Kṛṣṇa-ḥ   paca-ti   odana-m
        Krishna-Nom cook-3Sg rice-Acc
        'Krishna cooks rice.'
    b. Kṛṣṇ-ena   pac-ya-te   odana-ḥ
        Krishna-Instr cook-Pass-3Sg rice-Nom
        'Rice is cooked by Krishna.'   (Kiparsky 2002)

Although the *-m* suffix is a morphological reflex of the *karman* role, it does not appear in (1.5b) because the agreement suffix on a passive verb form is analysed as the morphological reflex of this role, for which reason the default nominative ending is used instead. In essence, this analysis claims that role identification in Sanskrit crucially involves both head marking and dependent marking. In combination with information from the passive morpheme or lack thereof, the verb's agreement morphology (i.e. head marking) is used to identify either the agent or the patient. The other roles are identified by the inflectional morphology on the dependents. Although *kārakas* necessarily conflate what can easily be conceived of as distinct roles, since only six of them are posited, they are nevertheless fundamentally semantic categories around which the rules of grammar revolve. In contemporary theories of grammar, these kinds of roles are generally either called THEMATIC ROLES/RELATIONS (sometimes abbreviated as 'θ-ROLES'), following Gruber (1965), CASE RELATIONS/ROLES, following Fillmore (1968), or simply SEMANTIC ROLES/FUNCTIONS.

Concepts such as subject, direct object, and indirect object, which are thoroughly ingrained in Western linguistic theories, have their roots in the notion of subject-predicate structure in logic and grammar from Aristotle's *Categories* and traditional grammars of Latin and Greek which, unlike Pāṇini's grammar of Sanskrit, take the dependent-marking morphology in these languages to stand essentially in a one-to-one correspondence with the primary grammatical-relation categories. In Latin, like in Sanskrit, which dependent is marked with so-called nominative morphology depends in part on whether the verb is in its passive form or not, as illustrated by the following sentences.

(1.6) a. Roman-i   null-os   tyrann-os   laudabant
        Roman-NomPl no-AccPl tyrant-AccPl praise.Imperf3Pl
        'The Romans used to praise no tyrants.'
    b. Null-i   tyrann-i   ab Roman-is   laudabantur
        no-NomPl tyrant-NomPl by Roman-AblPl praise.Imperf3PlPass
        'No tyrants used to be praised by the Romans.'

With an active verb, as in (1.6a), the patient is marked with the accusative ending, whereas the dependent with the same role is marked with a nominative ending when the passive form of the verb is used, as in (1.6b). Under the assumption that the dependent-marking morphology fundamentally announces the main grammatical relations, 'the Romans' (agent) and 'no tyrants' (patient) can alternatively play the same role, depending on the form of the verb. Since this role does not have a clear semantic characterization, one must either use a very schematic (or vague) label, such as 'subject', or a label with no other meaning at all, such as 'nominative'. Accommodating languages such as contemporary English in which the dependent-marking morphology traditionally designated by the word *nominative* plays a subordinate role to constituent order in indicating the role in question, the most common term for this role is 'subject'. In Latin, the subject of the sentence is said to be marked with nominative morphology and to determine verb agreement, etc. The direct object is said to be marked with accusative morphology; and the indirect object with dative morphology. These kinds of grammatical roles, which are less clearly amenable to a semantic characterization than roles such as agent and source, are often formally distinguished in theories of grammar and are alternatively called SYNTACTIC RELATIONS/FUNCTIONS or GRAMMATICAL RELATIONS/FUNCTIONS, in contrast with semantic roles.

As is made clear in what follows, there are theories or approaches to grammatical analysis, including that of Pāṇini discussed above, that fail to draw a clear distinction between syntactic functions and semantic roles, and not all theories that do draw a distinction do it in the same way. Moreover, one of the main concerns of theories that clearly distinguish syntactic functions and semantic roles is the nature of the principles governing the relationship between them, since NPs are conceived of as having both and the syntactic function is systematically related to the semantic role. For these reasons, in this book the term *grammatical relation* is used in a maximally general and inclusive way. The terms *semantic role* and *syntactic function* are used to draw a distinction where appropriate, with the understanding that different theories take varying stances about where, if at all, the boundary between the two categories lies and adopt varying terminological conventions. Nevertheless, syntactic functions such as subject and direct object, which are taken to be prototypical of the grammatical-relation category, constitute the main focus of attention.

1.2 Case, voice, and grammatical relations

Two morphological categories that are intricately involved in the identification of grammatical relations in many languages are CASE, that is morphological marking on or within NPs that provides information concerning grammatical relations (see Blake 1994), and VOICE (Klaiman 1990), that is inflectional morphology on a verb or other morphosyntactic marking that functions to indicate which of two or more alternative interpretations of the grammatical relations of its dependents is intended. Both of these categories were illustrated in the Sanskrit and Latin examples discussed above. Consider again the following Sanskrit sentences and Pāṇini's analysis (Kiparsky 2002).

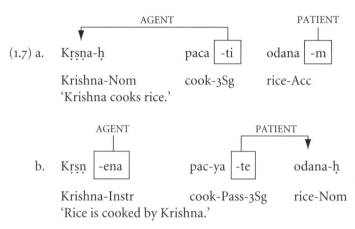

(1.7) a.   Kṛṣṇa-ḥ   paca -ti   odana -m

             Krishna-Nom   cook-3Sg   rice-Acc
             'Krishna cooks rice.'

    b.   Kṛṣṇ -ena   pac-ya -te   odana-ḥ

             Krishna-Instr   cook-Pass-3Sg   rice-Nom
             'Rice is cooked by Krishna.'

If the verb is in its active-voice form (indicated by absence of a passive morpheme), it agrees with the dependent bearing the agent role. The patient is identified by the accusative case marking. If the verb includes the passive-voice suffix, however, it agrees with the dependent bearing the patient role. The instrumental case suffix on the other dependent indicates that it bears the agent role. In both sentences, the dependent that agrees with the verb takes the nominative case suffix, for which reason nominative case itself does not specify a particular semantic role. An alternative analysis using the subject and direct object grammatical relations would go as follows. The nominative case suffix indicates the subject in both cases. The accusative case suffix indicates the direct object. If the verb is in its active-voice form, the dependent that bears the agent role is also the subject and the dependent that bears the patient role is the direct object. The passive-voice suffix on the verb indicates that the patient is the subject, for which reason the agent is neither the subject nor the direct object, but what is generally called an oblique, which happens to be marked with instrumental case. Whichever analysis one adopts, information from the case marking on the dependents and information from the voice marking on the verb function jointly to identify the grammatical relations (semantic and/or syntactic) of the dependents.

Because the morphological phenomenon known as case-marking functions primarily to indicate grammatical relations, the term *case* is sometimes used in one way or another in place of *grammatical relation*. In one trend, initiated in Fillmore (1968) and continued and developed in different ways in, for example, Localist Case Grammar (Anderson 1971, 1977) and Lexicase Grammar (Starosta 1988), *case relation/role* (or, sometimes, *deep case*) is used essentially as a translation of Pāṇini's *kāraka*. That is to say, case relations are considered to be very general semantic roles with grammatical import, which may or may not have an invariant or direct relationship with the morphological case categories used in the dependent-marking system of a language. For Pāṇini, for example, agent and instrumental are both among the recognized *kārakas*. The nominal suffixes of Sanskrit, however, do not correspond exactly, as the agent role is analysed as being indicated either by the agreement morphology on an active verb or the instrumental suffix (when the verb agrees with some other dependent, as in passive clauses). The instrumental suffix is used to either indicate the instrumental role or, sometimes, the agent role.

In Lexicase Grammar there is a universal set of semantically characterized case relations (agent, patient, locus, means, and correspondent) that form part of the underlying basis for the use of case forms (nominative, accusative, dative, etc.). Abstracting away from numerous representational idiosyncrasies of the theory, the Lexicase analysis of the Sanskrit active and passive sentences discussed above would go roughly as follows, where case relations are in uppercase letters and case forms are not.

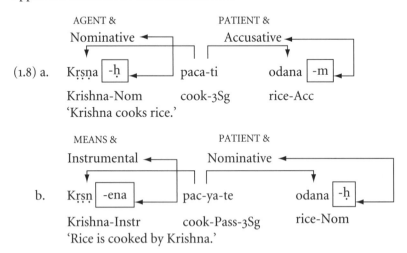

The idea is that the active verb in (1.8a) has a VALENCE (Hockett 1958, Tesnière 1959) or a set of specifications concerning what it can combine with, that includes a requirement for a dependent with the case relation agent (the perceived external instigator of an action or state) and the case form nominative, which the NP *kṛṣṇaḥ* satisfies. The nominative suffix is essentially a morphological realization on the NP of the nominative case form specified in the verb's valence. The NP *odanam* satisfies the verb's valence requirement for a dependent with the patient case relation (the perceived perceptual centre of an action or state) and an accusative case form. The passive verb, shown in (1.8b) has a different valence, which specifies that the patient dependent is linked with the nominative case form and the other dependent is interpreted as a means (the entity perceived as necessarily involved in an action or state affecting the patient) with the instrumental case form. Although case relations are essentially semantic roles,[3] case forms are not exactly the same thing as morphological case markers. The case form nominative, for example, is assumed to be universal and is therefore a feature in the valence of verbs in languages that do not have any kind of case-marking affixes on or within NPs. Thus, case forms are more abstract than case markers. They are, in essence, another form of grammatical relation, which in some languages have a direct morphological manifestation in the form of morphological case markers and in others may be manifested by other morphosyntactic means, such as constituent order.

In another trend, initiated in the Government-Binding Theory incarnation of Transformational Grammar (Chomsky 1981), the term *case* (often capitalized or called 'abstract case' to distinguish it from morphological case) is used in reference to a role-differentiation and dependent-licensing mechanism that works in terms of grammatical relations (see Chapter 5 for further details). The use of *case* to designate both morphological case categories in languages and grammatical relations is potentially confusing, inasmuch as the names of the individual cases do not differ for the two different uses. In essence, dependents bearing the subject role are said to be licensed by a nominative case relation that holds between them and an inflectional/functional element or position in a clause. Similarly, direct objects are licensed by an accusative case relation that holds between them and a verb (or, in some versions of the theory, an inflectional/functional element or position in a clause). In this theory, what are called nominative and accusative case features constitute one instantiation of the traditional subject and direct object grammatical relations. Although these relations occur across languages, the morphological reflexes of the abstract case features vary considerably. A language may or may not indicate them with either or both head marking (overt agreement) or dependent marking (overt case marking). Although *case*, in this grammatical-relation sense, is used for syntactic functions, in the form of nominative and accusative cases, also known as 'structural cases', it is also used for semantic roles, insofar as 'inherent' or 'semantic' cases such as instrumental, locative, partitive, and ablative are assumed to be licensed directly by semantic roles.

In view of the influence of analyses of case-marking distinctions in particular languages on the development of theories of grammatical relations as well as the various ways in which the term *case* has been used within different theories, it is important to point out that there are good reasons for clearly distinguishing grammatical relations and morphological case-marking categories, as suggested by such terminological contrasts as *Case* vs. *case* (Transformational Grammar), *case relation* and *case form* vs. *case marking* (Lexicase Grammar), and *deep case* vs. *surface case* (Fillmore 1968).

One particularly striking example of why grammatical relations and case-marking categories need to be distinguished comes from Icelandic—a language that is renowned for its nominative, accusative, dative, and genitive subjects (Zaenen *et al.* 1985, Van Valin 1991, Barðdal 2001, Sigurðsson 2002). Although Icelandic uses nominative case morphology for prototypical agent-subjects in active-voice clauses and accusative case morphology for prototypical patient-direct objects, there are various constructions which, for different reasons, show alternative case-marking patterns. For example, there is a rather large class of verbs having to do with psychological or emotive states that allows either the NP designating the experiencer of the state or the NP designating its stimulus (or target or cause) to function as the clausal subject. However, in both of these instances the case marking is determined by the experiencer vs. stimulus distinction, rather than by the subject vs. object distinction. The following examples show that the stimulus of the verb *henta* 'like, please' is in the nominative case form whether it precedes the verb of its clause or follows it, just as the experiencer is in the dative case form in either of these positions.

(1.9) a. Ég   veit   að   þetta   mun henta   mér.
       I   know that this.Nom will please 1SgDat
      'I know that this will be pleasing to me.'

   b. Ég   veit   að   mér   mun   henta þetta.
       I   know that 1SgDat will   like   this.Nom
      'I know that I'll be pleased with this.'   (Barðdal 2001)

Significantly, there is a general convention in Icelandic that restricts the preverbal position in clauses of the kind containing *henta* in these examples to the subject. That is to say, there is a constraint on preverbal position in clauses that is generally sensitive to a particular dependent of the verb—like various other constraints in the language, including conjunction reduction, subject–verb inversion, subject-to-subject raising, and reflexive anaphor ante-cedence. With typical verbs designating physical actions, only the nominative agent satisfies these constraints. Thus, the constraints are sensitive to some kind of role category like subject (or the most prominent or most privileged dependent of a clause, whatever this is called). Since with verbs like *henta* the nominative stimulus can be in preverbal position and also manifests the other subject properties, it follows that this dependent can be the subject of its clause. However, since the dative experiencer can also be in preverbal position and it too manifests the other subject properties, it follows that this depen-dent can be the subject of its clause as well. Needless to say, in Icelandic there is a role—ostensibly a subject role—that is identified by constituent order and other correlative syntactic phenomena rather than nominative case marking.

There are numerous similar phenomena in languages that make it difficult to maintain the view that case-marking categories reliably indicate syntactic functions such as subject and direct object. In Finnish, for example, accusative case can be used on certain constituents that are not direct objects and fails to be used on certain constituents that are direct objects. More specifically, accusative case is used for adjunct adverbial phrases, which are not direct objects, and is replaced by partitive case on direct objects in the context of imperfective sentential aspect, as illustrated by the following examples (from Megerdoomian 2000).

(1.10) a. Matti   luk-i   kirja-t   tunni-ssa
         Matti.SgNom   read-3SgPst book-PlAcc   hour-Iness
         'Matti read the books in an hour.' *perfective interpretation*
     b. Matti   luk-i   kirjo-j-a   tunni-n
         Matti.SgNom   read-3SgPst book-Pl-Part hour-Acc
         'Matti read books for an hour.' *imperfective interpretation*

As noted in Kiparsky (2001), accusative adverbial phrases, such as *tunni-n* in (1.10b) do not have the defining syntactic properties of direct objects, such as the ability to be expressed as the subject of a passive sentence or to control raising to object or secondary predication. Moreover, although the partitive vs. accusative distinction expresses something about the semantics of clauses, it apparently does not express a grammatical-relation distinction, since the partitive object has the defining syntactic properties of direct objects (Kiparsky 1998, Ackerman and Moore 1999). Thus, accusative case identifies neither all nor only direct objects.

The issue of mismatches between grammatical relations and morphological marking is considered further in Section 1.3 and in subsequent chapters.

Suffice it to say, for now, that one of the fundamental challenges for a theory of grammar is that, although there is a systematic relationship between grammatical relations and case-marking categories, the correspondence is not always straightforward.

1.3 Different theoretical approaches to grammatical relations

Theories of grammar differ not only with respect to how they categorize grammatical relations, but also with respect to how many and which relations are recognized, how individual relations are labelled, and, of course, how, precisely, the roles of dependents are assigned or determined.

1.3.1 *Subject and direct object*

If a theory recognizes the grammatical relations subject and direct object, there is a fair amount of consensus concerning what is meant by these terms. The basic idea is that the grammar of a language revolves primarily around two core roles. At least in the most common basic language type (known as an accusative language—see Section 2.1), of which English and most other Indo-European languages are examples, the most syntactically privileged of these two is the subject. Although dependents with various semantic roles can be subjects (depending on the voice of verbs among other things), the proto-typical subject is an agent (or the most active participant in an event) and the agent is the subject in a basic active-voice clause. Similarly, although dependents with various semantic roles can be direct objects, the prototypical direct object is a patient (or the primary target of an agent's action) and the patient is a direct object in a basic active-voice clause.

However, not all theories recognize subject and direct object grammatical relations. As noted above, these concepts played no role in Pāṇini's grammar of Sanskrit. In Lexicase Grammar, these labels are also not used, although the case form nominative is close to the same notion as subject. One key difference is that the grammatical relation subject, in theories that employ it, is not necessarily constrained to being associated with the NP that bears nominative case marking (or else there could be no such thing as dative subjects, for example), whereas the nominative case form in Lexicase Grammar is. The dependent that expresses the verb's nominative case form need not manifest a case feature morphologically; but if it does, this case feature cannot conflict with the case form. In fact the notion subject can be characterized in alternative ways in Lexicase Grammar. Consider, for example how dative subjects in Icelandic might be handled:

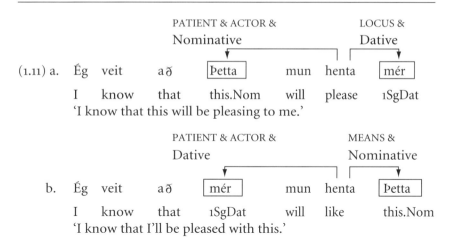

(1.11) a. Ég veit að [Þetta] mun henta [mér]

        I know that this.Nom will please 1SgDat
'I know that this will be pleasing to me.'

b. Ég veit að [mér] mun henta [Þetta]

        I know that 1SgDat will like this.Nom
'I know that I'll be pleased with this.'

Crucially, in this theory, case relations (semantic roles) need not be the same for corresponding NPs across paraphrases. How a speaker conceives of the situation described by a sentence is what counts—not what happens in the situation from an objective point of view. Thus, either the experiencer or the stimulus of the psychological state designated by *henta* can be conceived of as the perceptual centre of the state, that is the patient. If the stimulus is conceived of as the patient, as in (1.11a), the experiencer is naturally conceived of as the locus (i.e. the perceived abstract or concrete location of the action or state), for which reason the dative case form is appropriate, since it is one of the common choices for the locus role. In addition to the case relations and case forms, there is also a semantic macrorole called 'actor' (the entity perceived as instigating or carrying out an action or bearing the attributes of a state), which was omitted from the Lexicase analysis of Sanskrit active and passive pairs presented in Section 1.2, for the sake of simplicity.[4] Since there is no accusative case form in the verb's valence, the dependent bearing the patient role is, by general rule, assigned the actor macrorole, which always goes to one and only one of the dependents. The same analysis of case relations, case forms, and macrorole assignment would be appropriate for the English sentence *This is pleasing to me.* In (1.11b), the experiencer of the psychological state designated by *henta* is conceived of as the patient. The stimulus of the psychological state, which is an entity perceived to be necessarily involved in the state or action affecting the patient, plays the role of means. Again, since there is no dependent with an accusative case form, and this is therefore an intransitive clause, the patient has the actor macrorole. The case relations and macrorole assignment are the same as in *I am pleased with this.* What makes Icelandic different from English is that the case form specifications remain dative vs. nominative in both of the valence frames of *henta*, and the unmarked alignment of actor and nominative is abandoned in the dative subject construction.[5] Why then does the dative subject have the usual grammatical properties of subjects (case marking aside)? A plausible answer is that these phenomena are sensitive to the actor macrorole rather than the nominative case form. That is, the rule for constituent order, for example, specifies that the dependent bearing the actor macrorole occupies preverbal position in clauses.

In short, by appealing to a nontraditional set of grammatical relations without the usual subject and direct object categories, Lexicase Grammar makes possible alternative characterizations of what is generally thought of as the subject of a clause. One kind of 'subject' is the dependent linked to the actor macrorole; another kind is the dependent linked to the nominative case form. Although the actor macrorole and nominative case generally coincide, they need not. The traditional subject and object relations are also not employed in Role and Reference Grammar (Foley and Van Valin 1984, Van Valin and La Polla 1997, and see Chapter 4), which, like Lexicase Grammar, provides alternative ways of describing grammatical phenomena for which the traditional subject role is usually invoked, including the possibility of appealing to an actor semantic macrorole (a notion that in fact originates in this theory).[6]

1.3.2 *Indirect object*

Use of the indirect object grammatical relation and its characterization are also subject to considerable cross-theoretical variation. When such a category can be identified—which is not always the case—the prototypical role appears to be that of recipient in an act of giving, with other semantic roles such as beneficiary, addressee, perceiver, etc. being included in ways that vary across languages (Dixon and Aikhenvald 2000). One kind of evidentiary basis for an indirect object relation is that typological research on certain syntactic phenomena suggests a grammatical-relation hierarchy with a third core relation (in addition to subject and direct object). For example, languages are known to differ in terms of which types of clausal dependents can be targeted by their relative-clause formation strategies (Keenan and Comrie 1977). The key constraints can be formulated in terms of a hierarchy such as the following.

(1.12)   Subject > direct object > indirect object > oblique > possessor > object of comparison
   NP accessibility hierarchy (Keenan and Comrie 1977)

All languages appear to allow relativization of subjects.[7] Some languages, however, draw the line at subject; others at subject and direct object; others at subject, direct object, and indirect object; and so forth. The top end of the same hierarchy has been claimed to govern agreement systems in languages (Moravcsik 1974, Whaley 1997: Ch. 3), which come in four main types: no agreement (e.g. Lahu, Mandarin), agreement with the subject only (e.g. Russian, Turkish), agreement with the subject and direct object (e.g. Quiché, Ahmaric), or agreement with the subject, direct object, and indirect object (e.g. Abkhaz, Manam).[8] Implicit in these claims about the role of a grammatical-relation hierarchy in syntactic phenomena is the idea that the grammars of some languages revolve around three primary relations rather than one or two. However, the empirical research underlying such typological generalizations is based on the assumption that all languages have indirect objects, which can be identified on an *a priori* basis (for example, the recipient in a process of giving is an indirect object). In fact, there is considerable variation across languages in terms of the way dependents with a recipient role function in the grammar. Moreover, when a special grammatical relation with recipient as prototype can be identified in particular languages, different theoretical characterizations of this relation are possible.

The Romance language family provides good examples of a system that appears to have three primary grammatical relations. In Brazilian Portuguese there is a special pronominal form for direct objects. As the following examples show, a 3rd person pronominal direct object can either be placed in canonical direct object position following the verb, in the same unmarked form in which it appears when it is a subject or the object of a preposition (1.13a–b), or it can be realized as a verb-initial pronoun in an accusative form (1.13c), that is a form restricted to direct objects (technically a clitic, which the standard orthography doesn't indicate as such systematically).[9]

(1.13) a. Ela   mudou   ele.
           3SgFem   changed   3SgMasc
           'She changed him.'
       b. Ele   mora com   ela.
           3SgMasc   lives with 3SgFem
           'He lives with her.'
       c. Ela   o   mudou.
           3SgFem   3SgMascAcc   changed
           'She changed him/it.'

The primary evidence for an indirect object category is that there is another 3rd person pronominal object clitic form that is not used for direct objects, but for dependents of a verb that are conceived of as typically active, receptive participants in the event described by the verb (i.e. recipients, beneficiaries, addressees, or experiencers of cognition, perception or emotion), which is to say, more or less the typical class of participants that trigger dative case marking or indirect object agreement cross-linguistically. The following examples illustrate the use of dative *lhe*, which alternates with a phrase that is invariably marked with a preposition (usually *para* 'for/to' or *a* 'to'), as shown by (1.14a).[10]

(1.14) a. Ela   lhe   deu um   presente / deu um presente para ele.
          3SgFem 3SgDat gave a   present   gave a present to him
          'She gave him/her a present/gave a present to him.'

      b. Isso   lhe   parece doido.
          that 3SgDat   seems   crazy
          'That seems crazy to him/her.'

      c. Ela   lhe   falou   disso.
          3SgFem 3SgDat   spoke   of.this
          'She spoke to him/her about this.'

      d. *Ela   lhe   mudou.
          3SgFem 3sgDat   changed
          'She changed him/her.'

      e. *Ela   lhe   mora.
          3SgFem 3sgDat   lives
          'She lives with him/her.'

There are various ways in which the class of dependents that can be expressed as a dative pronominal clitic differs from the class of dependents that can be expressed as an accusative clitic (direct objects). For example, only the latter can be the subject of a passive clause or the pivot in the so-called *tough* movement construction and a certain kind of contrastive focus construction known as the pseudocleft construction (see Section 2.3.2). However, the dative class is distinguished from the class of obliques not only by the special pronominal form but also by the fact that, like direct objects and unlike obliques, its members can be the reciprocolization pivot (or omitted element) in the reflexive/reciprocal *se* construction:

(1.15) a. Eles   se   deram as   mãos.   (*indirect object pivot*)
          3MascPl 3Rec   gave   the hands
          'They held hands.' (Literally, 'They gave each other the hands.')

b. Eles   nunca   mais   se   falaram.   (*indirect object pivot*)
    3MascPl   never   more   3Rec   spoke
    'They never again spoke to each other.'

c. Eles   se   amam.   (*direct object pivot*)
    3MascPl   3Rec   love
    'They love each other.'

d. *Eles   se   moram.   (**oblique pivot*)
    3MascPl   3Rec   live
    'They live with each other.'

Thus, there are at least three main categories of non-subject dependents: obliques, direct objects, and a kind of dependent that is like a direct object in some ways and like an oblique in others.

As detailed in Chapter 3, in Relational Grammar (Perlmutter 1983, Perlmutter and Rosen 1984, Blake 1990), as in traditional analyses of English and Romance languages, there are three primary grammatical relations around which the grammars of languages are assumed to largely revolve: subject, direct object, and indirect object. Other dependents of verbs fall into the general category of obliques. Schematically, the analysis of Brazilian Portuguese non-subject dependents would be as follows.

                direct object   *indirect object*

(1.16) a. Ela   deu [um   presente] para [a   mãe   dela]
           3SgFem gave   a   present   to.the the mother of.3SgFem
           'She gave a present to her mother.'

                        oblique

b. Ela   mora com   [a   mãe   dela]
    3SgFem lives   with   the   mother   of.3SgFem
    'She lives with her mother.'

Accusative pronominal clitics are reserved for direct objects; dative pronominal clitics for indirect objects. The pivot of the *se* reciprocal/reflexive construction can be either a direct object or an indirect object—but not an oblique. It is, of course, unclear whether this is the only or best way of categorizing and labelling the non-subject dependents in Brazilian Portuguese.

There are languages in which there appears to be no evidence for an indirect object category. For example, in Kamaiurá, an indigenous language of Brazil of the Tupí-Guraraní family (Seki 2000), the grammar is organized around two core grammatical relations, corresponding roughly to subject and direct object in Brazilian Portuguese (see Section 2.1.3 on some precise differences in the conception of these). NPs with the semantic roles that are characteristic of what are often considered to be indirect objects in other languages, including recipient, beneficiary, and addressee, are marked with a postposition, like obliques and unlike subjects and objects, as illustrated by the following examples.

(1.17) a. ywyrapara   o-me'eŋ   kara'iwa   upe
          bow   3-give   foreigner   to
          'He gave the bow to the foreigner.'
      b. tata   atsã   e-monyk   je=upe
          fire   Dim   2Sg-light.Imper   1Sg=to
          'Please light the fire for me.'
      c. tarekaja'a   upi'a   o-mo'at   'ytsiŋa   'arim
          turtle   egg   3-lay   sand   on/in
          'The turtle laid eggs in the sand.'

Although various constituent orders are possible, if there are three verbal dependents, the subject and object, if either or both are expressed as NPs, normally occur in preverbal position without a postposition and other NP dependents of verbs normally occur in postpositional phrases in postverbal position, as in all three of the examples in (1.17). Grammatical relations may be indicated by head marking in the form of either prefixes or pronominal clitics (the latter being indicated by the '=' separator, following Seki's notation), which index (or agree with) either the subject or the object, the choice being determined first by which is higher on a hierarchy of person (1st person > 2nd person > 3rd person) and, when they are of the same rank by person, by a grammatical relation hierarchy on which subject outranks object. Postpositions can have the same person-sensitive morphemes on them, which index the NP that they go with. Thus, *upe* 'to' (or what Seki glosses as 'dative') in (1.17b) has the pronominal clitic *je* on it, indicating that its object, the recipient dependent of the verb, is 1st person singular. If the subject or object dependent of a verb or the object of a postposition is indicated with head-marking morphology and is pronominal, it need not be—and usually isn't— expressed as an independent pronoun. Significantly, *upe*-marked NPs, which might be analysed as indirect objects by virtue of the semantic roles that *upe* typically indicates, do not appear to have any distinguishing syntactic properties that make them more object-like than obliques.

Consider, for example, the phenomenon of recipricolization in Kamaiurá. As shown by (1.18a) the reciprocal prefix *jo-* appears on the verb when the reciprocal pivot (the dependent that is not syntactically expressed) is the direct object.

(1.18) a. a'e-wana   o-jo-u'u
         3Masc-Pl   3-Rec-bite
         'They bit each other.'

    b. karamemā   o-me'eŋ=awa   o-jo-upe
         present   3-give=Pl   3-Rec-to
         'They gave presents to each other.'

    c. o-jepe'a=awa   o-jo-wi
         3-separate=Pl   3-Rec-from
         'They separated from each other.'

The same prefix is used when the reciprocal pivot is a recipient. However, as shown by (1.18b), *jo-* appears on the postposition rather than the verb, just as it does when the reciprocal pivot is any oblique dependent, as in (1.18c). There are various further syntactic phenomena that distinguish direct objects from obliques, including passivization, reflexivization (for which a prefix different from *jo-* is used), and relative clause formation. In every case the *upe*-marked dependent behaves like an oblique. It is, of course, possible to maintain that *upe*-marked NPs in Kamaiurá are indirect objects, as would be the case in a standard Relational Grammar analysis. However, it appears that nothing in the grammar of the language suggests that this syntactic function is operative in a way that distinguishes it from a more general oblique function.

There are also languages in which there are alternative constructions for expressing NPs with recipient-type semantic roles and different potential analyses of the grammatical relations in such constructions. In English, for example, there are various potential ways of defining an indirect object category and a lack of consensus among theoreticians about how, if at all, to define it. For example, one might claim that indirect objects are identified by the preposition *to*, which is often used with NPs playing the same kinds of semantic roles as Brazilian Portuguese indirect objects. Under this analysis, the italicized NPs in the following examples would be indirect objects.

(1.19) a. I gave a present to *my sister*.
    b. They transferred the title to *the new owners*.
    c. The candidate promised very little to *the voters*.
    d. It seems to *me* that there is a serious problem.
    e. I'm going to drive Bill to *the supermarket*.

The problem with such a claim is that the indirect object relation would play no role in the grammar other than to account (vacuously) for the occurrence of the preposition *to*. One could just as easily say that the grammatical relation of indirect object is identified by the preposition *from* or *for*.

The overall class of NPs marked with the preposition *to* (or occurring in a PP with *to*) has no syntactic privileges or restrictions that do not extend to NPs marked with *from* or *for*. If there is an indirect object category in English, it appears not to be overtly marked. The prepositional system does not zero in on such a category. Moreover, it is marked neither by pronominal case (the *he* vs. *him* contrast only yields a distinction between nominative and non-nominative), nor agreement (only subjects trigger very limited agreement on verbs), nor even constituent order, as shown below. Thus, unlike in Brazilian Portuguese, the usual markers of the primary syntactic functions fail to announce an indirect object relation.

Another possibility is that *indirect object* names the subset of *to*-marked NPs (or P-marked NPs), that can appear alternatively as the first object (O1) in the so-called double-object construction,[11] illustrated by the following examples.

(1.20) a.   I gave $[_{O_1}$ my sister$]$ $[_{O_2}$ a present$]$.
     b.   The candidate promised $[_{O_1}$ the voters$]$ $[_{O_2}$ very little$]$.
     c.   *I'm going to drive $[_{O_1}$ the supermarket$]$ $[_{O_2}$ Bill$]$.
     d.   *They transferred $[_{O_1}$ the new owners$]$ $[_{O_2}$ the title$]$

Under this alternative analysis, *my sister* and *the voters* in (1.19a) and (1.19c), respectively, would be indirect objects, unlike the other italicized NPs in (1.19). *The new owners*, for example, would not be an indirect object in (1.19b), because it cannot be an O1 in the double-object construction, as shown by the ungrammaticality of (1.20d). The problem with this analysis is that indirect objects would only be identified by a single criterion: ability to be alternatively expressed as an O1 in the double-object construction. There appear to be no other syntactic phenomena for which a constraint needs to be formulated in terms of this precise class of dependents. Moreover, there are semantic and lexical constraints on the double-object construction (e.g. Green 1974, Pinker 1989, Gropen *et al.* 1989, Goldberg 1995) which obviate the need for an account in terms of an indirect object syntactic function. For example, (1.20c) is bad because the participant expressed as the O1 has to be conceived of as receiving something and supermarkets don't receive people that are taken to them in cars. On the other hand, although the potential O1 in (1.20d) is readily conceived of as receiving something, *transfer* belongs to a lexical class of Latinate verbs, which happens to dislike the double-object construction, for whatever reason.

A third possible approach is that *indirect object* names a class of dependents of verbs that can be defined as including both O1s in the double-object construction and all *to*-marked (or P-marked) NPs that have the same kind of semantic role as P-marked NPs that can be alternatively expressed as an O1.[12] Under this approach, all of the italicized NPs in the grammatical examples in (1.20) would be indirect objects, as would the italicized NPs in (1.19a–d). Although attempts at explicit definitions of the indirect object category in English are relatively rare, textbook introductions to grammar and linguistic analysis alike often assume a notion of indirect object something like this (e.g. Matthews 1997: 175, Barry 1998: ch. 3, Carnie 2002: ch. 3). There is, however, no preposition, case affix, or agreement affix that marks this putative class of NPs. There also appears to be no syntactic phenomenon in which this class of NPs demonstrably plays a role. Consider, for example, the passive construction. An O1 can be the subject of a passive clause (*My sister was given a present, The voters were promised very little*); but none of the *to*-marked NPs in (1.19) can (**My sister was given a present to, *I was seemed to that there was a problem*).

Based on distinctions that matter in the grammar of English, there seem to be two main categories of objects (i.e. non-subject dependents that are not marked by a preposition). A super-category of objects is identified by a constituent-order constraint and by a constraint on the passive construction. The constituent-order constraint says, in effect, that the (primary) object must be right-adjacent to the verb, without an intervening adverb, for example,[13] as illustrated by the following examples.

(1.21) a.   I left [$_{OBJECT}$ my keys] [$_{OBLIQUE}$ on the table] [$_{ADV}$ just now].
    b.   *I left [$_{ADV}$ just now] [$_{OBJECT}$ my keys] [$_{OBLIQUE}$ on the table].
    c.   *I left [$_{OBLIQUE}$ on the table] [$_{OBJECT}$ my keys] [$_{ADV}$ just now].

(1.22) a.   I sent [$_{O1}$ my mother] [$_{O2}$ some flowers] [$_{ADV}$ just now].
    b.   *I sent [$_{ADV}$ just now] [$_{O1}$ my mother] [$_{O2}$ some flowers].
    c.   *I sent [$_{O2}$ some flowers] [$_{O1}$ my mother] [$_{ADV}$ just now].

The O1 in the double-object construction and the sole object in any other construction are the dependents that are subject to the verb-adjacency constraint. These are also the dependents that can be alternatively expressed as the subject in the passive construction (at least in most dialects of English):[14]

(1.23) a.   My keys were left on the table.
    b.   *The table was left my keys on.
    c.   My mother was sent some flowers.
    d.   *Some flowers were sent my mother.

Given a choice between two non-subject dependents of a verb, the one that can be expressed as the subject in the passive construction is the same one that must appear right-adjacent to the verb otherwise.[15]

Based on these facts, it would appear that there is simply one category of primary object, which might simply be labelled 'direct object' and whose members are the O1 in the double-object construction and the sole object in any other construction. However, these two kinds of object are distinguished by other grammatical phenomena. For example, the object in a single object construction can be, and preferably is, placed at the rightmost edge of the clause (overriding the verb-adjacency constraint) just in case it has a complex internal structure, with an embedded relative clause, for example. This alternative constituent ordering, commonly known as heavy NP shift, is not possible for the O1 in the double-object construction (e.g. Stowell 1981, Larson 1988):

(1.24) a.   I should have left [OBLIQUE at home] [HEAVY OBJECT all those things that you're always telling me to get rid of].
      b.   *I should have sent [O2 some flowers] [HEAVY O1 all the people that deserve to be remembered for what they've done].

Similarly, the sole object of a verb can alternatively be expressed as a subject in the *tough*-movement construction, whereas an O1 cannot (Larson 1988, Siewierska 1991: 97), as shown by the following examples, in which the (b)-sentences in each pair illustrate *tough* movement.

(1.25) a.   It will be easy to leave [OBJECT these things] at home.
      b.   These things will be easy to leave at home.
(1.26) a.   It will be easy to send [O1 those people] [O2 some flowers].
      b.   *Those people will be easy to send some flowers.

Passivization and the verb-adjacency constraint operate in terms of what seems to be a super-category of objects, including O1s and the sole object in a clause with only one object. O1s are distinguished by certain other grammatical phenomena, in which they fail to behave like other objects and/or other non-subject dependents.[16]

The question is how to draw the necessary distinctions. It is possible to use a system of syntactic functions with three types of non-subjects: direct object, indirect object, and oblique, as in Relational Grammar. The key idea of the standard Relational Grammar analysis is that the double-object construction results from what can be viewed as a revaluation of grammatical relations: the indirect object is promoted to direct object, such that it is both an indirect object (at an underlying or initial level of representation) and a direct object (at a superficial or final level of representation). Ignoring various representational details, the analysis is as follows, where arrows represent the direction of the revaluation and chômeur is the final relation borne by a dependent whose initial grammatical relation has been 'taken over' by another dependent.

		direct object		*indirect object*	
(1.27) a.	My son gave	the flowers	to	his mother	
		indirect object	$\Rightarrow$	*direct object*	$\Rightarrow$
		direct object		*chômeur*	
	b. My son gave	his mother		the flowers	

The direct object properties of the O1 (right-adjacency to the verb, for example) are accounted for by its status as a final direct object. The ways in which the O1 differs from prototypical direct objects (inability to be the pivot in the *tough*-movement construction, for example) are accounted for by its initial indirect object status.

Another possibility, however, would be to say that there is simply a single syntactic category, (direct) object, which encompasses both O1s and the sole object in the single-object construction (as in Dryer 1986 and Siewierska 1991: 95). The special behaviour of O1s might be attributed to a semantic role difference between them and other direct objects. For example, suppose that the potential variety of semantic role distinctions is somehow collapsed into a small set of super-categories, along the following lines, as in Lexicase Grammar, discussed above, as well as various other theories.

(1.28)   Agent, Recipient, Patient, Instrument, Locative
          Generalized semantic roles

The idea would be that locative, for example, might include the more specific roles of source, as with the *from*-marked NP in *I removed this from the box*; goal or destination, as with the *to*-marked NP in *I drove my brother to the mall*; and location, as with the *on*-marked NP in *My keys are sitting on the table*. Similarly, recipient might include, among others, not only the prototypical role of recipient which gives the category its name, as with the O1 in *I gave my mother some flowers*; but also perceiver, as with the O1 in *I showed my mother the flowers*; and addressee, as with the O1 in *I told my mother a lie*. Under this kind of analysis, two kinds of English direct objects might be distinguished: those with a generalized recipient semantic role, that is O1s, and those with a generalized patient semantic role, that is the sole object in the single object construction. The grammatical relations of the non-subject dependents in the sentences in (1.27) might be as follows, where uppercase letters are used for semantic roles and 2nd object is the syntactic function of a patient that is neither an object nor an oblique.

		PATIENT &	RECIPIENT &
		object	*oblique*
(1.29) a.	My son gave	the flowers to	his mother
		RECIPIENT &	PATIENT &
		object	*2nd object*
b.	My son gave	his mother	the flowers

The verb-adjacency constraint and the main constraint on passive subjects could be sensitive to the object syntactic function. Non-patient or recipient direct objects would be excluded from certain phenomena, such as *tough* movement and heavy NP shift.

Lexical-Functional Grammar (Bresnan 1982*a*, 2000, Falk 2001 and see Section 3.4.1) adopts a theory of grammatical relations in which the syntactic function indirect object, as such, plays no role.[17] The analysis of English grammatical relations would be essentially as indicated in (1.29), various representational details aside.[18] In this kind of theory, all language-specific and typological evidence for a category such as indirect object must be accounted for in terms of (generalized) semantic roles or other semantic or grammatical distinctions among oblique dependents. For example, the grammatical relation hierarchies implicated by typological restrictions on relative clause formation strategies and verb agreement systems (see (1.12)) might be alternatively formulated to include the composite grammatical relation Obl$_{REC}$ (i.e. the syntactic function oblique and the semantic role recipient), in place of indirect object. By the same token, the grammatical relations of the Brazilian Portuguese examples in (1.16) might be as follows.

				PATIENT &		RECIPIENT &		
				object		*oblique*		
(1.30) a.	Ela	deu	um	presente	para	a	mãe	dela
	3SgFem	gave	a	present	to	the	mother	of.3SgFem
	'She gave a present to her mother.'							
					LOCATIVE			
					& oblique			
b.	Ela	mora	com	a	mãe	dela		
	3SgFem	lives	with	the	mother	of.3SgFem		
	'She lives with her mother.'							

Under this analysis, accusative pronominal forms are used for the object relation and dative forms for oblique-recipients. Given a grammatical relation hierarchy such as Subject > Object > Obl$_{REC}$ > Obl$_{INSTR}$ > etc., one might say that the pivot of the *se* reflexive/reciprocal construction cannot be lower than Obl$_{REC}$ on the hierarchy. Obl$_{REC}$ dependents fail to behave like direct objects in most respects because they simply have a syntactic function other than object. Of course, the Lexical-Functional Grammar approach to indirect objects extends straightforwardly to languages such as Kamaiurá, in which recipients behave like obliques, since they are, quite simply, categorized as a kind of oblique.

Returning to the question of indirect objects in English, there is at least one other kind of analysis in which the indirect object relation can be engaged. In recognition of the fact that the double-object construction evolved from an Old English construction with a dative-marked NP preceding an accusative object, one might simply analyse the O1 in the double-object construction as the only kind of indirect object (e.g. Jespersen 1927, Herriman 1995).[19] Like other PPs, *to*-phrases would simply be obliques. The direct object category would encompass the usual object in the single-object construction as well as the second object (O2) in the double-object construction. Thus, assuming the same generalized semantic roles, the grammatical relations of the non-subject dependents of the sentences in (1.27) and (1.29) might be characterized as follows.

			PATIENT &	*RECIPIENT &*
			direct object	*oblique*
(1.31)	a.	My son gave	the flowers to	his mother
			RECIPIENT &	*PATIENT &*
			indirect object	*direct object*
	b.	My son gave	his mother	the flowers

Under this analysis, a question arises as to why the indirect object rather than the direct object in (1.31b) patterns like the direct object in (1.31a) with respect to the verb-adjacency constraint and the constraint on the subject of passive clauses. The answer is that direct and indirect objects are two different kinds of object, as in Relational Grammar, for example. In essence, they are members of the class of dependents that are neither subjects nor obliques. Assuming also a ranking of semantic roles, as in Lexical-Functional Grammar and certain other theories (e.g. Jackendoff 1972, Grimshaw 1990), according to which recipient outranks patient, the constraints in question can be said to hold for the object with the highest-ranking semantic role, that is the object that is semantically most prominent.[20]

It should be clear that there are different ways of conceptualizing and labelling grammatical relations. If a theory utilizes the category of indirect object, it may characterize its relationship to the dependents of a verb in different ways. If a theory does not utilize a syntactic category of indirect object, it may utilize a generalized semantic role in its place. Although these different characterizations of the linguistic facts have potential ramifications, the extent to which the differences are ultimately just terminological remains unclear. Still, the contrasting approaches do seem to entail some different claims and predictions. Implicit in the Relational Grammar approach, for example, is the claim that there is no viable semantic characterization of the (final) indirect object relation. In principal, any dependent of a verb ought to be able to 'change' its initial syntactic function to indirect object. Implicit in the oblique-recipient approach, on the other hand, is the claim that although the oblique-recipient category may differ somewhat from language to language, given that semantic roles can have different precise conceptions, it nevertheless ought to be restricted to a narrow range of precise semantic roles, with some kind of similarity or shared feature, in a way that the subject and object categories are not.

1.3.3 *Oblique and other syntactic functions*

Dependents of verbs that do not have one of the primary syntactic functions are generally considered to be obliques,[21] as in the discussion above. For marking obliques, languages generally use adpositions or case markers that can be related to semantic roles in a wide variety of ways, although other marking devices are sometimes used, such as the relational nouns of Tzotzil and other Mayan languages (Aissen 1987). At one end of the spectrum are languages with a generalized oblique marker, such as Jarawara (Dixon 2000) and Halkomelem (Gerdts 1988*a*).[22] In Halkomelem, for example, the single adposition ʔə works for all obliques and, thus, fails to distinguish semantic roles in any way, as illustrated by the following examples.

(1.32) a. ni   ném?   ʔə   ɬə   sɬéni?   kʷθə   swəy?qe?
           Aux   go   Obl   Det woman   Det   man
           'The man went to the woman.'

       b. ni   ʔíməš   ɬə   sɬéni?   ʔə   kʷθə   sc'éšt
           Aux   walk   Det woman   Obl   Det   stick
           'The woman walked with a stick.'

       c. ni   cən   qʷál   ʔə   kʷθə   nə-télə
           Aux   1Subj   speak Obl   Det   1Pos-money
           'I spoke about my money.'

At the other end of the spectrum are languages like English with numerous prepositions for marking obliques or Hungarian with its sixteen or so oblique case-marking categories. Although semantic roles are reflected in the marking choices in such languages, the situation is complex. English, for example, uses *from* for NPs that have the source role (*I stole that from my brother, They came from Illinois*), *to* for NPs with the goal/destination semantic role (*I ran to the store, We drove the car to Chicago*), and *with* for NPs with the instrument role (*He sliced the bread with that knife, I made this with my own hands*). Hungarian has ablative, allative, and instrumental morphological case-marking categories to make roughly the same semantic distinctions (Rounds 2001). As with more generalized types of markers, such as nominative and accusative adpositions or case affixes, which can often be used for dependents with virtually any semantic role, there is generally some kind of role conflation with oblique markers as well, although the range tends to be more restricted. The range for English *to* is relatively large, as it is used not only for goal/destination but also for a variety of other roles (recipient, experiencer, perceiver, addressee, etc.) which for some analysts constitute an indirect object syntactic function rather than an oblique function (see Section 1.3.2). *With* has various uses in addition to its instrumental use, including a comitative use (*I went to the movies with my sister*), as well as what might be considered a comitative-addressee use (e.g. *Bill spoke with Tom about the problem* designates an event with Bill speaking TO Tom and Tom responding) and a comitative-locative use (e.g. *Sue lives with her mother* designates a state of affairs with Sue and her mother living together AT her mother's place). In some languages, such as the Greenlandic Eskimo-Aleut language Inuit (Woodbury 1977, Bittner 1987), the instrumental case marker is used not only for instruments but also agents in passive clauses and patients in antipassive clauses (see Section 4.2.1). Needless to say, the so-called instrumental marker does not have a unified meaning across or within languages.

Not only do oblique morphological cases and adpositions conflate semantic roles but they can also make very fine-grained semantic distinctions concerning details of an entity with a general semantic role. For example, various subtle differences in the conception of the referent of an NP with the goal role can be indicated by choice of preposition in a sentence such as *I loaded the hay onto/on/into the wagon*. Similarly, in Hungarian, in addition to a less specific ablative case category for the source role (corresponding to English *from*), elative case morphology can be used for a source conceived of as containing the moving participant (corresponding to English *out of*), and delative case morphology can be used for a source conceived of as supporting the moving participant (corresponding to English *off of*). Although there are regularities of various kinds, the relationship between semantic roles and oblique markers within and across languages can be complex.

In any case, there are essentially two theoretical stances to the notion of an oblique grammatical relation. In some theories, there is a formally recognized distinct oblique syntactic function, with a variety of semantically determined kinds that can be marked in different ways across languages, as in Lexical-Functional Grammar, for example. In other theories, oblique NPs simply lack the defining features of the core grammatical relations (e.g. by not occupying one of the privileged positions in syntactic structure) and are marked in a way that may or may not be semantically determined, as in Transformational Grammar (see Chapter 5) and Role and Reference Grammar (see Chapter 4). Under either approach, (at least most) adpositionally-marked dependents in both languages like English and languages like Halkomelem are treated as belonging to a different category than subjects and objects. The marking rule for Halkomelem is straightforward: (in a theory that utilizes the oblique relation) any kind of oblique is marked with the preposition ʔə; or (in a theory without an oblique relation) any kind of NP that is not a subject or object is marked with the preposition ʔə. For English, obliques are marked, following a complex schema, according to the kind of oblique relation borne; or any kind of NP that is not a subject or object is marked according to its semantic role, following a complex schema.

There is a bigger theoretical divide concerning the question of whether finer distinctions than oblique vs. core (subject/object) functions should be drawn, and, if so, how. One issue has to do with a distinction between oblique arguments and adjuncts, that is verb phrase modifiers such as *in the kitchen* in *I ate breakfast in the kitchen*, which specifies a setting for the event designated by *eat* rather than expressing one of the defining participants in the type of event specified by the verb. Another has to do with the analysis of constructions in which the default subject or object has been displaced by some other dependent of the verb or 'demoted'. For example, if the O1 in a double-object construction of the kind exemplified by *give* [$_{O1}$ *the boy*][$_{O2}$*a bike*] is the direct object, what is the relation of the O2 (or demotee from direct object)? Similarly, what is the relation of the agent (or demotee from subject) in the passive construction exemplified by *The dog was fed by the boy*?

Generally, some kind of distinction is drawn between adjuncts and what are often called 'arguments' of verbs, that is NPs or other phrases that express participant roles specified in the meanings of verbs. Relational Grammar, however, does not formally distinguish these, since all co-constituents of a clause are assumed to bear one or more relations to the clause rather than to verbs per se. Although the conceptual distinction between argument and adjunct is relatively clear, the empirical basis for it is problematic, even with respect to well-studied languages such as English. As noted in Whaley (1993), applying the available criteria to English yields more of a continuum than a clear-cut distinction between oblique arguments and adjuncts. From a cross-linguistic perspective, this murkiness is exacerbated by the fact that the same morphological marking is often used across the full range of constituent types, as evidenced, for example, by the Finnish use of accusative and inessive cases for both core and oblique arguments and what are presumably temporal adjuncts (see (1.10)) and the similar multiple use in English of such preposi-tions as *in*, which can mark a goal participant in an event designated by a verb (*put the toys in the box*), a locational setting for an event (*eat breakfast in the kitchen*), or even a temporal setting (*go to the store in the morning*). Consequently, not only is the issue of where and if to draw a line between adjuncts and oblique arguments a difficult one, but so is the question of how to categorize such demotees as the *by*-marked agent in the English passive construction and its analogues in other languages, since the murkiness of the adjunct vs. argument distinction can extend to them as well. Indeed, theories take various stances concerning *by*-marked agents: from an adjunct designa-tion in Lexical-Functional Grammar and Role and Reference Grammar, for example, to the Relational Grammar analysis, in which demotees of all kinds belong to an altogether distinct category, called 'chômeur'. Thus, modulo certain cross-linguistic differences in the primary or core grammatical rela-tions (considered in Section 2.1) and certain theory-specific implementation details (concerning the indirect object category, for example), the distinction between core and oblique relations is relatively uncontroversial. However, there is more uncertainty surrounding such potentially distinct categories as adjunct and demotee.

As an example of the adjunct vs. oblique argument problem, consider the following different kinds of *with*-marked NPs in English.

(1.33) a.   Sue lives *with her mother*.
     b.   Jake spoke *with us* about that.
     c.   I'm going to fill the glasses *with wine*.
     d.   You should slice the bread *with the serrated knife*.
     e.   I painted the house *with my sister*.

If the basic idea is that arguments express defining elements of the process or state designated by a verb, then it seems clear that *the bread* in *You should slice the bread in the kitchen* is an argument and *in the kitchen* is an adjunct. The meaning of *slice* is presumably something like 'x does something to y and because of this y becomes thin flat pieces.' Because *the bread* in *slice the bread* specifies the entity indicated by the variable y in the hypothesized meaning of *slice*, it is an expression of an argument of the verb. Since adding 'in someplace (*z*)' to the hypothesized definition would not serve to clarify the meaning of the verb in any way or to distinguish *slice* from other verbs, *in the kitchen* is presumably an adjunct. But what about the *with* phrases in (1.33c–d)? The difficulty is that the meanings of words are not available for direct inspection. Does *slice* really mean '*x* uses something sharp (*z*) to do something to *y* and because of this *y* becomes thin flat pieces'?

One kind of rationale for claiming that *wine* in (1.33c) is an argument goes as follows. First, this phrase has a theme or 'moving participant' meaning (see Section 1.3.4) as opposed to a standard instrument meaning. This is revealed by the possibility of adding an instrumental *with* phrase to (1.33d) (*I'm going to fill the glasses with wine with a funnel*). Ordinarily, two *with* phrases with a simple instrumental meaning cannot be added to the same clause (**I'm going to fill the glasses with a funnel with a pitcher*), although *with* phrases with different meanings can (*I'm going to fill the glasses with wine with my brother*). Hence, the *with* phrase in (1.33c) expresses the semantic role of theme (the entity conceived of as under-going motion) or, perhaps, instrumental theme, since wine is both used to fill and undergoes movement to a specified goal. Now, *with* phrases can have this theme meaning only in the context of verbs in the same semantic class as *fill*, that is verbs of goal-oriented caused motion (e.g. *load, pack, spray*, etc.). As the theme inter-pretation does not occur in other contexts, the *with* phrase is expressing a semantic argument of the verb. It is, therefore, not an adjunct.

The same kind of reasoning applies to the locative and addressee *with* phrases in (1.33a–b). For example, a sentence such as *Tom spoke with the children about that with his brother* can mean 'Tom and his brother spoke to the children about that' but not 'Tom and the children spoke to his brother about that'. The addressee role, which goes to the first *with* phrase, seems to come not from *with* per se but from the verb. An addressee interpretation occurs only with a *with* phrase that accompanies a verb of communication (*speak with, talk with, argue with, chat with*, etc.). It is less clear whether the same reasoning can be extended to cases like (1.33d). One could say that the instrumental meaning of *with* is contingent upon co-occurrence with a verb whose meaning entails the use of an instrument. *Slice*, for example, designates a process that ordinarily requires the use of a sharp implement. However, instrumental *with* phrases can be added to clauses with a wide array of verb types, not all of which designate inherently instrumental processes (e.g. *I filled the glasses with wine with a funnel, She spoke to the crowd with a bullhorn, He reads with a magnifying glass*).

Potential omissibility is another factor that can have a bearing on the adjunct issue. For example, the fact that *the bread* is not omissible in (1.33d) (**You should slice in the kitchen*) provides a clue that it is an argument. Prototypical adjuncts are rarely, if ever, required (e.g. *You should slice the* *bread (in the kitchen))*. Although not being able to be omitted provides evidence for argument status, omissibility does not provide evidence against argument status, since patient/direct object dependents of a verb that are clearly arguments based on other criteria are often omissible, as in the case of *I ate (a donut) in the kitchen, We drove (the car) to Chicago,* or *I can see (things) with these glasses*. Moreover, prototypical PP arguments are also often omissible (*That looks funny (to me), I stole some money (from him), He lied (to me)*), although not always (e.g. *in the refrigerator* is not omissible in *He put the beer *(in the refrigerator)*). As for the different types of *with*-marked dependents, the omissibility criterion is only applicable to the comitative-locative *with* phrase, which shows evidence of being an argument:

(1.34) a.   Sue lives *(with her mother).
   b.   Jake spoke (with us) about that.
   c.   I'm going to fill these glasses (with wine).
   d.   You should slice the bread (with the serrated knife).
   e.   I painted the house (with my sister).

Another kind of syntactic evidence come from the pseudocleft construction (Vestergaard 1977, Radford 1988: Ch. 5, Whaley 1993: Ch. 3), illustrated by the following examples.

(1.35) a.   What I'm going to do in the kitchen is *slice the bread.*
   b.   What I'm going to do in the kitchen is *dance.*
   c.   *What I'm going to do in the refrigerator is *put the beer.*
   d.   *What I'm going to do the bread (in the kitchen) is *slice.*

The generalization is that the focused verb phrase in the pseudocleft construction (i.e. the phrase appearing sentence-finally following the copula) must include the verb and any arguments that it may have. In (1.35a–b), *slice the bread* and *dance* can be in the sentence-final focus position because neither phrase is missing any of the arguments of its verb. Examples (1.35c–d), on the other hand, are ungrammatical because *put the beer* is focused without its goal argument and *slice* is focused without its direct object argument. The pseudocleft test confirms the argument status of the comitative-locative *with* phrase and differentiates the remaining types as follows.

(1.36) a.   *What I'm going to do with my mother is *live.*
   b.   *What Jake is going to do with us (about that) is *speak.*
   c.   What I'm going to do with the wine is *fill these glasses.*
   d.   What I'm going to do with the serrated knife is *slice the bread.*
   e.   What I'm going to do with my sister is *paint the house.*

Since, an ordinary comitative *with* phrase need not accompany a verb and any of its arguments in the pseudocleft focus position, as in (1.36e) as well as in the case of verbs without any non-subject arguments (*What I'm going to do with my sister is work/leave/play*), such phrases appear to be adjuncts. Also falling on the adjunct side of the divide by this criterion are the theme-instrumental *with* phrase accompanying transitive *fill* and the ordinary instrumental *with* phrase accompanying transitive *slice*, as shown by the grammaticality of (1.36c–d). The comitative-addressee *with* phrase accompanying *speak*, on the other hand, behaves like an argument (1.36b).

The placement of emphatic reflexives provides another possible means of distinguishing adjuncts and arguments (Radford 1988: ch. 5, Whaley 1993: ch. 3). An emphatic reflexive is an intonationally focused reflexive *Xself* form that does not itself express an argument of a verb and is necessarily construed with the subject, as in the following examples.

(1.37) a.   Tom's gonna slice the bread in the kitchen HIMSELF.
     b.   Tom's gonna slice the bread HIMSELF in the kitchen.
     c.   Tom's gonna put the beer in the refrigerator HIMSELF.
     d.   * Tom's gonna put the beer HIMSELF in the refrigerator.

As the contrast between (1.37b) and (1.37d) shows, it is possible to place an emphatic reflexive in a postverbal position before a prototypical PP adjunct but not before a prototypical PP argument. There appears to be a constraint to the effect that an emphatic reflexive cannot immediately follow a verb, independently of the adjunct/complement status of the following phrase (e.g. *Tom reads/studies/works/sleeps* HIMSELF *in the library*). For this reason, the emphatic reflexive criterion appears to be inapplicable to the *live with X* construction. It works as follows with the other *with* phrases under consideration here:

(1.38) a.   *Jack's gonna speak about that HIMSELF with us.
     b.   ?Jack's gonna fill the glasses HIMSELF with wine.
     c.   Jack's gonna slice the bread HIMSELF with the serrated knife.
     d.   Jack's gonna paint the house HIMSELF with a friend.

The key difference between the pseudocleft and emphatic reflexive criteria is that instrumental themes (*with wine* in *fill the glass with wine*) are only marginally adjunct-like with respect to the latter.

In short, these different kinds of *with*-marked NPs show varying degrees of argument/adjunct behaviour. In the case of *live with my mother*, all the available evidence suggests that *with my mother* is an argument. In the case of *paint the house with my sister*, *with my sister* displays relatively clear adjunct behaviour. *With wine* in *fill the glasses with wine* falls somewhere in the middle. It clearly satisfies only one adjunct criterion (omissibility in the VP pseudocleft construction). Phrases such as *with a serrated knife* in *slice the bread with a serrated knife* are often considered to be arguments, presumably because of the theoretical prominence of a semantic role category labelled 'instrument' (owing, for example, to Fillmore 1968), the relative importance of an instrumental case-marking category in languages with robust dependent-marking morphology, and the fact that instrumentally-marked dependents and/or subject and object dependents with an instrumental semantic role can be arguments sometimes.[23] However, at least in English, it seems hard to justify an argument classification for common instrumental *with* phrases.

Tagalog has what has been called an adjunct-fronting construction (Schachter and Otanes 1972, Kroeger 1993), which seems to announce which constituents of a clause are adjuncts. Tagalog is a verb-initial language in which, outside of special constructions, constituents follow the verb. In one such special construction adverbial phrases and other typical adjuncts are placed in sentence-initial position, followed by any pronominal dependents of the verb, as illustrated by the following examples, adapted from Kroeger (1993: ch. 2).

(1.39) a. [dahil   sa=iyo]   ako   nahuli
           because   Loc=you   1SgNom   late
           'Because of you, I was late.'

    b. *[ang=libro=ng   ito]   ko   binili   para   kay=Pedro
           Nom=book=Lnk   this   1SgGen   bought   for   Loc=Pedro
           'This book, was bought for Pedro by me.'

    c. *[ng=nanay]   siya   pinalo
           Gen=mother   3SgNom   spanked
           'By mother, he was spanked.'

    d. [para kay=Pedro]   ko   binili   ang=libro=ng   ito
           for   Loc=Pedro   1SgGen   bought   Nom=book=Lnk   this
           'For Pedro, this book was bought by me.'

    e. [sa=pamamagitan   ng=sandok]   siya   kumuha   ng=sabaw
           Loc=use   Gen=ladle   3SgNom   take   Gen=soup
           'With this ladle, I took some soup.'

    f. *[ng=papel   na   iyon]   niya   binalutan   ang=libro
           Gen=paper   Lnk   that   3SgGen   wrapped   Nom=book
           'With that paper, the book was wrapped by her.'

A prototypical adjunct, such as a 'because' phrase, can undergo adjunct fronting (1.39a), whereas a subject (marked with nominative case) for

example, cannot (1.39b).[24] Indeed, although the agent and patient can either
be the subject (if marked nominative) or not (if marked genitive), they can
never undergo adjunct fronting (1.39c). The distinction between NPs marked
with a case such as genitive and nominative and those contained in prepositional phrases seems to correlate with the possibility of adjunct fronting. A
beneficiary dependent marked with the preposition *para*, for example, can
undergo adjunct fronting (1.39d), as can an instrumental phrase headed by
the complex preposition *sa=pamamagatin* (1.39e). A genitive-marked instru-
ment(-theme), however, cannot (1.39f). Although both the use of a preposition and the possibility of adjunct fronting appear to be plausible adjunct
criteria, the situation is complicated by the fact that recipients, which are
marked with the all-purpose locative/dative case marker *sa*, can undergo
adjunct fronting:

(1.40) [sa=akin]   nila   ibinigay   ang=premyo
        Loc=me   3PlGen   given   Nom=prize
        'To me, the prize was given by them.'

Although Tagalog may indeed draw a line between arguments and adjuncts
with this fronting construction, the line is drawn quite differently than it
would be in English, in which the recipient dependent of a verb such as *give*
would quite clearly be an argument by all criteria. Another possibility is that
genitive and nominative are the cases for NPs with a core syntactic function
(object and subject respectively), whereas *sa* and prepositions mark oblique
dependents (independently of an adjunct/argument distinction), in which
case adjunct fronting is really oblique fronting. An interesting implication
of this analysis is that the functional equivalent of the English passive construction, as illustrated by (1.39c), has the non-subject agent as a core
dependent, rather than an oblique or adjunct. This issue is considered further
in Section 2.2.1.

Returning to the question of 'demotees', it seems pretty clear that the O2 in
the double-object construction in English is an argument, since it cannot be
omitted (*I gave my mother *(some flowers)*), must accompany the verb and the
O1 in the pseudocleft construction (*What I did was give my mother some
flowers* vs. *What I did some flowers was give my mother*), cannot be preceded
by an emphatic reflexive (*Tom sent Sue* HIMSELF *the flowers* vs. *Tom sent Sue
the flowers* HIMSELF), and only occurs with a limited class of verbs designating
events of transferring (of varying degrees of abstractness) in which its referent
plays the role of thing transferred. Still, it remains unclear whether it should
be categorized as a direct object, as in some traditional analyses (see Section
1.3.2), an oblique (in effect), as in certain Transformational Grammar analyses

in which it receives an 'inherent' rather than a 'structural' case (Larson 1988, Baker 1988b), or a non-oblique of a special category, such as the 2nd object of Lexical-Functional Grammar or the chômeur of Relational Grammar.

It is clear that in many languages with similar constructions, the analogue of the O2 is overtly marked like an oblique. Halkomelem, for example, uses the generalized oblique preposition ʔə in the corresponding construction in which the recipient has the direct object function:

(1.41) ni ʔám-əs-t-əs   kʷθə sqʷəmə́yʔ ʔə kʷθə sθ'ám?
       Aux give-Recip-Tr-3 Det dog   Obl Det bone
       'He gave the dog the bone.'

However, given the complexity of the relationship between morphological categories and grammatical relations within and across languages, there is no reason to assume that ʔə in Halkomelem, for example, is a reliable indicator of an oblique syntactic function. It could be said to work for all constituents in a clause that are not in the general subject/object category. Indeed, Gerdts (1988a) shows that although this kind of constituent generally behaves like an oblique with respect to syntactic phenomena, it is distinguished from other obliques in that its verb appears with a distinct nominalizing prefix when it is fronted in a question or focus construction. She suggests an analysis according to which it may either be a chômeur or an indirect object. The indirect object analysis is made possible by the fact that dependents with a generalized recipient semantic role necessarily bear one of the two primary grammatical relations, as in (1.41).

Whether the 'demoted' agent of a passive clause in English is an oblique argument, an adjunct, or a member of some special category such as chômeur is also a difficult question. Like an argument, it expresses what is clearly a semantic role of the verb it goes with. The omissibility criterion fails to establish such *by* phrases as arguments, however, since they are generally omissible. The pseudocleft test turns out not to be illuminating since VP pseudoclefting doesn't work well with passive clauses at all (**What the car was was sold by Max*/**What the car was by Max was sold*).[25] An emphatic reflexive seems only marginally possible preceding a passive *by* phrase (?*Max was sold a car* HIMSELF *by Tom*). However, this may simply be due to the marginality of a postverbal emphatic reflexive with a patient subject (?*Max was sold a car* HIMSELF). Again, it is unclear whether the choice between possible classifications can be established on solid empirical grounds. From a cross-linguistic perspective, the question is even more complex, since (as discussed in Section 2.2.1) languages mark the grammatical relation of passive agents in a variety of ways and they behave syntactically like subject arguments to varying degrees. Even in English, the passive agent behaves like an agent subject in that it can control a rationale clause (e.g. Roeper 1987, Roberts 1987: ch. 3). That is to say, just as the interpretation of the implicit subject of the bracketed rationale clause is controlled by the subject agent in (1.42a), it is controlled by the passive agent, whether this is overtly expressed or not, in (1.42b).

(1.42) a. *The owner* torched this house [Ø to collect on the insurance].
     b. This house was torched (by *the owner*) [Ø to collect on the insurance].

1.3.4 *Semantic roles*

As should be clear even from the few contrasting analyses of basic linguistic phenomena considered above, theories vary even more dramatically in their labelling and conceptions of semantic roles than in their treatment of syntactic functions. At one extreme of the spectrum of approaches, semantic roles are verb-specific and play no role in the grammar other than to relate the syntactic function of NPs to the correct semantic interpretation of a sentence relative to individual verbs, as in Head-Driven Phrase Structure Grammar (Pollard and Sag 1994). That is to say, in this theory the verb *love* has a 'lover' semantic role, a 'lovee' semantic role, and a lexical valence specifying that the lover role is that of an NP with the subject function; the verb *hate* has a 'hater' semantic role, a 'hatee' semantic role, and a lexical valence specifying that the hater role is that of an NP with the subject function; and so forth.

At the other extreme of the spectrum is Dowty's (1991) theory of semantic roles, according to which only two (generalized) roles are recognized: proto-agent and proto-patient. Two roles suffice because they only function to determine which dependent of a transitive verb is the subject and which is the object. No other function is attributed to semantic roles as such. Each of these two generalized roles is characterized by a list of several properties, such as volitional involvement in the event, sentience, independent existence, etc. for the proto-agent. A dependent of a verb can be more or less agent-like and more or less patient-like, according to which properties it has from each set. Among two dependents, the one with the most proto-agent properties is realized as the subject.

How semantic roles are defined also varies widely across theories. Dowty's approach in terms of semantic entailments stands somewhere in between theories such as Lexicase Grammar or Fillmore's (1968) Case Grammar, in which semantic roles are primitive elements that are only roughly characterized with prose definitions, and theories for which terms such as *agent* and *patient* are merely mnemonic labels for elements in a grammar of verb meanings, or a lexical-conceptual semantics, as in Localist Case Grammar

(Anderson 1971, Delancey 1991). The key idea of the so-called localist approach to semantic roles, which can be traced back to Gruber (1965) and is refined and developed in various ways in much subsequent work (especially Talmy 2000), is that the most basic types of events and states involve location and/or motion and all other types of events and states are metaphorical extensions of these. For Delancey the grammar of the semantics of states and events, in terms of which the core semantic roles of agent, theme, and location are defined, is characterized as follows:[26]

(1.43) a. theme AT location   (*state*)
   b. theme GO-TO location   (*change of state event*)
   c. agent CAUSE theme GO-TO location   (*caused change of state event*)

Death has the role of location in *They put the murderer to death*, just as *the mall* does in *I drove my brother to the mall*, by virtue of the very general metaphorical conception of states as locations, manifested not only in the routine use of locative prepositions for both states and locations, as in *I'm in shock* vs. *I'm in my room*, but also in such expressions as *fall asleep* and *go crazy*. The conceptual schema in (1.43c) is equally applicable to cognitive, emotional, and perceptual processes. For example, the verb *bug*, as in *The music is bugging me*, designates an event in which the subject (agent) is conceived of as causing the direct object (theme) to 'go' to an emotional state of displeasure. By general rule, if the agent is expressed it is encoded as subject and the theme is encoded as direct object. As in Lexicase Grammar (see Section 1.3.1), the construal of events is what dictates the roles of the participants designated by NPs. Thus, even though one might say that *the wagon* is the location in both (1.44a) and (1.44b), since both sentences describe events that from an objective perspective only have hay doing any moving, the generalization that themes are encoded as direct objects remains valid because (1.44b) encodes a construal of the event in which the wagon (metaphorically) moves into the state of being filled.

(1.44) a. They loaded hay onto the wagon.
   b. They loaded the wagon (with hay).

In (1.44b) *with hay* is analysed as an adjunct phrase (see Section 1.3.3) that expresses only a peripheral aspect of the event, rather than one of the core roles.

   Different approaches to lexical semantic structure and different degrees of commitment to an elaborated theory of verb meaning result in considerable theoretical variation in terms of number and kind of semantic roles and terminological conventions. Generally, roles such as agent and patient (or theme) are recognized in addition to at least several others (experiencer, goal, source, instrument, beneficiary, etc.). It is generally taken to be obvious that there is some kind of default or natural direct object semantic role. In Fillmore (1968) this role was labelled 'objective' and defined as the role assigned to an NP that does not have one of the other roles. The label is indicative of the preferred alignment of this role with direct object/accusative case. However, since roles for Fillmore remain constant across paraphrases and, more generally, across the alternative syntactic frames that a verb can appear in, *the ball* has the objective role in *He rolled the ball down the hill, The ball was rolled down the hill by him,* and *The ball rolled down the hill.*

Although what is meant by the term *patient* varies considerably, it is often used in effect as a synonym of *objective,* as in various analyses discussed above. Although the term *goal* is used most often for some kind of locative role (e.g. that which something moves to, perhaps encompassing the recipient role), it is sometimes also used with essentially the same meaning as *patient* or *objective* (e.g. Dik 1997), presumably owing to a conception of the role as the 'target' of the agent's action, for which reason *target* is also sometimes used (e.g. Dixon 1994). Probably the most popular term for this role, however, is *theme.* Transformational grammarians, in particular, have generally been drawn to the terminological conventions introduced in Gruber (1965) and refined and developed in various ways in the work of Jackendoff (1972, 1987, 1990). However, since the underlying theories of lexical-conceptual semantics that explicate and justify the terminology are not a standard component of Transformational Grammar, there is little terminological uniformity.

Jackendoff (1987, 1990) proposes a grammar of conceptual semantics in which roles of theme and patient are differentiated and can sometimes be associated with different NPs in a clause, although they generally go together. The basic idea is that there are two main aspects of the meaning of a verb that can be separated. One aspect encodes an elaborate version of the kind of localist grammar of events and states expressed in (1.43); the other encodes information about the main action, that is who or what is conceived of as acting and who or what is acted on. Avoiding Jackendoff's complex notational system, Delancey's simpler system can be augmented as follows to show the key idea, for one kind of caused-motion schema.

(1.45)   actor^x ACT-ON patient^y
        agent^x CAUSE theme^y GO-TO goal
        caused change of location event, with patient = theme

In a sentence such as *They loaded hay onto the wagon,* for which (1.45) is an appropriate conceptual structure, *hay* would be both the patient, by virtue of being the principal target of the action, and the theme, by virtue of being the moving entity in the event. In the case of *They loaded the wagon with hay, the wagon* still has the role of goal; but it also has the role of patient, as *load* has an alternative conceptual structure that differs from (1.45) in that *goal* and *patient*, rather than *theme* and *patient*, are co-indexed. The generalization about the relationship between semantic roles and syntactic functions is that the patient of a verb in the active voice is realized as the direct object.

Owing in part to an influential principle known as the Theta Criterion (Chomsky 1981), which says in effect that each NP bears one and only one semantic role (or 'theta-role'), and in part to the minimal burden of semantic roles in the theory, practitioners of Transformational Grammar generally don't embrace Jackendoff's semantic distinction between patient and theme, however much sense it may make. They operate with a small set of semantic roles, which are often not explicitly defined, and use the term *theme* (or *patient* or *theme/patient*) in much the same way that Fillmore uses *objective* or Delancey uses *theme*. Chomsky makes little attempt in his own work to explicate semantic role terms or to articulate or endorse a grammar of verb meaning to which semantic roles might be related. Textbook introductions to the theory generally just give lists of semantic roles of varying length with prose definitions, the content of which varies somewhat from author to author. Radford (1997: 326), for example, defines *theme/patient* as the role of an 'entity undergoing the effect of some action', thus designating something more like Jackendoff's patient role, while leaving the definition vague enough as to cover his theme role as well—reflective of common practice.

The same kind of terminological and definitional issues arise with most other semantic roles. However, the main differences between theories of grammar that make use of semantic roles have to do with whether or not they are precisely characterized in terms of an overall theory of verb meaning and whether or not they are considered to have a direct impact on grammatical phenomena. In theories with a well-articulated characterization of verb meanings, semantic roles are more likely to be used, at least to some extent, in place of syntactic functions. Theories that place most of the explanatory burden for grammatical phenomena on primitive syntactic functions or positions in phrase structure are more likely to work with an undefined or imprecise list of semantic roles.

In this book, the terminological conventions of theories or analyses under consideration are used and explicated as necessary. For general descriptive purposes where precision is not critical, the terms *agent* and *patient* are used to designate generalized semantic roles, more or less in the sense of Dowty's *proto-agent* and *proto-patient* or Delancey's *agent* and *theme*.

1.4 Theories of grammar

A main goal of this book is to provide an overview of the treatments of grammatical relations in different modern theories of grammar and to bring out similarities and differences and strengths and weaknesses by showing how they have dealt with or might deal with a range of the interesting and challenging phenomena involving grammatical relations in different languages. Although numerous theories are commented on along the way, the focus is necessarily limited to a subset of the available theories. The theories chosen for consideration reflect primarily a concern for covering a wide spectrum of approaches with representative examples of the main types of theories. Each theory has been sufficiently articulated as to have a clear stance on the typological issues concerning grammatical relations and has had sufficient appeal to theoreticians and descriptive linguists as to have yielded analyses of a broad range of the phenomena across the languages of the world that bear on the key matters surrounding grammatical relations.

Role and Reference Grammar (Foley and Van Valin 1984, Van Valin and La Polla 1997) broadly represents what has come to be known as the FUNCTIONAL approach to grammatical analysis, which is characterized by a concern for meaning and the functions that language performs and how these influence and are manifested in grammatical organization. It defines grammatical relations primarily in terms of a theory of verb meanings, that is a conceptual semantics of verbs. Semantic roles are therefore brought front and centre in its characterizations of grammatical phenomena. Although it can define dependent categories corresponding more or less to the primary traditional syntactic functions (subject and object), these are not primitive notions of the theory and are not held to play a role in all languages. An in-depth look at Role and Reference Grammar and how it analyses grammatical-relation phenomena in different kinds of languages is supplemented by shorter overviews of two other theories with a functional orientation: Functional Grammar (Dik 1978, 1980, 1997), which articulates a semantic-role based account of grammatical-relation phenomena in a somewhat different way than Role and Reference Grammar, and Cognitive Grammar (Langacker 1991, 1999), which subsumes grammatical structure in an all-encompassing theory of conceptual structure, yielding a cognitive characterization of syntactic functions and, therefore, no significant distinction between syntactic functions and semantic roles.

The other theories to be examined are probably best portrayed as falling somewhere on the other side of a presumed divide between the functional approach to grammar and the FORMAL approach, which emphasizes the role of linguistic form and syntactic structure in the organization of language and makes minimal appeal to meaning and the functions of language as a source of explanation for grammatical phenomena. Although these theories take varying approaches to the labelling, identification, and definition of semantic roles, none includes as an integral component a fully articulated conceptual semantics of verbs. They focus, instead, on syntactic functions (in some form), which are seen as playing a central role in the analysis of sentence structure in all languages. How these syntactic functions are characterized constitutes the key difference. In Transformational Grammar (Chomsky 1965, 1981, 1995) the constituents of a sentence are portrayed as being systematically arranged in a hierarchical structure expressible as a tree, which encodes lexical class membership (noun, verb, adjective, etc.), constituency (i.e. information about which words are parts of which phrases), and linear precedence. Syntactic functions are defined, in complex ways, in terms of specific positions in trees or relationships with certain positions in trees. NPs can change their positions in trees (or undergo transformations), which can give rise to changes in syntactic function. Relational Grammar (Perlmutter 1983, Perlmutter and Rosen 1984, Blake 1990) rejects the tree formalism for sentence structure, in favour of a representation that basically only calls attention to constituency and grammatical relations. However, the Transformational Grammar idea that NPs can bear more than one syntactic function (albeit due to 'promotion' or 'demotion' rather than 'movement') is an important component of the theory. Relational Grammar makes the most elaborate attempt of any theory to account for grammatical phenomena and linguistic typology primarily in terms of the traditional notions of subject, object, and indirect object. The chapter on Relational Grammar is supplemented by a shorter overview of Lexical-Functional Grammar (Bresnan 1982a, 2000, Falk 2001), which is the other main theory in which syntactic functions such as subject and object are conceived of as primitive, central, and universal elements in the grammatical organization of languages.

2

Grammatical relations across languages

There are essentially three broad classes of fact about languages for which a theory of grammatical relations needs to be responsible. First, it appears that, at least in terms of their head-marking and dependent-marking systems for indicating grammatical relations, most languages draw a fundamental distinction between two basic roles, corresponding roughly to a category with agent as prototype and a category with patient as prototype. However, the different ways in which these categories are defined constitute one of the main syntactic typologies of languages. Secondly, in addition to active vs. passive voice alternations (see Section 1.2) and alternations between an object + oblique construction and a corresponding double-object construction (see Section 1.3.2), there are various kinds of 'relation-changing' and voice constructions in languages that have important implications for an understanding of grammatical-relation systems. Thirdly, languages frequently have verb classes or constructions for which the dependents manifest some but not all of the properties of canonical subjects or objects (as, for example, with the dative-subject construction in Icelandic discussed in Section 1.2).

2.1 Grammatical relations and major typological parameters

For typological purposes, it has become customary to recognize three main kinds of syntactic functions, in terms of a distinction between transitive and intransitive clauses. In a transitive clause in English, for example, there is a more or less agent-like subject and a more or less patient-like direct object, as in *The boy touched the branches*. In an intransitive clause there is a subject and either no non-subject dependent of the verb (*The boy slept*) or an oblique (or at least a non-direct object) dependent of the verb (*The boy ran to the store*). Given this distinction, the three categories are subject of a transitive clause, or A (for agent-like dependent), subject of an intransitive clause, or S, and direct object, or O (for object; sometimes labelled P for patient-like dependent). In terms of their head-marking and dependent-marking systems for indicating grammatical relations, rarely do languages either systematically distinguish all three of these categories or distinguish none.[1] Rather, these three categories are generally made to fit into a two-category marking system.

As should be clear from the discussion in Chapter 1 of basic grammatical-relation distinctions in English, Latin, Brazilian Portuguese, and Sanskrit, these languages treat the O category (direct object or accusative) as one and collapse A and S into the other main category (subject or nominative). Languages of this type are generally known as ACCUSATIVE languages. ERGATIVE languages (Dixon 1979, 1994), exemplified by Mayan languages, indigenous Australian languages of the Pama-Nyungan group, Eskimo-Aleut languages, Caucasian languages, and Basque, among others, treat the A category (commonly labelled 'ergative') as one and collapse the S and O categories into the other main category (commonly labelled 'absolutive'). In SPLIT-INTRANSITIVE or ACTIVE languages (Sapir 1917, Merlan 1985, Van Valin 1990, Mithun 1991), which include primarily certain indigenous languages of the Americas but also such languages as Acehnese (Durie 1985, 1988) and Georgian (Harris 1982, 1990), A and O are the prototypes of the two main categories, with the sole main dependent of intransitive verbs either belonging to the A category or the O category, depending on how A-like or O-like it is on semantic grounds which vary somewhat from language to language. Split-intransitive languages are in some sense a compromise between the accusative and ergative choices. Indeed, they can be portrayed as either basically accusative languages with the wrinkle that some Ss are marked like members of the direct object category or as basically ergative languages with the wrinkle that some Ss are marked like members of the ergative category.

In short, the types of languages whose primary grammatical-relation marking mechanisms identify two main grammatical relations are as shown in Figure 2.1. Of course, this typology can be extended to account for variations among languages concerning a third primary relation, or indirect object (see Section 1.3.2), by adding presence or absence of an IO category as an independent parameter for each language type. Brazilian Portuguese, for example, is an accusative language in which the indirect object category plays a role, hence its primary grammatical relations are S/A, O, and IO. Languages such as Kamaiurá, in which the class of NPs marked with a 'dative' adposition behave systematically like other obliques, could be said to simply lack the IO category. Similarly, languages can vary with respect to the constitution of the O category, independently of whether they have indirect objects or not and independently of questions of ergativity. In a PRIMARY-OBJECT LANGUAGE (Dryer 1986), illustrated by Halkomelem, as discussed in Section 2.2.4, recipient and

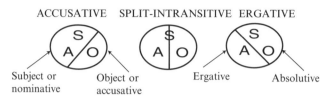

FIGURE 2.1. Types of languages with two main grammatical relations

beneficiary dependents are included in the O category, whereas in either an IO language such as Brazilian Portuguese or a non-IO language such as Kamaiurá they are necessarily excluded.

2.1.1 *Accusative languages*

Accusative languages are by far the most common (Dixon 1994: ch. 1). Moreover, languages of the ergative and split-intransitive types often show significant accusative tendencies of various kinds. Like most Indo-European languages, Brazilian Portuguese (see Section 1.3.2) manifests many of the key properties of accusative languages. The head-marking morphology identifies an A vs. O distinction. As shown by the following examples, a proclitic pronominal morpheme is used only for the O of a transitive clause, whereas a verbal agreement suffix indexes the A or the S, that is the subject.

(2.1) a. Eles   o   mudaram.
          3MascPl   3MascSgO   change.Pst3PlSubj
          'They changed it/him.'
      b. Ele   os   mudou.
          3MascSg   3MascPlO   change.Pst3SgSubj
          'He changed them.'
      c. Eles   caíram   /   gritaram
          3MascPl   fall.Pst3PlSubj   shout.Pst3PlSubj
          'They fell/shouted.'

An accusative classification of the language is justified by the fact that the main dependent of every type of intransitive clause is indicated by the indexing system in the same way as the A of a transitive clause. Moreover, to the extent that syntactic phenomena distinguish among the A, S, and O dependents of verbs, the lines are usually drawn in terms of an S/A vs. O distinction. For example, there is a constraint on the controller of the reflexive/reciprocal *se* construction, illustrated by the following examples.

(2.2) a. Eles   se   amam.   (*A controller; O pivot*)
          3MascPl   3Refl/Rec   love.Pres3Pl
          'They love each other/themselves.'

     b. Eles   nunca mais   se   falaram.   (*S controller; IO pivot*)
          3MascPl   never   more   3Rec   speak.Pst3Pl
          'They never again spoke to each other.'

     c. Ele   não   se   mostrou   aos   hóspedes.
          3MascPl   Neg   3Refl   show.Pst3Sg   to.the   guests
          'He didn't show himself to the guests.'   (*A controller; O pivot*)
          *'He didn't show the guests each other.'   (**IO controller; O pivo*t)

As noted in Section 1.3.2, the pivot of this construction, that is the omitted
dependent whose interpretation is keyed to another dependent, must be the
direct or indirect object. In (2.2a), the pivot is the O, which is not expressed
other than by the presence of the reflexive/reciprocal clitic *se*. Its interpretation is controlled by the A of the sentence.[2] Example (2.2b) shows that the
controller can also be an S (the clause is intransitive because the addressee
functions as IO). Example (2.2c) shows that an indirect object, for example,
cannot be the controller. The generalization is that the controller must be a
member of the S/A category.

Another phenomenon whose understanding depends on the same
grammatical-relation category is what is generally known as control of
infinitival complements. There is a class of verbs with prototype *querer*
'want' that can have a clausal complement, as illustrated by (2.3a). If it
designates the same participant as the subject of *querer*, the subject of the
embedded verb, which is necessarily in infinitival form, is not expressed, as in
(2.3b).

(2.3) a. Quero   [que ele   compre   um   carro].
          want.Pres1Sg   that 3MascSg   buy.PressSjunct3SgSubj   a   car
          'I want him to buy a car.'

     b. Quero   [Ø comprar um carro].   (*controllee = A of embedded V*)
          want.Pres1Sg   buy.Inf   a   car
          'I want to buy a car.'

The constraint of interest in this context has to do with which dependent of
the embedded verb can be the controllee, that is the missing element. Example
(2.3b) shows that it can be the A of the embedded verb. It can also be an S, but
not an O (or any other non-subject):

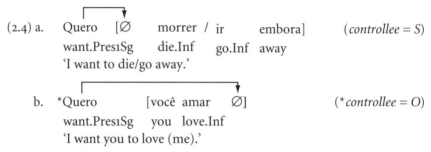

(2.4) a.   Quero   [Ø   morrer / ir   embora]   (*controllee* = S)
           want.Pres1Sg   die.Inf   go.Inf away
           'I want to die/go away.'

      b.   *Quero   [você amar   Ø]   (**controllee* = O)
           want.Pres1Sg   you love.Inf
           'I want you to love (me).'

The generalization is that the controllee must be the S/A dependent of the embedded verb.

It is important to bear in mind that languages are often not all or nothing with respect to the typology in Figure 2.1. Some grammatical phenomena in a language of one type may work in a way expected for another type. Although the overall orientation of Brazilian Portuguese is that of an accusative language, there are some grammatical phenomena that suggest a split-intransitive orientation. For example, the main constraints on constituent order are sensitive to different classes of intransitive verbs. In general, and ignoring constructions with emphatic focus in particular, subjects (S/A) must precede the verb, whereas other dependents follow the verb, with a strong preference for direct object first, as illustrated by the following examples.

(2.5) a.   O vizinho comprou um carro para mim.   (*A V O oblique*)
           'The neighbour bought a car for me.'
      b.   *Comprou o vizinho um carro para mim.   (**V A O oblique*)
           'Bought the neighbour a car for me.'
      c.   O vizinho foi para o supermercado.   (*S V oblique*)
           'The neighbour went to the supermarket.'
      d.   *Foi o vizinho para o supermercado.   (**V S oblique*)
           'Went the neighbour to the supermarket.'
      e.   O vizinho não trabalha.   (*S V*)
           'The neighbour doesn't work.'
      f.   *Não trabalha o vizinho.   (**V S*)
           'Doesn't work the neighbour.'

The problem is that the S/A category is not monolithic with respect to constituent order. The postverbal position is often preferred for an S that is conceived of primarily as a participant—particularly an inanimate one—that undergoes a change of state or location and, thus, is O-like:[3]

(2.6)a.   De repente aparece o vizinho na porta.   (*V S oblique*)
           'Suddenly shows up the neighbour at the door.'

   b.   Acabou o fósforo.   (*V S*)
       'Ran out the matches.'
   c.   Não saiu a mancha.   (*V S*)
       'Didn't come out the stain.'

The postverbal position is restricted to a category of verb dependents that includes all Os and a certain kind of S, whereas the preverbal position is required for a category of dependents that includes all As and other kinds of Ss.

At least with respect to basic constituent order, Brazilian Portuguese appears to take a split-intransitive rather than a strictly accusative approach to grammatical relations. This is not uncommon for accusative languages, as various kinds of phenomena implying a split-intransitive organization occur in such otherwise accusative languages as Japanese (Kishimoto 1996), French (Legendre 1989*b*), and Italian (Perlmutter 1989, Van Valin 1990), among others. The broad implication is that which combinations of the A, S, and O categories a language uses in its overall grammar is not necessarily determined by which combinations define its main system for marking grammatical relations morphologically (with case and agreement).

2.1.2 *Ergative languages*

In Ergative languages one or more of the main grammatical-relation marking mechanisms works in terms of two categories that are defined differently than in the accusative scenario. The O and S categories are collapsed into one, for which the case-marking category is generally called 'absolutive.'[4] The other category (ergative) is restricted to the A dependent. Unlike with most accusative languages, the A vs. S/O distinction is sometimes only used in the head-marking or dependent-marking morphological system (or both) and does not figure in the grammar otherwise. Such languages are said to be morphologically ergative. Even syntactically ergative languages will also often have mixtures of accusative-type marking, using the ergative system for dependent marking, for example, and the accusative system for head marking, or showing ergative marking in the past tense or main clauses and accusative marking in non-past tenses or subordinate clauses. This phenomenon is generally known as split ergativity.

Basque is an example of a morphologically ergative language whose overall syntactic organization appears not to be ergative (Ortiz de Urbina 1989). The following examples show that the head-marking morphology on the tense auxiliary agrees with both the A and the O in transitive clauses and with the S in intransitive clauses and that the dependent-marking morphology treats O and S in the same way and A differently—with the ergative suffix -*k*.

(2.7) a. zu-k   hura   hil   zenuen
          2Sg-Erg   3Sg.Abs   die/kill   2SgA3SgOAux
          'You killed him.'

     b. zu   hil   zen
          2Sg.Abs   die/kill   2SgSAux
          'You died.'

Outside of the morphology, neither the absolutive nor the ergative grammatical relations appear to play a role in syntactic phenomena. Conjunction reduction is the phenomenon whereby one of two co-referential NPs is omitted in one of the conjuncts of two or more conjoined clasues (e.g. *[[Susie$_i$ went to the store] and [Ø$_i$ bought something]]*). In Basque, the S/A category is what matters, as in accusative languages such as English:

(2.8) [Ø seme-a   eskolan   utzi]   eta   [klasera   joan   zen]
      A son-Abs   at.school leave   and   to.class   go   3SgSAux
      'X left his/her son at school and X went to class.'

That is to say, the interpretation of the omitted A of the first clause is controlled by the agreement-identified S of the second clause. The omitted NP (or pivot) in such a conjunction-reduction construction would be in the S/O category in a syntactically ergative language. Other languages reputed to be strictly or mainly morphologically ergative include Warlpiri (Bittner and Hale 1996*b*), Khinalug (Comrie 1978), Abkhazian (Anderson 1976), and Walmatjari (Dixon 1979), among many others.

   The Australian language Dyirbal (Dixon 1972, Dixon 1994) is probably the best known example of a syntactically ergative language. As the following examples show, the case-marking system on full NPs draws a distinction between A (ergative *-ŋgu* suffix) and S/O (absolutive, with no suffix). (Here and below, Dyirbal examples are from Dixon 1994: ch. 6).

(2.9) a. ŋuma   miyanda-nʸu   (*Absolutive S*)
          father.Abs laugh-Nonfut
          'Father laughed.'

     b. ŋuma   yabu-ŋgu   bura-n   (*Absolutive O; Ergative A*)
          father.Abs mother-Erg   see-Nonfut
          'Mother saw father'.

Although this A vs. S/O dependent-marking system works for all intransitive verbs and across all tenses and in both main and subordinate clauses, Dyirbal does show a split for the distinction between pronominal and full NPs, the former being marked on an accusative basis:

(2.10) a. ŋana   miyanda-nʸu   (*Nominative S*)
           we all.Nom   laugh-Nonfut
           'We all laughed.'

   b. ŋana   nʸurra-na   bura-n   (*Accusative O; Nominative A*)
       we all.Nom   you all-Acc   see-Nonfut
       'We saw you all.'

   c. nʸurra   ŋana-na   bura-n   (*Accusative O; Nominative A*)
       you all.Nom   we all-Acc   see-Nonfut
       'You all saw us.'

Now, in spite of this morphological ergative/accusative split, the syntax of Dyirbal is fundamentally ergative. This can be seen, for example, in conjunction reduction. As the following example shows the interpretation of the omitted NP in the second conjunct is controlled by the O of the first clause and not the A.

(2.11) [ŋuma   yabu-ŋgu   bura-n]   [∅ banaga-nʸu]
        father.Abs mother-Erg see-Nonfut   S return-Nonfut
        'Mother saw father and he/*she returned.'

The S/O (absolute) category is operative in a similar way in control of purposive clauses. In the purposive control construction, a suffix (*-ygu* or *-li*) is added to the verb of a subordinate clause and a dependent of the subordinate verb is omitted and interpreted as being the same as (or is controlled by) the S/O of the main clause:

(2.12) a. ŋuma   banaga-nʸu   [∅ yabu-ŋgu   bura-li]
           father.Abs return-Nonfut   O mother-Erg see-Purp
           'Father returned in order for mother to see him.'

   b. yabu   ŋuma-ŋgu giga-n   [∅ gubi-ŋgu   mawa-li]
       mother.Abs father-Erg tell-Nonfut O doctor-Erg examine-Purp
       'Father told mother to be examined by the doctor.'

   c. yabu   ŋuma-ŋgu giga-n   [∅ banaga-ygu]
       mother.Abs father-Erg tell-Nonfut   S return-Purp
       'Father told mother to return.'

The controller can be either an O, as in (2.12b–c) or an S, as in (2.12a); but cannot be an A. At least with these main clause verbs, the same situation would obtain in English. What is significantly different about Dyirbal is that the pivot or controllee must also be an S or O and cannot be an A. The absolutive category also plays a crucial role in relative clause formation, as the relativized position is restricted to S/O. Other languages with both morphological and robust syntactic ergativity include Hurrian (Anderson 1976), Inuit (Bittner and Hale 1996b), Sama (Foley and Van Valin 1984).

Many languages have a complex blend of ergative and non-ergative properties, both morphologically and syntactically, as in the case of Chukchee (Comrie 1978), Tzotzil (Aissen 1987), Tongan (Dixon 1994), and various Salish languages, as documented in some detail for Coast Tsimshian (Mulder 1994), Coeur d'Alene (Doak 1998), and Halkomelem (Gerdts 1988a), for example. As for dependent marking, Halkomelem only indicates A/S/O vs. oblique (or non-core), as noted in Section 1.3.3. The preposition ʔə is used for obliques; other NP dependents of verbs are unmarked. The head-marking morphology is much more complex. In essence, 1st and 2nd person S/A pronominals are realized in preverbal position, whereas (nonemphatic) 3rd person A and 1st and 2nd person O pronominals are realized as verbal suffixes and 3rd person S/O pronominals are not overtly expressed, as shown by the following examples.[5]

(2.13) a. ni   ʔiməš   (*3rd person S = Ø*)
           Aux   walk
           'He/she/it walked.'

       b. ni   cən   ʔiməš   (*1st person S = S/A pronoun*)
           Aux   1Subj walk
           'I walked.'

       c. ni   cən   qʼʷáqʷ-ət   (*1st person A = S/A pronoun;*
           Aux   1Subj club-Tr   *3rd person O = Ø*)
           'I clubbed him/her/it.'

       d. ni   qʼʷáqʷ-ət-əs   (*3rd person A = ergative suffix;*
           Aux   club-Tr-3A   *3rd person O = Ø*)
           'He/she clubbed him/her/it.'

       e. ni   qʼʷáqʷ-əθ-ám?š-əs   (*3rd person A = ergative suffix;*
           Aux   club-Tr-1O-3A   *1st person O = O suffix*)
           'He/she clubbed me.'

The system is accusative with respect to 1st and 2nd person, as evidenced by the use of preverbal *cən* 'I' for both S (2.13b) and A (2.13c) as opposed to a verbal suffix for O (2.13e). Ergativity comes into play only for 3rd person, which is Ø for both S (2.13a) and O (2.13c–d) but a verbal suffix (-*əs*) only for A (2.13d–e). The system is split-ergative not only in terms of person but also in that even the 3rd person category works on an accusative basis in subordinate clauses.

Certain syntactic phenomena are only sensitive to the A/S/O vs. oblique distinction. For example, clefting, question, and relative clause constructions use a simple fronting strategy if the pivot is any kind of A/S/O dependent. When the pivot in these constructions is an oblique, on the other hand, the verb of its clause must be nominalized. There are also phenomena that suggest a split-intransitive orientation, such as a constraint (essentially) limiting synthetic causativization to intransitive verbs whose subject is in control of the action designated by the verb. The pivot in the raising-to-object construction, on the other hand, is restricted essentially to the S/A category, including the 'logical A' in the passive construction but excluding O (see Section 2.2.1). Among the phenomena suggesting syntactic ergativitiy are quantifier float and possessor extraction. In the quantifier float construction, instead of being expressed within the NP that it modifies, the quantifier 'all' can be placed in clause-initial position as illustrated by the following examples.

(2.14) a. ni   x̌ʷelenčénəm   mə́kʼʷ   kʷθə   sƛ̓əlʔíqəɬ
        Aux   run.Pl   all   Det   children
        'All the children ran.'

     b. mə́kʼʷ   niw   x̌ʷelenčénəm   kʷθə   sƛ̓əlʔíqəɬ
        all   Aux.Lnk   run.Pl   Det   children
        'The children all ran.'

In (2.14b) the quantifier is fronted or 'floated' from an S. If a quantifier is floated in a transitive clause it can be associated with the O but not the A, as shown by (2.15). Thus, the generalization is that only an absolutive NP can be associated with a floated quantifier.

(2.15) mə́kʼʷ   niw   qʼʷál-ət-əs   tθə   sƛ̓əlʔíqəɬ   kʷθə   səplíl
        all   Aux.Lnk   bake-Tr-3A   Det   children   Det   bread
        'The children baked all the bread/*All the children baked the bread.'

Possessor extraction in the form of clefting, which puts a dependent in contrastive focus, is shown for the possessor of an S dependent in (2.16a). Although it is possible to cleft the possessor of an O, as well (2.16b), it is not possible to cleft the A of a transitive clause (2.16c). The constraint is, therefore, that only the possessor of an absolutive dependent can be clefted (or, more generally, fronted in an extraction construction).

(2.16) a. ʔə́ːnʔθə   ni   qʼáy   kʷθə   nə-sqʷəmə́yʔ
            1Emph   Aux   die   Det   1Pos-dog
            'It was me whose dog died.'

   b. nə́wə   ni   ʔáː-t-ʔéːnʔ   θə   ən-stáʔləs
       2Emph   Aux   call-Tr-1SgSubj   Det   2Pos-spouse
       'It was you whose wife I called.'

   c. *nə́wə   ni   ʔáː-θ-ámʔš-əs   θə   ən-stáʔləs
       2Emph   Aux   call-Tr-1O-3A   Det   2Pos-spouse
       'It was you whose wife called me.'

The key facts about ergativity that any theory of grammatical relations needs to be able to account for are the following.

- One or more of the main morphological grammatical-relation marking devices in a language can work in terms of a distinction between A and S/O categories, that is on an ergative basis.
- Languages with ergative morphological marking devices generally have at least some morphological marking devices that work on an accusative (or non-ergative) basis and may or may not have any syntactic phenomena whose constraints operate on an ergative basis.
- In syntactically ergative languages the most prominent grammatical relation is generally absolutive, that is the S/O category.

2.1.3 *Split-intransitive languages*

In split-intransitive languages the S, A, and O categories are collapsed, at least for one or more of the main grammatical-relation marking phenomena, into two primary categories: A with some A-like Ss (henceforth S_a) and O with some O-like Ss (henceforth S_o). As with languages generally classified as being ergative, split-intransitive languages tend to vary quite a bit in terms of how pervasive their defining two-category system is in the grammar. In some languages head marking and/or dependent marking operates on a split-intransitive basis, although other grammatical phenomena are by and large insensitive to the A/S_a vs. O/S_o distinction. In other languages, the A/S_a vs. O/S_o distinction is the only one that matters, not only for the head and dependent marking but also for other grammatical phenomena that depend on distinctions among A, S, and O dependents.

Kamaiurá (Seki 2000), discusssed in Section 1.3.2, has a split-intransitive system that appears to be limited to the marking of grammatical relations on verbs. Two main grammatical relations are indicated by head-marking (agreement) morphology realized on the verb, as well as by a preferred preverbal ordering and no postposition marking.[6] If a clause has both A and O constituents, the preferred order is A O V (oblique). If a clause has an S constituent, the preferred order is S V (oblique). Thus, in terms of constituent order, there is an A vs. O distinction; but there is no way of knowing whether S is considered to be in the A category (as in an accusative language) or the O category (as in ergative languages). The verb morphology, however, draws the grammatical-relation lines in a split-intransitive way. In transitive clauses, prefixes or clitics on the verb generally index either the A or O, the choice being contingent first on which is higher on a person hierarchy (1st > 2nd > 3rd) and, otherwise, on which is higher on a grammatical-relation hierarchy (A > O).[7] Thus, in (2.17a) the *o*-prefix indicates that the A is 3rd person, whereas in (2.17b) the *je* clitic indicates that the O is 1st person singular. If the A is 1st person, the prefix *a*- appears on the verb instead of *je* as shown by (2.17c).

(2.17) a. ywyrapara o-me'eŋ kara'iwa upe
           bow   3-give   foreigner to
           'He gave the bow to the foreigner.'
       b. kunu'uma   je=retsak
           child   1Sg=see
           'The child saw me.'
       c. kunu'uma   a-retsak
           child   1Sg-see
           'I saw the child.'

The crucial fact with respect to the core grammatical-relation typology is that with some intransitive verbs the A-indexing kind of morphology (*a-* = 1st person singular, for example) is used for the S dependent, whereas with other verbs, the O-indexing kind of morphology is used (*je* = 1st person singular, for example), as shown by the following examples.

(2.18) a. a-ja'eo   (*S marked like A*)
           1Sg-cry
           'I cried.'
       b. je='amot   (*S marked like O*)
           1Sg-be homesick
           'I'm homesick.'
(2.19) a. kunu'uma   o-wawak   (*S marked like A*)
           child   3-wake up
           'The child woke up.'
       b. je=yar   i-katu   (*S marked like O*)
           1Sg=canoe 3-be good
           'My canoe is good.'

In general, the A-marking (or nonstative) verbs designate actions or events (walk, eat, sing, die, fear, speak, break, fall, roll, etc.); the O-marking (or stative) verbs designate states (long, short, tall, happy, hard, soft, old, black, etc.). Although the stative verbs correspond typically to what would be adjectives in languages like English, they behave like verbs in Kamaiurá, as they cannot occur, for example, with a copula unless they are transformed into a noun and they can occur with verbal imperative morphology and with the same nominalizing affixes that are otherwise only used with transitive and nonstative intransitive verbs.

Split-intransitive languages cross-linguistically show a similar pattern semantically, with the A-marking vs. O-marking distinction correlating generally either with a nonstative vs. stative distinction or some kind of controlled action/state vs. uncontrolled action/state distinction (Mithun 1991).[8] In the North-American Muskogean language Choctaw (Davies 1986), for example, an S determines A head marking if the action or state the verb designates is conceived of as having a participant that is in control of it, as shown in Table 2.1.[9] Unlike in Choctaw, verbs such as 'sweat' and 'break' take A marking in Kamaiurá, because stativity, rather than participant control, is criterial.

Some theoreticians (e.g. Foley and Van Valin 1984: ch. 3, Dixon 1994: ch. 4) systematically distinguish a sub-type of split-intransitive case-marking system in which intransitive verbs alternate between A marking and O marking, depending on a situational interpretation. Choctaw, for example, displays the 'fluid-S' property, insofar as at least some intransitive verbs, such as *ttola*-'fall' and *habishko*-'sneeze,' take A marking to designate intentional actions and O marking otherwise. It is unclear, however, from Davies' description how fluid Choctaw is. Although intransitive verbs are not fluid in this sense in Kamaiurá, they become fluid when nominalized for the purpose of forming relative clauses, for example. More specifically, although nominalized stative verbs show only O-indexing morphology, nominalized nonstative verbs can show either A-indexing or O-indexing morphology, depending on whether the S is interpreted as being in control or not, as in the following examples.

(2.20) a. o-je'eɲ-uma'e   (*S marked like A; nonstative verb root*)
            3-speak-Nominal.Neg
            'one who (deliberately) doesn't speak.'

       b. i-je'eɲ-uma'e   (*S marked like O; nonstative verb root*)
            3-speak-Nominal.Neg
            'one who doesn't speak.'

       c. i-pituw-uma'e   (*S marked like O; stative verb root*)
            3-lazy-Nominal.Neg
            'one who isn't lazy.'

TABLE 2.1. Choctaw A vs. O marking and intransitive verb classes

A and S$_a$ marked with -*li*	O and S$_o$ marked with *sa*-
chi-bashli-**li**-tok	is-**sa**-bashli-tok
2SgO-cut-1SgA-past	2SgA-1SgO-cut-past
'I cut you.'	'You cut me.'
hilha-**li**-tok	**sa**-hohchafoh
dance-1SgA-past	1SgO-be hungry
'I danced.'	'I'm hungry.'
A-marking intransitive Vs	*O-marking intransitive Vs*
eat	break
play	hurt
run	suffer
go	be lost
arrive	be cold
work	sweat
jump	be ashamed
walk	be tall

This kind of fluidity extends to large classes of intransitive verbs in such languages as Acehnese (Durie 1985), discussed below, and Tsova-Tush (Holisky 1987).

Looking beyond what the head-marking morphology indicates about grammatical relations, syntactic phenomena in Kamaiurá appear to be sensitive to various groupings of the A, O, and S dependents. For example, there is a phenomenon, generally known as 'possessor raising', wherein the S or O of a verb is interpreted as the possessor of the referent of a noun that is incorporated into the verb. More specifically, there are alternative ways of treating the possessor of S and O dependents. In the (a)-examples in (2.21)–(2.23) the possessor is a dependent of the NP, indicated by indexing verbal morphology on the head N itself. The (b)-examples, which illustrate the possessor-raising phenomenon, have the head N incorporated into the verb and the NP that is interpreted as its possessor functioning as the O-marked dependent of the verb, as indicated by the pronominal prefix on the verb.

(2.21) a.   ne=atua   a-perek
            2Sg=nape   1Sg-hit
            'I hit your nape.'
      b.   oro-atua-perek
            1Sg2Sg-nape-hit
            'I hit you on the nape (of the neck).' (Literally, 'I nape-hit you.')[10]

(2.22) a.   ne='ajura   n=i-huku-ite
            2Sg=neck   Neg=3-be long-Neg
            'Your neck isn't long.'

     b.   na=ne='aju-wuku-ite
            Neg=2Sg=neck-be long-Neg
            'Your neck isn't long.' (Literally, 'You're not long-necked.')

(2.23) a.   ne=rea   o-jektosī
            2Sg=eye   3-roll
            'You rolled your eyes.' (Literally, 'Your eyes rolled.')

     b.   ne=rea-jektosī
            2Sg=eye-roll
            'You rolled your eyes.' (Literally, 'You eye-rolled.')

Significantly, possessor raising (with associated incorporation) is only possible from an O or S dependent and it can occur both with stative verbs, as in (2.22b), and nonstative verbs, as in (2.23b), although if the possessor is 'raised' from the S of a nonstative verb it is indexed with O marking on the verb rather than the usual A marking. Possessor raising is thus restricted to the S/O category, which is to say the absolutive dependent.

Although the way possessor raising works implies an ergative syntax, other phenomena operate in terms of other relational categories, which do not imply ergativity. For example, there are different precise strategies for forming relative clauses depending on the grammatical relation of the relativized position. With respect to relativization, the following categories of verb dependents are distinguished: A, S, O, and oblique. The Ss of both stative and nonstative intransitive verbs are relativized in the same way (with a distinct relativizing affix on the verb and retention of the pronominal prefix or clitic that indexes the relativized consitutent), whereas the A and O of transitive verbs are relativized in different ways (each having its own relativizing affix on the verb and neither being indexed by a pronominal prefix or clitic). On the other hand, with respect to reciprocalization and clause-internal reflexivization, there are constraints on the controller that put the A and S into the same category, that is the subject or nominative category.

Choctaw, which shows an A/S_a vs. O/S_o distinction with respect to head-marking morphology on the verb, also fails to work primarily in terms of an A/S_a vs. O/S_o split. For example, according to the analysis presented in Davies (1986), the controller of reflexivization has to be either an A or any kind of S. Similarly, the nominative case-marker that occurs on NP dependents puts the A and S together into the same category, as indicated by the following examples.

(2.24) a. ofi-yat   towa-yã   ilhioli-tok
         dog-Nom   ball-Obl   chase-Pst
         'The dog chased the ball.'

      b. issoba-yat   ĩpa-tok
         horse-Nom   eat-Pst
         'The horse ate.'

      c. chim-alla-t   cha:ha-h
         2Pos-child-Nom   tall-Pred
         'Your child is tall.'

Head marking doesn't occur in these examples because the A, S, and O dependents are all third person and therefore the verbs show no overt agreement. Nominative case marking obligatorily occurs on S/A dependents; oblique case marking occurs optionally on all other dependents, including Os. As can be seen from (2.24a), the A takes the nominative case marking, whereas the O takes the oblique suffix. The S of verbs in the 'eat' class, which show A agreement, and the S of verbs in the 'tall' class, which show O agreement, both take the nominative suffix, as shown by (2.24b–c) (the *-t* vs. *-yat* difference reflects phonologically-conditioned allomorphy). Although the constraint on the controller of reflexivization and the subject case-marking imply an accusative syntax, there are some phenomena that operate in other terms. Unlike in Kamaiurá, which allows possessor raising from both O-marked and A-marked Ss, Choctaw restricts possessor raising to O and S_o, thus showing more of a tendency toward syntactic split-intransitivity.

The Austronesian language Acehnese, spoken in Indonesia (Durie 1985, 1988, Van Valin and La Polla 1997: ch. 6), also draws a distinction between two categories: A/S_a and O/S_o, as can be seen from (2.25). (The analysis and examples here and below are adapted from Van Valin and La Polla 1997.[11])

(2.25) a. lôn   lôn=mat=geuh
         1Sg   1Sg=hold=3
         'I hold him/her.'

      b. gopnyan   geu=mat=lôn
         3Sg   3=hold=1Sg
         'He/she holds me.'

      c. geu=jak   gopnyan
         3=go   3Sg
         'He/she goes.'

      d. lôn   rhët=lôn
         1Sg   fall=1Sg
         'I fall.'

e. *lôn lôn=rhët
    1Sg fall=1Sg
    'I fall.'

The 3rd person and 1st person singular free-standing pronouns (*gopnyan* and
lôn), whose morphological form is insensitive to the A vs. O distinction, may
be expressed in addition to pronominal clitics (which are sometimes hom-
ophonous with the free-standing pronouns) as in the examples above, although often only one or the other is expressed. The morphological form of
the pronominal clitics is also insensitive to the A vs. O distinction (*geuh*, in
(2.25a) being a phonologically-conditioned allomorph of *geu*). What is significant with respect to grammatical relations is the placement of the pronominal clitics. The generalization is that a proclitic (i.e. verb-initial clitic) involves
A-marking (2.25a–b) or S_a-marking, as with an intransitive verb such as *jak*
(2.25c) whose main dependent is typically conceived of as being in control of
the action. An enclitic involves O-marking (2.25a–b) or S_o-marking, as with an
intransitive verb such as *rhët* (2.25d) whose main dependent is not typically
conceived of as being in control. Example (2.25e) is ungrammatical because
the 1st person clitic is expressed as a proclitic, inappropriately marking the 1st
person dependent like an A.

What makes Acehnese different from languages such as Kamaiurá and Choctaw is that there appear to be no grammatical phenomena for which syntactic
functions need to be defined in terms of a three-way distinction between A, S,
and O, an accusative-type distinction between O and subject (S/A), or an
ergative-type distinction between A and absolutive (S/O). The two categories
A/S_a and O/S_o appear to suffice for any phenomena requiring a distinction
among the A, S, and O categories. Consider, for example, the 'possessor raising'
construction. Like in Kamaiurá, a possessor of an O or S can either be expressed
as a constituent of the NP, as in the (a)-examples in (2.26)–(2.27) or can function
as a dependent of the verb, in which case the head (possessed) N is incorporated
or compounded with the V, as in the (b)-examples.

(2.26) a. seunang [até   lôn]
           happy   liver   1Sg
           'I'm happy.' (Literally, 'My liver (is) happy.')
       b. lôn   seunang-até
           1Sg   happy-liver
           'I'm happy.' (Literally, 'I'm liver-happy.')

(2.27) a. ka   lôn-tët   [rumoh   gopnyan]
           Asp   1SgA-burn house   3Sg
           'I burned his/her house.'

　　　b.　　gopnyan　ka　　lôn=tët-rumoh
　　　　　　3Sg　　　　Asp　　1SgA=burn-house
　　　　　　'I burned his/her house.' (Literally, 'Him/her, I house-burned.')

(2.28)　　* gopnyan　　ka　　　aneuk-woe
　　　　　　3Sg　　　　　Asp　　child-return
　　　　　　'His/her child returned.'

The key fact is that a possessor can only 'raise' from an O (2.27b) or S$_o$ (2.26b); not from an S$_a$, as shown by the ungrammaticality of (2.28). Thus, the phenomenon is keyed to neither the O category (accusative), nor an S/O category (absolutive), but to an O/S$_o$ category.

　　As an example of a phenomenon keyed to the A/S$_a$ category, consider control of a verb phrase embedded under the verb 'want'. In English, as in Brazilian Portuguese (see Section 2.1.1), an infinitival verb phrase can be embedded under verbs such as *want*, in which case the subject dependent of the infinitival phrase is not expressed if it is the same as the subject dependent of the main verb (e.g. *I want* [*to die/fall down/go home/see a movie*]). Similarly, in Acehnese the A of the verb *taguen* 'cook' is not overtly expressed if the phrase *taguen bu* 'cook rice' is embedded under *tém* 'want' and the experiencer of *tém* is understood to be the same participant as the A of *taguen*:

(2.29)　　gopnyan　geu-tém　[Ø　taguen　bu]　(*controllee = A of embedded V*)
　　　　　　3Sg　　　　　3=want　　　　cook　　rice
　　　　　　'He/she wants to cook rice.'

Thus, the interpretation of the unexpressed dependent of the embedded phrase is 'controlled' by the experiencer of *tém*. The question is which dependent of an embedded verb can be controlled in this construction. As the following examples show, unlike in English and typical accusative languages, the controllee can be an S$_a$ dependent of an intransitive verb, but not an S$_o$ dependent.

　　　　　　　　　　　　　　　　　　　　　　　　(*controllee = S$_a$ of embeded V*)
(2.30) a.　　gopnyan　geu-tém　[Ø　jak]
　　　　　　　3Sg　　　　　3=want　　　　go
　　　　　　　'He/she wants to go.'

　　　b.　*gopnyan　geu-tém　[Ø　rhët]　(**controllee = S$_0$ of embeded V*)
　　　　　　3Sg　　　　　3=want　　　　fall
　　　　　　'He/she wants to fall.'

Other syntactic phenomena generally do not systematically distinguish among A, S, and O dependents. The lack of any phenomena sensitive specifically to O or S/A categories poses a potential challenge to theories built around the traditional subject and direct object categories of accusative languages.

The main features of split-intransitive languages can be summarized as follows.

- At least with respect to a principal role-marking mechanism—typically head-marking morphology—a distinction is drawn between the A dependent and the O dependent and the S category is split into A-patterning and O-patterning Ss.
- There is generally a fairly clear underlying semantic motivation for the S-category split, typically based on a distinction between event-designating verbs (with S_a) and stative verbs (with S_o) or between participant in control (S_a) and participant not in control (S_o).
- Although in some languages the only distinction among A, S, and O categories that any morphosyntactic phenomena are keyed to is the A/S_a vs. O/S_o distinction, in other languages this distinction is mainly or only manifested morphologically (in the form of head or dependent marking) and other grammatical phenomena are sensitive to grammatical-relation distinctions of either the accusative kind or the ergative kind or both.

2.2 Voice and grammatical-relation alternations

As should be clear from the analyses of grammatical-relation marking parameters sketched in the previous section, categories such as A, S, and O and the grammatical relations defined in terms of these (subject, object, absolutive, etc.) play an important role in the grammatical phenomena of many languages. Languages generally provide their users with ways of doing such things as explicitly contrasting one of the participants in a state of affairs being talked about with some other. For example, one person says she thinks Bill likes Melissa; another wants to make clear that Ralph rather than Bill is the one who likes Melissa. Generally, one of the NPs or other phrases can be placed in a special position, at the beginning of the sentence for example, in order to signal contrastive focus of the desired kind. Perhaps a focus-suffix, particle or auxiliary verb will be added as well and the main clause may be put in a special subordinate form. Thus, one might get something such as:

(2.31)   It was Ralph that [Ø kissed Melissa].

Since the subordinate clause is in some sense missing one of the dependents of its verb because it has been placed in the special position, in order to get the right interpretation of a sentence such as (2.31), it is necessary to know that the displaced NP 'counts' as the missing NP. Now, in English the AVO constituent-order convention and the relevant convention concerning the relationship between semantic roles and the A and O categories make it clear that the missing NP in the subordinate clause plays the kisser role. That is to say, the A of *kiss* is associated with the kisser role and since there is a gap between the subordinating complementizer *that* and the verb *kissed* it can be inferred that the A is what is missing.

Suppose, however, that English had, instead, a VAO basic order for its clauses. It would not be possible in that case to tell whether (2.31) means 'Melissa kissed RALPH' or 'RALPH kissed Melissa', since a gap preceding or following *Melissa* would sound the same:

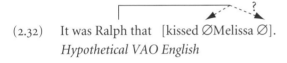

(2.32)   It was Ralph that [kissed ∅Melissa ∅].
         Hypothetical VAO English

This kind of ambiguity can arise for such a construction in languages with verb-initial, verb-final, or free constituent order. Of course, the problem could be solved by having a dependent-marking system or, perhaps, requiring the use of a pronoun in the position of the gap (*It was Ralph that kissed he Melissa*, for example, would work in a VAO language). In any case, one way that grammars manage to facilitate the correct interpretation of such constructions is by placing grammatical-relation constraints on them. For example, if by general convention the missing NP in the subordinate clause in such a construction had to be the subject, *Ralph* would automatically be interpreted as the kisser in (2.32).

Although the grammatical conventions that languages adopt can be complex and do not always have such transparent functional motivations, they do often work essentially in this way for all intents and purposes. One of the problems for a language such as hypothetical VAO English with a subject-only constraint on the contrastive focus (or 'cleft') construction is that there would be no way to say the equivalent of *It was Melissa that Ralph kissed*. It turns out, however, that languages often have mechanisms for changing the relationship between semantic roles and syntactic functions, such that the kissee, for example, can have the syntactic function that by default gets assigned to the kisser. Thus, by using the passive-voice construction in the subordinate clause, the interpretation 'It was Melissa that Ralph kissed' can be achieved, without violating the subject constraint on clefting. That is, hypothetical VAO English could just use *It was Melissa that was kissed by Ralph*.

In some languages, voice has a somewhat different effect. Rather than primarily maximizing the availability of syntactic privilege to NPs with different semantic roles, voice marking can provide information about the intended semantic role interpretation of the participants in the event/state designated by the verb, while allowing a faithful alignment of the privileged syntactic function with the cognitively most salient verb dependent. Languages frequently place constraints on which syntactic function can be associated with NPs whose referents are ranked highly in some way on a prominence hierarchy that operates primarily in terms of person and animacy (e.g. 1st/2nd person > human > animate > inanimate) (Silverstein 1976, Delancey 1981, Aissen 1999*b*). The person part of this kind of hierarchy is operative in Kamaiurá (as discussed in Section 2.1.3)—but without restricting syntactic functions per se. The head-marking morphology on a verb only indexes one of the A/S/O dependents, in most circumstances. For example, if one is 3rd person and the other is 1st or 2nd person, the 1st or 2nd person dependent is the only one indexed, irrespective of its syntactic function (A or O). In some languages, however, the A-marked dependent simply cannot be outranked by the O-marked dependent in terms of person/animacy or, in some cases, discourse saliency. Thus, in a hypothetical English with such a constraint, *I kissed her* would be possible, because the 1st person A is higher on this hierarchy than the 3rd person human O. But, there would be no way to say *She kissed me* without violating the constraint. A passive-voice construction (*I was kissed by her*), for example, makes it possible to express the meaning 'She kissed me', without violating the constraint. The 1st person dependent is the S, which is interpreted as the kissee because the S in a passive construction is interpreted as having the patient semantic role.

Voice alternations, such as passive vs. active in English, constitute a crucial component of the grammatical-relation systems in many languages and, consequently, are one of the main issues of concern for theories of grammatical relations. Just as there are different varieties of languages according to which grammatical relations tend to be privileged, that is S/A (in accusative languages) vs. S/O (in ergative languages), for example, there are correlative differences in kinds of voice constructions and kinds of grammatical-relation alternations. In languages with an accusative syntax in which S/A is often the most privileged category, the passive construction takes on a special significance, since, although it may have other motivations, one of its main effects is to allow dependents with the patient semantic role (and sometimes other roles) to have the privileged subject function. In languages such as Dyirbal, the ANTIPASSIVE voice construction is of special importance, since it allows the agent to have the absolutive function by demoting the patient to an oblique (or other non-core) function. In many languages a critical line is drawn between the core syntactic functions (S/A/O) and oblique relations. Correspondingly, some languages have multiple voice constructions (locative, instrumental, benefactive, etc.) or what are generally known as APPLICATIVE constructions, which have the effect of increasing the privileges or grammatical salience of dependents with such semantic roles as beneficiary, recipient, goal, instrument, and location, by putting them in the O (or S/O) category. Although much rarer, an INVERSE voice construction can allow the A-marked and O-marked dependents to have the semantic roles of patient and agent, respectively, which is the inverse of the alignment found in the direct voice. Although inverse voice may have other motivations, one effect can be to increase the privileges or grammatical salience of the patient (in a basically accusative language), while keeping the agent in one of the core functions.

2.2.1 *Passive voice*

As with all of the different kinds of voice categories, there are potentially different ways of defining the category designated by *passive*. The prototypical transitive active clause has an agent in the A function and a patient in the O function. As schematized in the contrasting valence structures in (2.33), the prototypical passive paraphrase is intransitive, with the patient in the S function, the agent omitted or in an oblique function, and some overt morphosyntactic marking of the voice difference.

(2.33) a. $\text{Verb}_X < A_{\text{AGENT}} \; O_{\text{PATIENT}} >$
         Active Voice
      b. $\text{Verb}_X\text{-Pass} < S_{\text{PATIENT}} \; (\text{Obl}_{\text{AGENT}}) >$
         Passive Voice

It is unclear, however, which, if any of the prototypical properties of the passive construction should be made criterial for taxonomic purposes, and whether anything of theoretical significance hinges on the choice. Presumably one would not want to exclude the English passive construction, simply because rather than having a verbal affix dedicated to announcing passive voice, it announces it with a unique combination of multifunctional markers, that is the *be* auxiliary together with a past-participle form of the verb. Suppose, however, a language had a specially-marked construction, differing from an active transitive clause in form but not meaning, in which the agent were marked like and behaved syntactically like the O of a transitive clause rather than an oblique. Would that construction be classified as passive? That is to say, consider a hypothetical English with active and non-active paraphrases of the following kind:

(2.34) a.   This person helped my mother.
       b.   My mother was helped this person.

This hypothetical English would have a special voice construction in which the patient is promoted to A rather than S and the agent is demoted to O rather than oblique. A theory of grammatical relations would have to have a way of characterizing the situation and accounting for the syntactic properties of the non-active construction, whether it is called passive or not. One could distinguish it from the prototypical passive by calling it 'reversal passive'. Although this general kind of voice construction in fact appears to exist, it is classified in this book as an instantiation of what is generally known as inverse voice (see Section 2.2.3). Taken to be criterial for the passive designation of a construction are the following properties:

(2.35)   *A clause is said to be in passive voice if it*
       a.   is an intransitive clause of a type that functions as a systematic alternative to some more basic transitive clause type, and
       b.   the dependent that would be the A in the basic clause type does not have any A/S/O function.

There are various constraints on syntactic phenomena in English that operate in terms of the S/A category. For example, the pivot of conjunction reduction must be the S/A of the second of two conjoined clauses (*[Sam went there] and [Ø interviewed Chris]* vs. **[Sam went there] and [Chris interviewed Ø]*). Another construction, commonly known as the 'raising to subject' construction, allows a dependent of an infinitival phrase embedded under certain verbs such as *seem* to be overtly expressed only as the subject of *seem*. As illustrated by the following examples, only an A or S dependent of the embedded verb can be the subject of *seem* in this construction.

A of embedded V = subject of seem

(2.36) a.   This drug seems [Ø to help people]

*O of embedded V = subject of seem

       b.   *People seem [this drug to help Ø]

S of embedded V = subject of seem

       c.   People seem [Ø to know about this drug]

In order to express the meaning of (2.36b), it is necessary for the patient of the embedded verb to have either the A or the S syntactic function. The passive construction makes this possible, since the patient (or what would otherwise be the O) is expressed as the S and the agent is omitted or expressed as an oblique (or 'adjunct'):

S of embedded passive V = subject of seem

(2.37)   People seem [Ø to helped by this drug]

Similarly, the meaning and effect of *[*Sam went there*] and [*Chris interviewed Ø*] can be achieved by passivizing the second conjunct ([*Sam went there*] *and* [*Ø was interviewed by Chris*]). Thus, one of the effects of the passive construction in English is to increase the syntactic privileges of the patient dependent.

The passive construction of the Tanoan native American language Southern Tiwa (Allen and Frantz 1983) works like English in that it can increase the syntactic prominence of the patient, as illustrated by the following examples.

(2.38) a.   seuanide   hliawra-mu-ban
            man   lady-see-Pst
            'The man saw the lady.'

      b.   hliawrade   mu-che-ban   seuanide-ba
            lady   see-Pass-Pst   man-Instr
            'The lady was seen by the man.'

Southern Tiwa is a typical polysynthetic language (Baker 1996), with noun incorporation and a robust head-marking system for marking A/S/O syntactic functions. Dependent marking is used only for oblique constituents, which bear case suffixes. Example (2.38a) is a transitive active clause, with the O incorporated in the verb, as it must ordinarily be.[12] There is no agreement morphology on the verb because 3rd singular animate S or A and O trigger null agreement. Example (2.38b) is the passive version of the same proposition. The perceiver (or agent) dependent is expressed as an oblique, marked with instrumental case; the percept (or patient) dependent is expressed as the S. There is a complex set of agreement (or pronominal) prefixes that index the S, A, and O dependents, including portmanteau markers for numerous A-O combinations. Although there are prefixes for combinations of A and O such as 1st person singular A and 3rd person O, there is no prefix that indexes the combination 3rd person A and 1st or 2nd person O. There is a prominence hierarchy (1st/2nd > 3rd) that prevents such a combination. The A of a clause cannot be lower on the person prominence hierarchy than the O of the same clause. Thus, there is no way to express the meaning of English *The lady saw me*, except by using the passive construction, as illustrated by the following examples.

(2.39) a. *hliawrade   †-mu-ban   † = *any potential prefix or no prefix*
           lady   3SgA1SgO-lady-see-Pst
           'The lady saw me.'
      b. hliawrade-ba   te-mu-che-ban
           lady-Instr   1SgS-see-Pass-Pst
           'I was seen by the lady.'

There is considerable variation across languages with respect to how the default A (or agent) is expressed in the passive construction and the extent to which it displays the typical syntactic properties of A/S/O dependents. The following examples illustrate some of the kinds of variation in passive agent expression, beyond the *by*/instrumental marking of Southern Tiwa and English, for which there are analogues in many languages.

(2.40)   *Kamaiurá* (Seki 2000)
      a. 'aŋ   hoka   i-'awyky-pyr-era   morerekwara   upe
           this   house   3-make-Nominal-Pass   chief   to/for/by
           'This house was made by/for the chief.'
           Halkomelem (Gerdts 1988a)
      b. ni   qʷə́l-ət-əm   ʔə   θə   sɬéniʔ   tθ̣ə   scéːɬtən
           Aux   bake-Tr-Intr   Obl   Det   woman   Det   salmon
           'The salmon was baked by the woman.'
           Seri (Marlett 1984, Farrell *et al.* 1991)
      c. m-yo-aː?-kašni
           2SgSubj-Dist-Pass-bite
           'You were bitten.'

In Kamaiurá the passive-voice form of the verb is nominalized and suffixed with a passive marker. The agent is expressed as an oblique, marked with the postposition *upe* that is also used for recipient and beneficiary dependents. Since the agent can be omitted, (2.40a) is ambiguous between a reading on which the *upe*-marked NP is interpreted as the agent and a reading with an implicit agent and an *upe*-marked beneficiary. From Seki's description, the *upe*-marked agent of a passive clause has the syntactic behaviour typical of any oblique. As shown by (2.40b), the Halkomelem passive voice is marked on the verb by a general intransitive marker that follows the transitive marker. As expected for an intransitive clause with a 3rd person S, the verb does not show any agreement. The S of passive clauses behaves in all respects like an S dependent (see Section 2.1.2). The agent is marked by the all-purpose oblique preposition. Seri, a Hokan language of Mexico, differs from these other languages in that the passive agent *must* be omitted, as in (2.40c).

Although the passive agent is marked like an oblique in Halkomelem, its syntactic behaviour is A-like in at least one respect. There is a raising-to-object construction, illustrated by the following examples, that generally allows only the S/A of the embedded clause to precede the embedded clause and function as the object of the main clause verb *x̌ec-* 'wonder, figure out, check out'.

A of embedded clause = O of x̌ec-

(2.41) a. ʔi   cən   x̌éc-t   tθə swə́yʔqeʔ
       Aux 1Subj wonder-Tr   Det man
              [ʔu   ni-ʔəs   ceʔ   ʔu   c'ew-ət-ál ʔxʷ-əs   Ø]
           Lnk   Aux-3SgSubj Fut   Lnk help-Tr-1P1O-3Ssubj
       'I'm checking out the man if he will help us.'

S of embedded clause = O of x̌ec-

   b. ʔi   cən   x̌éc-t   tθə   xʷələnítəm
     Aux 1Subj wonder-Tr   Det   white men
            [ʔu   ni-ʔəs   cəlkʷstaʔmət   Ø]
         Lnk Aux-3SgSubj   do
       'I wonder what the white men will do.'

*O embedded clause = O of x̌ec-

   c. * ʔi   cən   x̌eʔx̌cí-t   kʷθə nít
      Aux 1Subj wonder.Cont-Tr Det   3Emp
             [ʔu   ni:n   cəʔ λəwəɫ lə́m-nəxʷ   Ø]
           Lnk Aux1SgSubj fut again see-LcontrTr
       'I am wondering if I will see that one again.'

However, if a passive clause is embedded under this raising verb, either the S or the demoted agent can be raised:

S of embedded passive clause = O of x̌ec-

(2.42) a. ʔi   cən   x̌eʔx̌cí-t   kʷθə Bob
       Aux 1Subj wonder.Cont-Tr Det   Bob
            [ʔu   ʔi-ʔəs   lə́ʔləm-ʔət-əmʔ ʔə-x̌ John Ø]
          Lnk Aux-3SgSubj look-Tr-Intr   Obl-Det John
       'I am wondering if Bob is being watched by John.'

Agent of embedded passive clause = O of x̌ec-

b. ʔi   cən   x̌eʔx̌cí-t   kʷθə John
    Aux   1Subj wonder.Cont-Tr   Det John
         [ʔu   ʔi-ʔəs   lɔ́ʔləm-ʔət-əmʔ∅ kʷθə Bob
         Lnk   Aux-3SgSubj   look-Tr-Intr   Det Bob
    'I am wondering if Bob is being watched by John.'

Languages vary with respect to how many and what kind of S-/A-like privileges the agent in a passive clause may have. In French, for example, the oblique-
marked agent of a passive clause behaves like an S/A with respect to control of
certain kinds of adverbial phrases (Ruwet 1972, Legendre 1987, 1990), suggesting
the need to recognize essentially the same S/A/Obl$_a$ category that is needed for
Halkomelem raising to object. There are certain phenomena involving control
(or antecedence) of reflexive pronouns that work in terms of the same kind of
category in the Indo-Aryan language Marathi (Rosen and Wali 1989).

    In Seri, even though it cannot be overtly expressed, the agent of a passive
verb takes precedence over the S for the purposes of switch-reference marking—a morphological marking system for keeping track of the reference of
'subjects' across main and adverbial subordinate clauses. The following examples (adapted from Farrell *et al.* 1991) illustrate the possibility of using the
different-subject (DS) marker with both active and passive clauses of different
kinds.[13]

2Sg A in subordinate clause; 2Sg S in main clause; *DS
(2.43) a. [[mi-naiɬ kom m-po-ki:xk   (*ta)-x] ʔata:p   ko-m-si-a:
    2Pos-skin the 2SgSubj-Irr-wet DS-Aux mucus   3Obl-2SgSubj-
                                                          Irr-be

    ʔa=ʔa]
    Aux=Decl
    'If you wet your skin, you will be with mucus.' (i.e. 'get a cold')
    3Sg A in subordinate clause; 1Sg S in main clause; DS
    b. [[ʔim-t-kašni   ma-x]   ʔp-yo-o:ʔa]
    1SgO-Real-bite DS-Aux   1SgSubj-Dist-cry
    'Since it bit me, I cried.'
    ∅$_{AGENT}$ in main PASSIVE clause; 2Sg A in subordinate clause; DS
    c. [m-yo-a:ʔ-kašni   [kokašni šo m-t-aʔo   ma]]
    2SgSubj-Dist-Pass-bite snake   a   2SgSubj-Real-see DS
    'You were bitten, after you had seen a snake.'

ø_{AGENT} *in subordinate* PASSIVE *clause;* ø_{AGENT} *in main* PASSIVE *clause;*
*DS

d. [[ʔaːt   kiʔ   p-aːʔ-kaː   (*ta)-x]   ʔeːpoɬ   kiʔ   mos
     limberbush   the   Irr-Pass-seek   DS   -Aux ratany   the   also
     si-aːʔ-kaː   ʔa=ʔa]
     Irr-Pass-seek   Aux=Decl
     'If limberbush is looked for, white ratany should be looked for also.'

Seri is an accusative AOV head-marking language with agreement/pronominal markers on verbs for S/A, O, and oblique dependents. Third person S/A and O agreement is zero. The DS marker (*ta* in irrealis clauses and *ma* in realis clauses) appears in clause-final position of a subordinate clause, possibly affixed to a tense auxiliary element, if and only if its 'subject' is not the same as the 'subject' of the main clause. In (2.43a) the DS marker cannot be used because the A of the subordinate clause and the S of the main clause both refer to the same 2nd person. In (2.43b), on the other hand, the DS marker must be used because the A of the subordinate clause refers to a 3rd person, whereas the S of the main clause refers to the speaker. Even though the S of the passive main clause refers to the same singular person as the S of the subordinate clause, a DS marker must be used in (2.43c) because the implicit agent of the passive clause refers to a 3rd person. By the same token, a DS marker cannot be used in (2.43d), in spite of the fact that the Ss of the two passive clauses refer to different 3rd person entities, because the implicit agents refer to the same person. The privileged category of dependents for purposes of switch-reference marking is the agent or the S of an active clause, which can have any semantic role, including that of patient, as in (2.43a).

Languages such as Seri and Halkomelem, in which the 'demoted' agent of a passive clause has subject properties of various kinds, pose potential challenges for theories of grammatical relations. Even though languages, by and large, operate in terms of the same syntactic categories that head-marking and dependent-marking systems recognize, that is A, O, S/A, S/O, O/S$_o$, and A/S$_a$, grammatical phenomena also appear to work in terms of more complex categories.

2.2.2 *Antipassive voice*

Passive voice changes the default alignment of semantic roles and syntactic functions in such a way as to increase the syntactic privileges of the patient, or, more generally, the dependent that would otherwise be the O. Because the agent is either not overtly expressed or is realized as an oblique in a passive clause, the patient has the syntactic function of S rather than O. This increases its prominence and privileges in a syntactically accusative language, since the

S/A category is more privileged than the O category. In a syntactically ergative language, a promotion from O to S has less of an effect since the privileged syntactic category (S/O) already encompasses the O. Because the S/O function typically has more privileges than the A function in ergative languages, there is more functional motivation for a voice that promotes the default A to S. The antipassive version of a clause with an agent and patient is intransitive by virtue of the demotion of the patient to oblique (or, possibly, indirect object or second object), such that the agent is the S. Schematically, proto-typical active and antipassive clauses have the following contrasting valence structures.

(2.44) a. $\text{Verb}_x < \text{A}_{\text{AGENT}} \text{ O}_{\text{PATIENT}}>$
          Active Voice
       b. $\text{Verb}_x\text{-Antipass} <\text{S}_{\text{AGENT}} \text{ Obl}_{\text{PATIENT}}>$
          Antipassive Voice

There are various construction types in languages that approximate the prototypical antipassive construction in one or more ways. In this book, the properties taken to be criterial are as follows.

(2.45)   *A clause is said to be in antipassive voice if it*
       a.   is an intransitive clause of a type that functions as a systematic alternative to some more basic transitive clause type, and
       b.   the dependent that would be the O in the basic clause type does not have any A/S/O function.

In Section 2.2.3 it was noted that there are various syntactic phenomena in Dyirbal that are constrained to occur with S/O dependents. For example, the controller and pivot in the conjunction-reduction construction must both be either the S or the O of their respective clauses, as illustrated by (2.11), repeated here as (2.46).

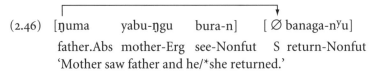

(2.46) [ŋuma   yabu-ŋgu   bura-n]   [Ø banaga-nʸu]
       father.Abs mother-Erg see-Nonfut S return-Nonfut
       'Mother saw father and he/*she returned.'

In order to say the equivalent of English *Mother saw father and returned, yabu* 'mother' has to be in S function and, therefore, in absolutive case. This can be accomplished by putting the verb in antipassive voice, in which case the patient is marked dative and does not function as the O. Since an antipassive clause is intransitive, the agent is the S and can control conjunction reduction:

(2.47) [yabu bural-ŋa-nʸu   ŋuma-gu] [∅ banaga-nʸu]
   mother.Abs see-Antipass-Nonfut father-Dat S return-Nonfut
   'Mother saw father and she/*he returned.'

Antipassive voice in Dyirbal systematically allows agents of transitive clauses to have the S/O syntactic privileges of the language, not only with respect to conjunction reduction, but also relativization and control of purpose clauses as discussed in Section 2.2.3.

 Languages often have both passive and antipassive voice constructions. This makes sense primarily because both kinds of construction can have functions other than increasing the syntactic privileges of the default A or O. As noted above, the passive construction, for example, also or alternatively functions to background or lower the grammatical prominence of the agent. The antipassive construction does the same for the patient.[14] Halkomelem is an example of a language that has both passive and antipassive voices. The following examples (adapted from Gerdts 1988*a*) illustrate the contrasting morphological properties of the alternative ways of saying that the children baked the bread.

(2.48) a. ni q'ʷə́l-ət-əs tᶿə sX̌əlʔíqəɬ kʷθə səplíl
    Aux bake-Tr-3A Det children Det bread
    'The children baked the bread.'
  b. ni q'ʷə́l-əm tᶿə sX̌əlʔíqəɬ ʔə kʷθə səplíl
    Aux bake-Intr Det children Obl Det bread
    'The children baked the bread.'
  c. ni q'ʷə́l-ət-əm ʔə tᶿə sX̌əlʔíqəɬ kʷθə səplíl
    Aux bake-Tr-Intr Obl Det children Det bread
    'The bread was baked by the children.'

In an active voice clause with agent and patient (2.48a), the verb is marked for transitivity with the -*ət* suffix and A agreement with the -*əs* suffix—if the A is 3rd person. Antipassive voice (2.48b), like passive voice (2.48c), is indicated by lack of A agreement on the verb and intransitive marking. Passive marking is distinguished by retention of the transitivity suffix. Furthermore, the agent is in the oblique function (indicated by the preposition *ʔə*) in the passive clause, whereas the patient is in the oblique function in the antipassive clause.

 As in Dyirbal, one effect of antipassive is to increase the syntactic privileges of the agent. As noted in Section 2.2.3, possessor extraction and quantifier float are restricted to the S/O dependent. The agent can undergo these syntactic processes only in antipassive voice (in which case it has the S function), as illustrated by the following examples for quantifier float, that is clause-initial placement of a quantifier.

*Quantifier floated from O-patient/*A-agent of active clause*

(2.49) a. mə́kʷ niw qʼʷə́l-ət-əs tᶿə sƛ̓əlʔíqəɬ kʷθə səplíl
       all Aux.Lnk bake-Tr-3A Det children Det bread
       'The children baked all the bread/*All the children baked the bread.'
       *Quantifier floated from S-agent/*Obl-patient of antipassive clause*

    b. mə́kʷ niw qʼʷə́l-əm tᶿə sƛ̓əlʔíqəɬ ʔə kʷθə səplíl
       all Aux.Lnk bake-Intr Det children Obl Det bread
       'All the children baked the bread/*The children baked all the bread.'

2.2.3 Inverse voice

An inverse-voice system is one in which there are two kinds of transitive clause, each of which is characterized by a different association of semantic roles and (at least some of) the morphological markers of the A and O functions. In the direct voice a given morphosyntactic marker of type $M1$, typically a verbal pronominal/agreement affix, might index, say, the dependent with the agent semantic role, and another marker of type $M2$ might index the dependent with the patient role. The inverse voice clause has the alignment of roles and marker types reversed, typically with some overt voice marking, as schematized in (2.50).

(2.50) a. $\text{Verb}_x \ M1_{\text{AGENT}} \ M2_{\text{PATIENT}}$
      Direct Voice

    b. $\text{Verb}_x\text{-Inverse} \ M1_{\text{PATIENT}} \ M2_{\text{AGENT}}$
      Inverse Voice

The inverse voice phenomenon can be defined more generally as follows.

(2.51) *A clause is said to be in inverse voice if it*
    a. is a transitive clause of a type that functions as a systematic alternative to another more basic transitive clause type,
    b. it has the patient marked in the way that the agent is marked in the more basic clause type, and
    c. both the agent and patient have some A/S/O function.

Typically, there are limited paraphrase possibilities in the alternative voices in an inverse system, since the possibility of inverse vs. direct voice constructions for a given meaning is governed by a person/animacy hierarchy in some way. The following examples from the Chilean language Mapudungun (from Arnold 1998: ch. 2) illustrate the basic situation.

(2.52) a. mutrüm-fi-n ñi ñuke
       call-3O-1SgSubj Pos mother
       'I called my mother.'

b. mutrüm-e-n-ew   ñi   ñuke
  call-Inverse-1SgSubj-3O Pos   mother
  'My mother called me.'

The dependent with the agent role is coded on the verb with the S/A-indexing 1st person singular suffix in the direct-voice clause in (2.52a); and the patient is coded with a 3rd person O-indexing suffix. In the inverse-voice clause in (2.52b) the 1st person patient is marked with the same suffix that is used for the agent in the direct-voice alternative; and a different O-indexing suffix is used for the 3rd person agent. The indexing suffix combination together with the presence of the inverse suffix indicate that the dependent with the S/A marking in (2.52b) is to be interpreted as having the patient role. The choice between direct and inverse voice is governed by a prominence hierarchy of the kind operative in the Kamaiurá verb agreement system in a somewhat different way (see Section 2.1.3). The hierarchy for Mapudungun is as follows.

(2.53) 1st > 2nd > 3rd proximate > 3rd obviative
   Prominence hierarchy for Mapudungun

As is typically the case in inverse systems, the relative prominence of two 3rd person dependents is determined by obviation (e.g. Aissen 1997), that is cognitive salience due to discourse factors. In essence, a 3rd person dependent is proximate if its referent is an established topic of the preceding discourse and otherwise is obviative. The constraint on inverse vs. direct voice is that the dependent that is S/A-indexed on the verb must be ranked higher on the prominence hierarchy than the dependent that is O-marked. Thus, 'My mother called me', for example, can only be expressed in the inverse voice, as in (2.52b), since the 1st person dependent needs to be S/A-marked.

 The Algonquian language family is perhaps the most well known for its inverse voice system. The main differences between Mapudungun and Algonquian are that the latter has overt verb suffixes for both direct and inverse voice, often only has an overt marker for one of the dependents, and draws the relevant distinction only for a certain class of transitive verbs with animate dependents. The prominence hierarchy is 1st/2nd > 3rd proximate > 3rd obviative (Klaiman 1993). The following Plains Cree examples (from Wolfart and Carroll 1981) illustrate the phenomenon.

(2.54) a. ni-sēki-ā-nān   atim
    1-scare-Direct-1Pl   dog
    'We scared the dog.'

b.   ni-sēki-iko-nān   atim
     1-scare-Inverse-1Pl   dog
     'The dog scared us.'

In (2.54a), the person/number affixes indicate that this transitive verb has a 1st person plural dependent. Example (2.54b) has precisely the same person/ number affixes; but the semantic role they are associated with is different. The prominence hierarchy dictates that the 1st person dependent gets the primary, and in this case only, marking on the verb. The direct suffix indicates that the highest-ranking dependent on the hierarchy (i.e. the 1st person dependent) has the agent semantic role; the inverse suffix indicates that this same dependent has the patient role.

This kind of system is characteristic of Algonquian languages in general, including Algonkin (Henderson 1971), Ojibwa (Rhodes 1976), and Fox (LeSourd 1976), and has been claimed to exist, in some form, in various other languages or language families, including Tanoan (Klaiman 1993), Kinyarwanda (Kimenyi 1980, Ura 2000), and Tzotzil (Aissen 1999*a*). There are essentially two analytical approaches to the general phenomenon. On one approach, adopted, for example by Dahlstrom (1991) for Cree and Klaiman (1993) for Tanoan and Algonquian, the agent is the A and the patient is the O in both constructions. The voice morphology simply indicates alternative interpretations of the indexing morphology. That is, as a function of the voice, the 1st person plural affixes in (2.54a), for example, index the A, whereas in (2.54b), the same affixes index the O. Since the direct and inverse clauses are claimed to have the same alignment of syntactic functions and semantic roles (i.e. agent A and patient O), this kind of analysis involves only inverse morphology, as schematized in (2.55).

(2.55)   Inverse morphology analysis of (2.54)

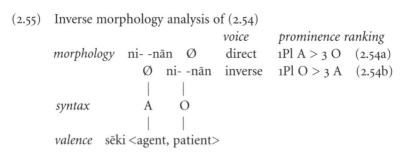

On the alternative inverse syntax approach, adopted by Rhodes (1976) and Permlutter and Rhodes (1988) for Ojibwa, Arnold (1997, 1998) for Mapudun-gun, and (in essence) Ura (2000) for Kinyarwanda, the marking on the verbs is a direct reflection of (surface) syntactic functions. The A of the Mapudungun direct-voice clause in (2.52a), for example, is the agent and the patient is the O. The alignments of syntactic functions and semantic roles are reversed in the inverse-voice clause in (2.52b), as schematized in (2.56).

(2.56)   Inverse syntax analysis of (2.52)

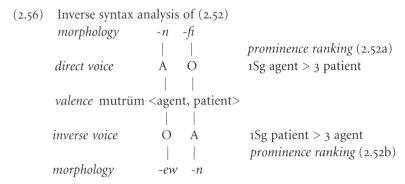

In other words, inverse voice is essentially a special kind of passive voice. The key difference between the passive and inverse constructions is that the inverse agent is 'demoted' to O rather than being omitted or realized as an oblique. This kind of analysis presents a potential challenge for theories of grammar, which differ with respect to whether and in what way the A and O functions are distinguishable from 'agent' and 'patient'. An analysis with A–O reversal entails that 'A' cannot really mean anything like 'agent' or 'most agent-like'. It has to simply mean 'highest ranking of the two core syntactic functions of a transitive clause'.

Although the issue has engendered some controversy, inverse voice has generally been analysed as a purely morphological phenomenon in Algonquian and certain other language families, due to a lack of clear behavioural differences between inverse and direct clauses with respect to S/A-sensitive syntactic phenomena. In some languages, however, there exists compelling evidence for a reversal of syntactic functions in inverse clauses. The Amazonian language Jarawara (Dixon 2000), for example, has what can be considered a kind of inverse construction that illustrates in an interesting way why an inverse syntax (or reversal) analysis of some kind might be entertained. A/S/O dependents are distinguished in several ways from obliques. The latter are expressed more peripherally in the clause and are marked with a postposition. The former are not postpositionally marked, have special slot-restricted pronominal forms (except for 3rd singular) that are obligatorily expressed even if a full NP which they agree with is also expressed, and determine agreement on verbs and auxiliary verbs in several ways. The following examples illustrate the differences between oblique and A/S/O dependents.[15]

(2.57) a. [otaa   nijaa]   mee bosa   na-meke-hete-ke
           1NsgExcl Obl   3Nsg get.up.early Aux-follow-TnsFem-DeclFem
           'Then they got up early on us.'

       b. otara   mee   bosa   ka-na-hani
           1NsgExclO   3Nsg   get.up.early   Appl-Aux-TnsFem
           'Then they got-up-early-on us.'

In (2.57a) the oblique maleficiary dependent is marked with a postposition.
Example (2.57b) has a transitive paraphrase derived with the applicative voice
prefix *ka-* (see Section 2.2.4) that indicates that the maleficiary is O. The S in
(2.57a) and the A in (2.57b) are expressed as an A/S/O pronoun that must
occupy the pronominal position in a transitive clause that is closest to the
verb. In certain cases, depending on person and number, the 'closest' pronominal is actually realized as a verbal prefix. The O in (2.57b) is expressed as
an accusative pronoun which must occupy the first pronominal position in a
transitive clause. All pronominal elements are closer to the verb than any
other dependent constituents. Because all of the core dependents in both of
these sentences are pronominal, the gender agreement morphology is the
default feminine.

If both A and O dependents are 3rd person singular, gender agreement,
manifested in the form of the verb and/or a mood suffix is the primary and
often the only morphological manifestation of distinctions among the A and O
dependents, since the pronominal form for 3rd singular subject and object is null.
The following intransitive sentences illustrate S-indexing gender agreement.

(2.58) a. Mioto   ki-joma-ke-ka
           Mioto(Masc)   be.in.motion-through.gap-coming-DeclMasc
           'Mioto (a man) came in.'

       b. Watati   ki-joma-ke-ke
           Watati(Fem)   be.in.motion-through.gap-coming-DeclFem
           'Watati (a woman) came in.'

With a transitive verb, there is generally a choice between two constructions
to express the same propositional meaning, provided that both dependents
are not 1st/2nd person:

(2.59) a. Mioto   Watati   awa-ka
           Mioto(Masc) Watati(Fem)   see-DeclMasc
           'Mioto saw Watati.'

       b. Watati   Mioto   hi-wa   hi-ke
           Watati(Fem)   Mioto(Masc)   Inv-see   Inv-DeclFem
           'Mioto saw Watati.' (or, 'Watati was seen by Mioto.')

In the construction shown in (2.59a), henceforth the direct voice construction (= Dixon's 'A-construction'), gender agreement is with the agent, which preferably comes first if two A/S/O full NPs are expressed. In the alternative construction shown in (2.59b), henceforth the inverse voice construction (Dixon's 'O-construction'), gender agreement is with the patient, which preferably comes first if two A/S/O full NPs are expressed. The choice between constructions is determined by discourse considerations of the obviation kind. In essence, the prominence hierarchy for Jarawara is proximate > obviative. When there is a choice between direct and inverse voices, the construction which puts the proximate (discourse-salient) dependent of the verb in the privileged syntactic function is chosen.

Recall that in a language with an accusative syntax such as English the conjunction-reduction pivot must be the S/A dependent, whereas in a language with an ergative syntax, such as Dyirbal, the pivot must be the S/O dependent (see Section 2.1.2). In Jarawara the dependent that determines the gender of the mood suffix is also the one that is the pivot in the conjunction-reduction construction, as illustrated by the following examples.

Direct clause agent controller; Direct clause agent pivot

(2.60) a. [Mioto   kijomake-ka]   [∅   Watati   awa-ka]
           Mioto(Masc) come in-DeclMasc   Watati(Fem)see-DeclMasc
           'Mioto came in and saw Watati.'

Direct clause agent controller; Inverse clause patient pivot

  b. [Watati   kijomake-ka]   [∅ Mioto   hi-wa   hi-ke]
      Watati(Fem) come in-DeclFem   Mioto(Masc) Inv-see Inv-DeclFem
      'Watati came in and Mioto saw (her).' (or 'was seen by Mioto.')

When an infinitival clause is embedded under the 'raising' verb *seem* in English (see Section 2.2.1), the S/A of the embedded verb (whether in passive or active voice) functions as the subject of *seem*:

Agent of embedded active V = subject of seem

(2.61) a. This drug seems [∅ to help people]

Patient of embedded passive V = subject of seem

  b. People seem [∅ to be helped by this drug]

Similarly, if a clause is embedded under *awine/awa* 'seem, in my opinion' in Jarawara, the latter shows gender agreement with the agent of a direct clause and the patient of an inverse clause, as illustrated by the following examples:

Direct verb agent controls gender agreement on 'seem'

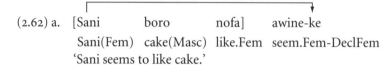

(2.62) a. [Sani   boro   nofa]   awine-ke
            Sani(Fem) cake(Masc) like.Fem   seem.Fem-DeclFem
            'Sani seems to like cake.'

Inverse verb patient controls gender agreement on 'seem'

    b. [boro   Sani   hi-nofe]   awia-ka
            cake(Masc) Sani(Fem) Inv-like.Masc   seem.Masc-DeclMasc
            'Sani seems to like cake.' (or, 'Cake seems to be liked by Sani.')

What appears otherwise to be a clear case of syntactic function reversal for the agent and patient dependents in the alternative voices (or construction types) is complicated by the fact that the pronominal expressions of syntactic functions are only partially reversed. For example, a 1st person singular S/A pronoun is expressed as a prefix on verbs. As the following examples show, the same pronominal prefix on the verb that is used for the agent/S in an intransitive or direct transitive clause is used for the agent in an inverse clause.[16]

Direct voice; feminine mood suffix because agent is 1st person
(2.63) a. Okomobi   o-nofa   o-ke
            Okomobi(Masc)   1SgSubj-like   1Sg-DeclFem
            'I like Okombi.'
Inverse voice; masculine mood suffix because patient is masculine
    b. Okombi   o-nofa   o-ka
            Okomobi(Masc)   1SgSubj-like   1Sg-DeclMasc
            'I like Okombi.'

Inverse voice is indicated in (2.63b) only by the gender agreement on the mood suffix, since the inverse-voice prefix *hi-* only occurs when both A and O are 3rd person. As the following examples show, both the A and O preverbal pronominal slots are filled when neither the agent nor the patient is 3rd singular.

Direct voice; feminine suffixes because both pronominal slots are filled

(2.64) a.   aba   mee(-ra) otaa   kaba-haro otaa   ama-ke
        fish(Masc) 3Nsg(-O)1NsgExcl eat-TnsFem 1NsgExcl extent-DeclFem
        'We were eating fish.'

Inverse voice; feminine suffixes because both pronominal slots are filled

   b.   aba   mee(*-ra) otaa   kaba-haro mee   ama-ke
        fish(Masc) 3Nsg(-O)1NsgExcl eat-TnsFem 3Nsg extent-DeclFem
        'We were eating fish.' (or, 'Fish was being eaten by us.')

One generalization concerning pronouns in transitive clauses is that the first slot is reserved for the patient and the second slot for the agent, independently of voice. A second is that the pronoun that gets obligatorily copied into the slot preceding what Dixon calls the 'secondary' verb (*ama*) expresses the agent in direct voice but the patient in inverse voice. Indeed, the only overt morphological indication of inverse voice in (2.64b) is the form of the copied pronoun preceding *ama-ke*. A third restriction, is that although the first pronominal slot is occupied by a pronoun expressing the patient in both inverse and direct voices, if this pronoun is 3rd person it can only take the morphologically accusative form (i.e. be suffixed with -*ra*) in the direct clause.

   Summarizing, the key morphosyntactic facts about grammatical relations and voice constructions that an analysis of Jarawara needs to account for are as shown in Table 2.2. Any analysis has to be able to account for the fact that, independently of voice, both the patient and agent are associated with the two core syntactic functions of the language, as evidenced by the fact that in both voices these determine the content of the two preverbal pronominal slots, are not marked by postpositions, and occupy the two central NP constituent positions in the clause. Moreover, in the inverse voice the patient, by and large, has the syntactic privileges and most of the morphological properties that the agent has in the direct voice (and that the S has in intransitive clauses), as indicated by the shaded cells in Table 2.2. At the same time, it is necessary to account for the fact that the direct and inverse voices treat the agent and patient in the same way with respect to the preverbal pronominal slots.

   One analysis would take the preverbal pronominal forms as the primary indicators of syntactic functions. Both voices would be transitive and the agent would be the A and the patient the O in both. The difference between the voices could be attributed to a dual syntax: accusative with respect to direct voice and ergative with respect to inverse voice. That is to say, the agent is syntactically privileged in the direct voice because it is in the S/A (nomina-

TABLE 2.2. Jarawara voice and grammatical-relation phenomena

Grammatical phenomena	Direct voice		Inverse voice	
	Patient	Agent	Patient	Agent
Preverbal pronominal slot	1st	2nd/prefix	1st	2nd/prefix
Full NP order preference	2nd	1st	1st	2nd
Conjunction-reduction pivot	no	yes	yes	no
Verb/mood gender agreement	no	yes	yes	no
Agreement on 'seem'	no	yes	yes	no
Pronoun preceding secondary V	no	yes	yes	no
3NsgAcc pronominal form	yes	no	no	no

tive) category; the patient is syntactically privileged in the inverse voice because it is in the S/O (absolutive) category. The problem with this approach, which is the one taken by Dixon, is that it necessitates disjunctive characterizations of most of the key phenomena. That is to say, the rules for constituent order, conjunction reduction, and verb/mood gender agreement, for example, would have to be formulated as follows:

(2.65) a. The preferred constituent order is AOV in the direct voice and OAV in the inverse voice.

b. The conjunction-reduction pivot is the S/A dependent in the direct voice and the O dependent in the inverse voice.

c. Verb/mood gender agreement is controlled by the S/A dependent in the direct voice and the O dependent in the inverse voice.

Under this analysis, Jarawara is a typological anomaly. Not only is it characterized as alternating between two basic kinds of syntactic organization (i.e. ergative and accusative) with respect to the same phenomena, but it also has two different basic word orders: AOV (when accusative) and OAV (when ergative).

An alternative, which avoids positing such unusual typological properties, is to analyse the language as fundamentally accusative with the inverse voice associated with syntactic-function reversal. Although A/O reversal is itself rare, it does plausibly occur in other langues, as noted above, and simply amounts, in some sense, to a variation on the passive construction. It is clear that the inverse voice is more marked morphologically (as there is a verbal prefix for it in clauses with 3rd person dependents), is less commonly used (only 30 per cent of the transitive clauses in Dixon's textual sample), and serves one of the key functions of passive clauses in accusative languages (increasing the prominence and privileges of the patient). On the syntactic inversion analysis, the agent and patient reverse their alignments with the

A and O categories, as illustrated by the following analysis of the semantic role/syntactic function alignments of the examples in (2.59).

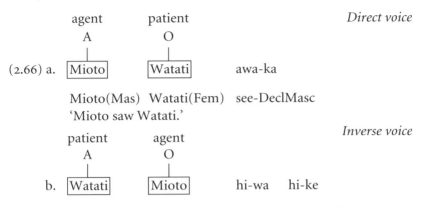

Given this kind of an inverse syntax analysis of the inverse-voice construction, the generalization about preverbal pronominals is that they are determined directly by the agent vs. patient distinction. Rather than being formulated in voice-specific ways, the other constraints can also be characterized as working for the language as a whole:

(2.67)   a.   The preferred constituent order is AOV.
         b.   The conjunction-reduction pivot is the S/A dependent.
         c.   The S/A dependent controls verb/mood gender agreement.

Thus, it is possible to characterize Jarawara as a mostly unremarkable accusative language whose grammatical phenomena work in terms of the categories S/A and O. It is necessary, however, to recognize an inverse-voice construction with some kind of A–O reversal and to be able to formulate morphosyntactic constraints in terms of either 'underlying' A and O categories or the kinds of generalized semantic roles that are implicitly envisioned here in the use of the terms *agent* and *patient* and which have more precise characterizations in certain theories (e.g. the actor and undergoer macroroles of Role and Reference Grammar, discussed in Section 4.1.2, or the proto-agent and proto-patient categories of Dowty 1991).

2.2.4 *Applicative constructions*

Passive and inverse voices can function to give S/A syntactic privileges to dependents whose default syntactic function is O. Antipassive voice can function to give S/O syntactic privileges to a dependent whose default syntactic function is A. Applicative constructions, which could be viewed as instantiating a kind of voice, differ primarily in that they target the O syntactic function, giving O or S/O syntactic privileges to dependents that are neither the default O nor the default A. Schematically, the valence structures of a prototypical applicative and a corresponding basic construction are as in (2.68); the applicative phenomenon can be defined as in (2.69).[17]

(2.68) a. $\text{Verb}_x <\text{S/A}_{\text{AGENT}} \dots >$
        Basic construction

     b. $\text{Verb}_x\text{-Appl} <\text{A}_{\text{AGENT}}\ \text{O}_{\text{NON-PATIENT}} \dots >$
        Applicative construction

(2.69)   *A clause is said to be of the applicative type if*
     a. it is a transitive clause that contains an overt marker to distinguish it from other clause types and/or is a systematic alternative to some other available clause type, and
     b. a non-patient dependent has the O function.

In Halkomelem (see Section 2.1.2 and Gerdts 1988a) such key grammatical phenomena as relativization, clefting, and *wh*-question formation, grant special privileges to dependents with any of the S/A/O functions. The S/O category is privileged for other phenomena, including quantifier float and possessor extraction. Given this system, it is not surprising that Halkomelem has both a way of getting the agent in the S category (i.e. an antipassive construction) and ways of getting dependents with various semantic roles in the O category. The applicative construction is characterized by a verbal affix signalling that a non-patient has the O function, and the patient, if there is one, does not. Since S/O is the most privileged syntactic function, 'promotion' to O in an applicative construction is essentially functionally equivalent to promotion to S via passive in an accusative language.

Halkomelem has four distinct applicative clause types, as illustrated by the following examples.[18]

(2.70) a. ni   ʔám-əs-t-əs   kʷθə sqʷəméyʔ ʔə kʷθə sθ'ámʔ
          Aux give-Recip-Tr-3A Det dog   Obl Det bone
          'He gave the dog the bone.'

     b. ni   qʷ'əl-əɫc-t-əs   ɫə   sɫéni   ʔə kʷθə səplíl
          Aux bake-Ben-Tr-3A Det woman   Obl Det   bread
          'He baked the bread for the woman.'

     c. ni   θ'ʷeykʷ'ʷ-méʔ-t-əs kʷθə sqʷəméyʔ
          Aux startle-Stim-Tr-3A Det   dog
          'He was startled by the dog.'

d. ni   yə?é?wə?-n-əs-əs   ɫə   sɫéni
Aux   come-Goal-Tr-3A   Det   woman
'He came toward the woman.'

Examples such as (2.70a–b) are, of course, similar to the English double-object construction (see Section 1.3.2), except with a recipient or benefactive suffix on the verb. One other difference is that the recipient and beneficiary objects are harder to analyse as indirect objects in Halkomelem because the patient is clearly an oblique, or at least a non-object, by multiple criteria and the recipient and beneficiary dependents are therefore the only objects. That they are indeed members of the O category is indicated, among other things, by the transitive suffix on the verbs, the A 3rd person suffix on the verb (indicating that these are transitive clauses and that there is thus an O), and the fact that, if they were 1st or 2nd person, the recipient and beneficiary would be indexed like an O on the verb, with an object pronominal suffix, as shown in (2.71), which summarizes the meanings of the full array of potential morphological markers.

(2.71)   O = BEN V HAS A & O   O = 1ST PERSON A = 3RD PERSON   PATIENT=OBLIQUE

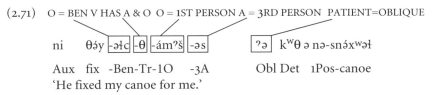

ni   θə́y -əɫc -θ -ám?š -əs   ?ə   kʷθ ə nə-snə́xʷəɫ
Aux   fix -Ben-Tr-1O   -3A   Obl Det   1Pos-canoe
'He fixed my canoe for me.'

Halkomelem also differs from English in that it does not have an alternative construction in which the recipient and beneficiary can be expressed as an oblique (or indirect object). What this means is that the most basic transitive clause type, which has the patient as O, is systematically ruled out for a verb with a recipient or beneficiary dependent. This appears to reflect a prominence hierarchy constraint that is, at some level of analysis, analogous to what happens with verbs that have a 3rd person agent and a 1st person patient in Southern Tiwa (see Section 2.2.1). In Southern Tiwa the potential active-clause realization of such a verb is ruled out, because the A cannot be outranked in terms of person prominence by the O. In Halkomelem the beneficiary and recipient dependents appear to always be animate and the patient appears to be typically inanimate. As Gerdts notes, there is an animacy hierarchy effect operative with the O category that is also manifested with the stimulus and goal applicative constructions illustrated by (2.70c–d). Goal and stimulus dependents can be alternatively expressed as obliques—and indeed have to be if they are inanimate:

(2.72) a.   ni   cən   c'ə́q'   ʔə   kʷθə   sx̌t'ə́kʼʷ-s   (*Inanimate oblique*)
           Aux 1Subj astonished Obl Det   carving-3Pos
           'I was astonished at his carving.'

       b.   ?*ni   cən   c'ə́q'-mé?-t   kʷθə   sx̌t'ə́kʼʷ-s   (?**Inanimate O*)
           Aux 1Subj astonished-Stim-Tr Det   carving-3Pos
           'I was astonished at his carving.'

       c.   ?? ni   cən   c'ə́q'   ʔə   kʷθə   sqʷəmə́y? (??*Animate oblique*)
           Aux 1Subj astonished Obl Det   dog
           'I was astonished at the dog.'

       d.   ni   cən   c'ə́q'-mé?-t   kʷθə   sqʷəmə́y?   (*Animate O*)
           Aux 1Subj astonished-Stim-Tr Det   dog
           'I was astonished at the dog.'

(2.73) a.   ni   ném   ʔə   kʷθə   stá?lu?   (*Inanimate oblique*)
           Aux   go   Obl   Det   river
           'He went to the river.'

       b.   *ni   ném-n-əs-əs   kʷθə   stá?lu?   (**Inanimate O*)
           Aux   go-Goal-Tr-3A   Det   river
           'He went to the river.'

       c.   ni   ném   ʔə-ƛ̓   John   (*Animate oblique*)
           Aux   go   Obl-Det   John
           'He went to John.'

       d.   ni   ném-n-əs-əs   kʷθə   John   (*Animate O*)
           Aux   go-Goal-Tr-3A   Det   John
           'He went to John.'

The situation with syntactic functions for non-patient dependents of a verb can be summed up as follows. Inanimate NPs cannot be an O, whereas animate NPs are preferentially expressed as an O, with the strength of the preference being determined by the inherent animacy of their semantic role (Rec/Ben > Stim > Goal). That is to say, the prototypical goal is a place rather than an animate participant; the recipient and beneficiary roles are necessarily associated with animate participants; and the stimulus role is neutral with respect to animacy. Ensuring that dependents with the higher cognitive salience associated with animacy have higher grammatical salience, and, therefore, maximal syntactic privilege, appears to be the main functional motivation for the system. Since the semantic role of the O can vary considerably, the applicative morphology on the verb serves to provide role information in the same way that prepositions and case markers do for constituents in dependent-marking languages.

Of crucial importance to understanding the grammatical correlates of applicative verbs in Halkomelem is that with respect to the phenomena for which only A/S/O dependents have special privileges, the oblique-marked patient fails to behave like an O, unlike the non-patient O-marked dependents, which show most O properties. For example, as noted in Section 2.1.2, a quantifier such as 'all' can only be floated (i.e. separated from the NP that it is associated with) from an absolutive (S/O) dependent and only a core dependent (A/S/O) can be put in contrastive focus in the cleft construction. The beneficiary rather than the patient behaves like an O with respect to quantifier float in (2.74a). The contrast between (2.74b) and (2.74c) shows that the recipient—not the patient—behaves like a core dependent with respect to clefting.

(2.74) a. mə́k'ʷ niw   ʔíləq-əɬc-t-ʔeːnʔ   kʷθə nə-méʔmənʔə ʔə kʷθə
           all   Aux.Lnk buy-Ben-Tr-1SgSubj Det 1Pos-offspring Obl Det
           qʷɬə́yʔšənʔ
           shoe
           'I bought all my children shoes/*all the shoes for my children.'
       b. niɬ   kʷθə Bob ni xʷàyəm-əs-t-ʔeːnʔ ʔə kʷθə nə-léləm-ʔə
           3Emph Det   Bob Aux sell-Rec-Tr-1SgSubj Obl Det 1Pos-house-Pst
           'It was Bob that I sold my house to.'
       c. *niɬ   kʷθə nə-léləm-ʔə   ni xʷàyəm-əs-t-ʔeːnʔ kʷθə   Bob
           3Emph Det 1Pos-house-Pst Aux sell-Rec-Tr-1SgSubj Det   Bob
           'It was my house that I sold to Bob.'

The non-patient dependent in every type of applicative construction shows parallel properties. It behaves like an O rather than an oblique, not only with respect to quantifier float and clefting, but also with respect to possessor extraction, relativization, and *wh*-question formation.[19]

Although the non-patient objects have many of the O properties of the language, they do differ from patient Os with respect to certain phenomena, such as reflexivization. If the agent and the patient are co-referential, a person-neutral reflexive suffix is added to the verb, making it intransitive, as shown in (2.75a–b). If a non-patient argument (normally expressed as an oblique) is co-referential with the agent, the reflexive suffix cannot be added to the verb (2.75c); instead, an emphatic oblique-marked pronominal form must be used (2.75d).

(2.75) a. ni   cən   xíq'-əθət
           Aux   1Subj   scratch-Refl
           'I scratched myself.'

b. ni   q'áy-θət
   Aux   kill-Refl
   'He killed himself.'

c. *ni   cən   čxʷmé:mʔ-θət
   Aux   1Subj   speak-Refl
   'I spoke about myself.'

d. ni   cən   čxʷmé:mʔ   ʔə-ƛ̓   ʔé:nθə
   Aux   1Subj   speak   Obl-Det   1Emph
   'I spoke about myself.'

In all of the applicative constructions, the O-marked dependent does not behave like a patient with respect to reflexivization. The reflexive suffix cannot be added to an applicative verb, as shown for the benefactive case in the following example.

(2.76) *ni   cən   θəy-əłc-θət   ʔə   kʷθə   snə́xʷəł
        Aux   1Subj   make-Ben-Refl   Obl   Det   canoe
        'I made myself a canoe.'

Non-patient Os also fail to behave like patient Os with respect to reciprocalization, which works in essentially the same way as reflexivization, but with a distinct suffix, and antipassive voice, which effectively demotes patients to oblique (see Section 2.2.2).

Although it has its own unique mix of complexities, which pose interesting analytical challenges, Halkomelem displays properties that are not atypical of applicative constructions cross-linguistically. In an applicative clause, a non-patient is marked like a member of the O category and takes on many of the syntactic privileges of the O category. In cases where the verb also has a patient dependent, it has none of the O privileges and is marked like an oblique. Halkomelem is, thus, an applicative language of an asymmetric type (Bresnan and Moshi 1990, McGinnis 2002), like Chichewa (Alsina and Mchombo 1990), Tzotzil (Aissen 1983), Chamorro (Gibson 1980), and many other languages, including (many dialects of) English, whose double-object construction is, from a typological perspective, a kind of applicative construction, modulo the possible interpretation of the O1 as an 'indirect object' rather than O (see Section 1.3.2). In languages of the symmetric type, such as Kinyarwanda (Kimenyi 1980, Dryer 1983) and other Bantu languages, such as Chi-Mwi:ni (Kisseberth and Abasheikh 1977) and Kichaga (Bresnan and Moshi 1990), both the patient and the non-patient dependents are bare NPs and behave syntactically like an O in most ways (at least with certain combinations of patient and non-patient). Kinyarwanda can have as many as three NPs with the morphosyntactic properties and privileges of an O in one clause. The examples in (2.77) and (2.78) (from Kimenyi 1980) illustrate the phenomenon. With verbs such as 'give' and 'ask', the recipient/addressee cannot be an oblique and does not require applicative marking, as shown in (2.77a) and (2.78a). An instrumental can be an oblique (2.77a); but can also be an O, in which case an instrumental marker must appear on the verb (2.77b). Beneficiaries can be added relatively freely to clauses but cannot be oblique and require an applicative suffix, as shown in (2.78a). Examples (2.77b) and (2.78a) show that there can be as many as three non-subject bare NPs, all of which have such A/S/O or O-restricted privileges as being able to be relativized, to be the subject in a passive clause, and to be realized as an object pronominal prefix on the verb, the latter possibility being illustrated by (2.78b).

(2.77) a. Úmwáana   y-a-sab-ye   umugóre   ibíryo   n'íntoki
           child   Subj-Pst-ask-Asp   woman   food   with.hands
           'The child asked the woman for food with his hands.'

    b. Úmwáana   y-a-sab-iish-ye   umugóre   ibíryo   intoki
        child   Subj-Pst-ask-Instr-Asp   woman   food   hands
        'The child asked the woman for food with his hands.'

(2.78) a. Umugóre   a-rá-hé-er-a   umugabo   ímbwa   ibíryo
           woman   Subj-Pres-give-Ben-Asp   man   dog   food
           'The woman is giving food to the dog for the man.'

    b. Umugóre   a-rá-bi-yí-mu-he-er-a
        woman   Subj-Pres-it-it-him-give-Ben-Asp
        'The woman is giving it to it for him.'

Languages with applicative constructions also differ with respect to the range of non-patient dependents that can be expressed as an O. The English applicative O is restricted to recipient-type semantic roles, as is the case for Korean (Park 2002), for example. Bantu languages, particularly Kinyarwanda, on the other hand, allow applicative Os to have a large range of semantic roles, including not only recipient and beneficiary, but also instrumental, locative, possessor of patient, and even 'adverbial' or adjunct roles of certain kinds. Other languages fall in between these extremes in various ways, although recipient applicative Os seem to always be at least one of the options. The use of overt verbal applicative marking also varies considerably. Languages like English and Korean, with only a kind of recipient applicative construction, seem generally not to have a morpheme dedicated to announcing the construction, whereas languages such as Kinyarwanda and Halkomelem, with various kinds of non-patient Os tend to favour overt marking. Whereas, Halkomelem has markers for recipient, benefactive, stimulus, and goal applicative Os, Kinyarwanda has distinct markers for instrumental, goal, and benefactive Os and no overt marking for recipient Os. Other Bantu languages, such as Chichewa, only have a single marker.

Partially independently of their syntactic behaviour, patient and non-patient dependents in applicative constructions can be marked in different ways. In English, Korean, and Bantu languages they both look like objects, that is they are bare NPs in English and Bantu and are both marked with an accusative case morpheme in Korean. In Chamorro and Halkomelem only the non-patient is a bare NP; the patient is marked with a general-purpose oblique preposition. However, even in languages that mark both in the same way, the applicative O never appears to be outranked by the patient O in terms of grammatical prominence, as evidenced by ability to participate in phenomena that are restricted to Os or dependents in the A/S/O categories.

Finally, languages differ with respect to whether certain non-patient semantic roles are obligatorily expressed as an O in an applicative construction or not. In Halkomelem, as discussed above, animate non-patients other than goal cannot be realized as obliques. In Tzotzil (Aissen 1983), recipients can only be an applicative O, whereas beneficiaries can either be an oblique/adjunct or an applicative O. In Chamorro, Korean, and English (for the most part), applicative Os of all types have an alternate oblique (or indirect object) realization. If there is a regularity, it seems to be that more animate or more cognitively salient event participants (e.g. recipient/beneficiary > location/instrument) are more likely to be restricted to an O realization.

Summarizing, some of the various possibilities for applicative constructions and some languages instantiating them are as in Table 2.3.[20]

TABLE 2.3. Some variable features of applicative constructions

	A	B	C	D	E
Kinyarwanda	yes	some	3	yes	yes
Kichaga	yes	some	1	yes	yes
Chichewa	no	some	1	yes	yes
Halkomelem	no	some	4	yes	no
Tzotzil	no	some	1	no	no
Chamorro	no	yes	1	yes	no
English	no	yes	0	no	yes
Korean	no	yes	0	no	yes

Legend: A: symmetric; B: oblique/O alternations; C: verbal morphemes; D: RECIP/BEN O + other non-patient Os; E: patient marked like O.

2.2.5 *The Philippine voice system*

Austronesian languages such as Tagalog, Cebuano, and Ilokano have often been analysed as having a unique voice system. The reason for this is that these languages generally have one primary privileged dependent in each clause and multiple voices (each with an associated verbal morphology), whereby dependents with various semantic roles can have the privileged function. The morphological form of the verb identifies, at least roughly, the general semantic role of the privileged NP. Although there are clear parallels with applicative-voice languages such as Halkomelem, discussed above, and, as noted below, it is possible to treat the Philippine system as one with some combination of applicative constructions and passive or antipassive constructions that function to promote various dependents to either O or S, the problem is that it is unclear that the primary privileged function is appropriately characterized as S/O. The basic system can be illustrated with the following Tagalog examples, adapted from Kroeger (1993).

(2.79) a. bumili   ang=lalake   ng=isda   sa=tindahan
           buy.Perf.Act ≻=man   Gen=fish   Loc=store
           'The man bought fish at the store.'

     b. binili   ng=lalake   ang=isda   sa=tindahan
           buy.Perf.Obj Gen=man   ≻=fish   Loc=store
           'The man bought the fish at the store.'

     c. binilhan   ng=lalake   ng=isda   ang=tindahan
           buy.Perf.Loc Gen=man   Gen=fish   ≻=store
           'The man bought fish at the store.'

     d. ipinambili   ng=lalake   ng=isda   ang=pera
           buy.Perf.Instr Gen=man   Gen=fish   ≻=money
           'The man bought fish with the money.'

     e. ibinili   ng=lalake   ng=isda   ang=bata
           buy.Perf.Ben Gen=man   Gen=fish   ≻=child
           'The man bought fish for the child.'

NPs are marked for case with one of three markers, for which different labels are used by different analysts. Although there are various uses for the *sa* case marker, it is generally associated with semantic roles such as location, source, goal, and recipient, for which reason I use the gloss 'Loc(ative)', following Foley and Van Valin (1984). The privileged NP, whose general semantic role is indicated by the voice marking on the verb, is marked with *ang*, which has been glossed in various ways by different analysts, including 'nominative', 'focus', and 'absolute'. However, since a particular analysis of the construction is implicit in the usual choices, I simply use the arbitrary symbol ➤, which is meant to indicate only that this is the special or privileged dependent. Dependents of verbs which are not marked with *ang* or *sa* are marked with *ng*. I follow Kroeber and others in calling this 'Gen(itive)', since it is also used to mark the possessor relation within NPs. It is not uncommon in languages for the possessor-marking device to be extended to various clause-level dependency relationships. In these examples, the verb root is *bili*. Various combinations of infixes, prefixes, and suffixes are used to indicate aspect and voice. I make no attempt here to segment and individually label the different components of the verb stem. The key fact is that the form of the verb correlates with which dependent is marked with *ang*. Although there are idiosyncrasies of various kinds, the general system can be summarized as follows. Active voice is used with an *ang*-marked agent (2.79a). Objective voice is used with an *ang*-marked patient (2.79b). Locative, instrumental, and benefactive voices are used with *ang*-marked NPs with a generalized locative, instrumental, or beneficiary role, respectively (2.79c–e). For the most part, grammatical relations are indicated by the combination of information from the voice marking on the verb and the sparse case marking information. Although the NP constituents can appear in various orders, there are certain preferences, such as agent first and, otherwise, *ang*-marked NP last.

The phenomenon known as quantifier float illustrates how the *ang*-marked dependent is the privileged one. Although certain quantifiers, such as *lahat* 'all', normally appear within the NP that they modify, for purposes of emphasis they can also be placed right after the verb, dislocated from their associated NP. As the following examples show, in every voice *lahat* must be interpreted as modifying the *ang*-marked NP (or ➤ dependent).

(2.80) a. sumusulat   lahat ng=mga=bata   ang=mga=liham
           buy.Imperf.Obj   all   Gen=Pl=child   ➤=Pl=letter
           'The/some children are writing all the letters.'
         * 'All the children wrote the letters.'

       b. sinusulat   lahat ang=mga=bata   ng=mga=liham
           buy.Imperf.Act   all   ➤=Pl=child   Gen=Pl=letter
           'All the children are writing letters.' Not: 'all the letters'

       c. binigyan   lahat ng=mga=guro   ng=pera   ang=mga=child
           give.Perf.Loc all   Gen=Pl=teacher Gen=money   ➤=Pl=child
           '(The) teachers gave money to all the children.'
           Not: 'all the teachers/money.'

Relativization also works in terms of the same privileged constituent. A relative clause in Tagalog is simply a clause with a missing constituent that modifies the NP that it immediately follows. The modified NP controls the interpretation of the missing NP, as shown by the following examples. (The *ni* and *kay* case markers are the allomorphs of *ng* and *sa*, respectively, that are used with proper names.)

(2.81) a.   ang=bata=ng [nanuksu   Ø   kay=Josie]
            ⪰= child=Lnk tease.Perf.Act   Loc=Josie
            'The child that teased Josie.'

   b.   ang=bata-ng [tinuksu   Ø   ni=Josie]
            ⪰= child=Lnk tease.Perf.Obj   Gen=Josie
            'The child that Josie teased.'

If the relative clause is in the active voice, the gap in the relative clause is necessarily interpreted as the agent, which is the ⪰ dependent, as shown by (2.81a). If the verb of the relative clause is in any other voice, the gap must be interpreted as the ⪰ dependent in that voice, as shown for objective voice in (2.81b).

Other phenomena that are restricted to the ⪰ dependent, like quantifier float and relativization, include control of secondary predication, possessor raising, number agreement, raising to object from an embedded clause, and conjunction reduction. There are also phenomena that are sensitive to other categories of dependents. Consider, for example, control of participial complements of verbs such as 'leave', 'catch', and 'find', which in Tagalog take the form of a clause with a verb in a non-completive aspect and a 'missing' dependent, as illustrated by the following examples.

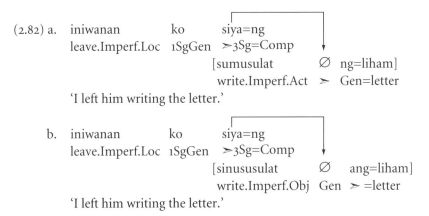

(2.82) a.   iniwanan   ko   siya=ng
            leave.Imperf.Loc 1SgGen   ⪰3Sg=Comp
                              [sumusulat   Ø   ng=liham]
                              write.Imperf.Act   ⪰   Gen=letter
            'I left him writing the letter.'

   b.   iniwanan   ko   siya=ng
            leave.Imperf.Loc 1SgGen   ⪰3Sg=Comp
                              [sinususulat   Ø   ang=liham]
                              write.Imperf.Obj Gen   ⪰   =letter
            'I left him writing the letter.'

c. inabutan   ko   si= Manuel
    catch.Imperf.Loc 1SgGen   ➤= Manuel
                    na   [hinahalikan   ng=katulong   ∅]
                    Comp   kiss.Imperf.Obj   Gen=maid   ➤
            'I caught Manuel being kissed by the maid.'

Although the controller has to be the ➤ dependent, the controllee can either be the agent or the ➤ dependent. The controllee is the ➤ dependent and the agent in an active voice clause in (2.82a), the agent and genitive dependent in an objective voice clause in (2.82b), and the patient and ➤ dependent in an objective voice clause in (2.82c). Under no circumstance can the controllee be anything but an agent or the ➤ dependent. A similar constraint is operative with respect to the controller of a participial adjunct construction (Kroeger 1993: 42).

As discussed in Section 1.3.3, there is a so-called adjunct-fronting construction that privileges the following class of constituents: adverbials, prepositional phrases (expressing, for example, causal, instrumental, or beneficiary roles), and NPs marked with locative case. The class of constituents excluded from adjunct fronting consists of the ➤ dependent and all NPs marked with genitive case, including some NPs with the instrumental role, agents with verbs not in the active voice, and patients with verbs not in the objective voice. With this in mind, the grammar of Tagalog seems to operate with the syntactic categories shown in Figure 2.2.

The classification of the ➤ dependent is the key question in some sense. One approach, worked out in some detail for the very similar grammar of Cebuano in Bell (1976, 1983; see also Bloomfield 1917, Perlmutter and Postal 1984) takes the ➤ dependent to be S/A, or subject, in an accusative language, with all voices other than active being variations on passive voice. On the accusative analysis, the ➤ dependent category is more specifically that of final (or surface) subject, whereas the α category in Figure 2.2 is that of any kind of subject (final or initial/logical). The genitive marking with the β category is attributed to the multifunctionality of genitive case (= accusative case, demoted agent case, instrumental case, etc.). It is unclear how the γ category might be accounted for.

Another approach takes languages of this sort to be basically ergative languages (e.g. Dryer 1978, Payne 1982, De Guzman 1988, Cooreman *et al.* 1988, Gerdts 1988b, Blake 1990: ch. 7, Farrell 1994a: ch. 4). The ➤ dependent is the S/O or absolutive NP. In all transitive clauses with voices in which it is marked genitive, the agent is simply the A. The active voice is actually antipassive voice (see Section 2.2.2), with the patient demoted, such that the agent is the S. The instrumental, benefactive, and locative voices are simply applicative constructions (see Section 2.2.4),[21] with the patient demoted such that NPs with various semantic roles can be the O. Under this approach, the phenomena restricted to the ➤ dependent, are restricted to the S/O category, the α category in Figure 2.2 is that of A/S/O. The genitive marking with the β category is attributed to the multifunctionality of genitive case (= ergative case, demoted patient case, instrumental case, etc.). It is unclear how the γ category might be accounted for.

A third general approach takes languages of the Tagalog kind to be neither accusative nor ergative. There is one main distinction: ➤ vs. other dependents. The various voices are, in some sense, different varieties of an inverse voice of the kind suggested for Jarawara in Section 2.2.3, inasmuch as the agent is expressed as a core constituent rather than an oblique in the voices in which it is not the ➤ dependent. The ➤ dependent is called either the topic (Schachter 1976), the subject (Kroeger 1993), or the pragmatic pivot (Foley and Van Valin 1984). Relativization, quantifier float, raising to object, etc., are constrained to work with the subject or pragmatic pivot (=the ➤ dependent as indicated by the voice of the verb). All other constituents of the clause are either core arguments (=the β category in Figure 2.2) or non-core constituents, including obliques and adjuncts (=the γ category). Adjunct fronting works only for non-core constituents. Genitive marking is used for non-subject core dependents of the verb. The category α is that of agent/S/A.

In any case, whether Philippine languages are ultimately amenable to a standard accusative or ergative analysis or not, the complexity of the voice system and its interaction with case marking and the unique ways in which the categories of syntactically privileged constituents are constituted pose interesting challenges for typologies of grammatical relations and theories of syntax.

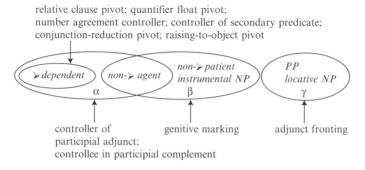

relative clause pivot; quantifier float pivot;
number agreement controller; controller of secondary predicate;
conjunction-reduction pivot; raising-to-object pivot

➤ *dependent*   *non-*➤ *agent*   *non-*➤ *patient*
instrumental NP   *PP*
locative NP

α   β   γ

controller of   genitive marking   adjunct fronting
participial adjunct;
controllee in participial complement

FIGURE 2.2. Tagalog syntactic categories

2.3 Function splitting and quasi-subjects/objects

As should be clear from the discussion in the previous sections of voice constructions and the typological parameters of grammatical-relation marking systems, defining the role categories that the grammars of languages operate with is a non-trivial matter. In an ideal system, the head-marking, dependent-marking, and constituent-order devices of a language would identify a uniform set of grammatical relations in a consistent way and syntactic phenomena such as relative clause formation, quantifier float, control, raising, and conjunction reduction would operate straightforwardly in terms of the same categories. Natural languages, however, tend to be more complex—presumably for good reasons that remain somewhat obscure. Often, alternative relation-marking devices mark the same dependent of a verb as having different grammatical relations. In Choctaw, for example, under certain conditions an NP that is case-marked nominative (S/A) can be indexed on the verb with the affix that is used for the O of a transitive clause (see Section 2.1.3). Morphologically ergative languages, in fact, generally employ relation-marking systems that are partially at odds with each other (see Section 2.1.2). Even more remarkably, in one voice construction in Jarawara the preverbal pronominal indexing mechanism seems to identify as A and O the same dependents that the constituent-order and gender-agreement mechanisms identify as O and A, respectively (see Section 2.2.3). It seems, however, that when all of the marking information is taken into account and interpreted, a coherent system of grammatical relations can invariably be discerned, although sometimes there may be viable alternative analyses. Even so, the syntactic processes of a language may not operate entirely in terms of the same system of grammatical relations. For example, in Kamaiurá (see Section 2.1.3) the morphological marking devices indicate that the main categories are A/S_a and O/S_o, with subjects of intransitives splitting into two distinct classes. For the purposes of relative clause formation, however, there are different strategies to relativize A, S, O, and oblique functions. Thus, S is treated as a uniform category, distinct from both A and O. Similarly, possessor raising is constrained to occur with S/O rather than just O/S_o dependents.

An even more complex issue is that grammatical phenomena within and across languages work in terms of complex and hybrid categories of grammatical relations, some of which are quite different than those that the primary marking systems ever indicate. In Halkomelem (see Sections 2.1.2 and 2.2.1), although certain grammatical phenomena are constrained to occur with such syntactic functions as S/O or any A/S/O function, which the marking devices of the language explicitly indicate, others are not. For example, the pivot in the raising to object construction must be either the S/A of the embedded clause or the passive oblique agent, suggesting that the apparently oblique agent is subject-like to some extent and that the category of relevance to the phenomenon is different from and more complex than any of the categories that the head-marking and dependent-marking devices indicate. Similarly, in Tagalog (Section 2.2.5) most syntactic phenomena are restricted to the *ang*-marked dependent (generally considered to be the S/A or S/O). However, the controller of participial adjuncts, for example, can be either the *ang*-marked dependent or a genitive agent. It turns out that, across languages, demoted agents frequently have at least some S/A properties. Thus, a subject-sensitive function can sometimes be split between two different dependents. In what follows, the general kind of a dependent that has a restricted subset of the morphosyntactic properties of a subject, is referred to as a QUASI-SUBJECT. This term is not meant to designate a particular grammatical relation; it is merely a theory-independent and analysis-neutral label for a type of dependent that has subject syntactic privileges to some limited extent.

Similarly, the 'demoted' patient in applicative constructions (see Section 2.2.4) is O-like to varying degrees across languages. In certain Bantu languages, such as Kinyarwanda, it generally has both the morphological marking and syntactic privileges of an O. In Halkomelem, it appears to have no O properties at all, although it also differs partially from similarly marked non-patient obliques. In English, on the other hand, although the patient (or second object) in the double-object construction is not O-like in that it cannot be placed right-adjacent to the verb and generally cannot be the subject in a passive clause (at least for most speakers—see Section 1.3.2), it is like a prototypical patient O in that it is not marked by a preposition and, unlike oblique complements (2.83b) and like Os (2.83a), it can, at least under certain circumstances (e.g. Bolinger 1971: ch. 4), precede a preposition functioning as a so-called particle (i.e. a discontinuous part of a compound or 'phrasal' verb), as shown by (2.83c).

(2.83) a.   I want you to give the exams *back* to them.
       b.   *I want you to give the exams to them *back*.
       c.   I want you to give them the exams *back*.

Although there are various analyses and labels that have been used for the second object in this construction, it is, from a descriptive and typological perspective, a QUASI-OBJECT, since it has a restricted set of the O-defining properties of the language.

Even outside of the standard voice and 'relation-changing' constructions, in many languages the dependents of certain verb classes can be marked in ways that are at odds to varying degrees with what their overall grammatical behaviour suggests about their syntactic function. In some cases, as with Icelandic dative subjects (often called 'quirky subjects'), discussed briefly in Section 1.2, the syntactic behaviour of the dependent in question is system- atically subject-like, in spite of the dependent-marking or head-marking morphology. Icelandic dative (and accusative or genitive) subjects have most of the many S/A syntactic privileges of the language. They essentially only fail to behave like subjects with respect to morphological marking, that is case marking and verb agreement. In other languages, certain similar kinds of dative-marked NPs may have only a small set of the various syntactic privil- eges of the prototypical subject. Although it is not entirely clear how to draw a line or whether one should be drawn, this latter type, considered to be a quasi-subject, is distinguished here from the Icelandic type, which is called an OBLIQUE SUBJECT (or dative subject, accusative subject, etc.).[22] Although possibly less common and certainly less well-studied, the same kind of variation appears to occur with objects. Some languages use alternatives to O-marking with dependents that otherwise have essentially all the syntactic privileges of objects and are thus OBLIQUE OBJECTS, whereas other languages have quasi-objects, often with certain verbs or verb classes, that have a much more restricted set of object properties and may or may not be marked like an oblique.

2.3.1 *Quasi-subjects and oblique subjects*

Beyond the passive agents of some languages, there are various kinds of syntactic constructions that could be characterized as having quasi-subjects. In English, for example, the P-marked location-designating NPs in the fol- lowing sentences occupy the preverbal slot normally reserved for S/A depend- ents, whereas the postverbal NP determines the presence or absence of the 3rd singular S/A-indexing -s suffix.

(2.84) a.   At the top of that mountain sits an eagle's nest.
       b.   In this grave lie the remains of a great man.

In this so-called LOCATIVE INVERSION construction (Coopmans 1989, Levin and Rappaport Hovav 1995: ch. 6, Bresnan 1994, Ura 2000: ch. 5), both dependents are quasi-subjects, by virtue of the fact that each has at least one S/A property and neither has all of the S/A properties. Numerous positions have been taken on if either of the dependents is the 'true' subject. Any analysis that attempts to portray either as the true subject runs into difficulties with the fact that neither, for example, can undergo subject-Aux inversion (2.85), be construed with a 'floated' quantifier (2.86), for which there is an S/A constraint, or be the subject of a raising verb such as *seem* (2.87), a possibility restricted to the S/A of the embedded infinitival phrase (see Section 2.2.1).

(2.85) a.   Did these children see the movie?
     b.   * Does at the top of the mountain sit an eagle's nest?
     c.   * Does an eagle's nest at the top of the mountain sit?

(2.86) a.   These children *both* watched the movies.
     b.   * In these graves *both* lie those great men.

(2.87) a.   These children seemed [$\emptyset_A$ to like the movie].
     b.   ??At the top of the mountain seems [$\emptyset$ to sit an eagle's nest].
     c.   *An eagle's nest seems [at the top of the mountain to sit $\emptyset$].

Many languages have an analogous construction in which the locative dependent has varying degrees of subject properties, with Bantu languages such as Chichewa apparently having an oblique subject in the Icelandic sense (Bresnan and Kanerva 1989). English also has a locative PP subject in a copular non-verbal predicate construction that only superficially resembles the preverbal locative inversion quasi-subject, and which might be designated an oblique subject, as shown by the following examples:

(2.88) a.   Behind the couch is a good place to hide.
     b.   Is behind the couch a good place to hide?
     c.   Behind the couch and under the bed are *both* good places to hide.
     d.   Behind the couch seems [$\emptyset_s$ to be a good place to hide].

Probably the most well-studied kind of quasi-subject is the verb or verb-class restricted dative kind that is found in many languages of different families and types, including Germanic languages (Allen 1995, Sigurðsson 2002), Russian and Polish (Dziwirek 1994, Franks 1995, Moore and Perlmutter 2000), Marathi, Newari, and Hindi (Joshi 1993, Rosen and Wali 1989, Mohanan 1994, Bickel and Yādava 2000), French and Italian (Perlmutter 1984, Belletti and Rizzi 1988, Legendre 1989a), Choctaw (Davies 1986), K'ekchi (Berinstein 1990), and Korean and Japanese (Ura 1999, 2000). Although these languages are often claimed to have dative subjects in the Icelandic sense, the dependent type in question in many of these languages has relatively few syntactic subject properties, as noted by Moore and Perlmutter (2000).

In addition to a certain class of psychological verbs—discussed briefly in Section 1.2—whose experiencer and stimulus dependents are always marked dative and nominative, respectively, but which alternate freely between subject and non-subject (Barðdal 2001). Icelandic has verbs and other predicates of certain classes that have a dative, accusative, or genitive dependent that is a non-alternating subject (i.e. S or A). Most of these are either passivized verbs or psychological verbs of some kind. The following examples (adapted from Sigurðsson 2002) illustrate a few kinds of dative subjects, to which attention is limited here.

(2.89) a. Mér   höfðu alltaf   virst   stelpurnar   vera gáfaðar.
           1SgDat had.3Pl always   seemed girls.FemPlNom to.be intelligent
           'The girls had always seemed to me to be intelligent.'

       b. Mér   var   hjálpað.
           1SgDat   was   helped
           'I was helped.'

       c. Ólafi   leiddist.
           Olaf.Dat   bored
           'Olaf was bored.'

Neither the case morphology nor the verb agreement marks the preverbal NP in clauses like these as the S/A dependent. In (2.89a), for example, the postverbal nominative NP rather than the 1st person dative subject is indexed by the agreement morphology on the auxiliary verb. When there is no nominative NP, the predicate (auxiliary/verb/adjective complex) is in a non-agreeing or 3rd singular form. The following examples highlight the agreement contrast between dative and nominative subjects with a predicate that alternates between dative and nominative subjects, correlative with a difference in meaning.

(2.90) a. Strákarnir   höfðu   verið   illir.
           boys.MascPlNom   had.3Pl been   bad.MascPlNom
           'The boys had been angry.'

       b. Strákunuum   hafði   verið   illt.
           boys.Dat   had.3Sg been   bad.NeutSg
           'The boys had been ill/felt badly.'

Since agents of volitional action-denoting predicates are invariably agreement controllers in nominative form, as are the experiencers of many verbs of psychological experience, it is perhaps tempting to consider the preverbal dative NPs in examples like (2.89) and (2.90b) to be topicalized or fronted constituents in clauses with no subject, or with a postverbal subject in the case of (2.89a). However, with respect to numerous syntactic phenomena (as many as sixteen according to Sigurðsson, including reflexive antecedence, subject-verb inversion, raising, complement control, and conjunction reduction) only the preverbal NP in such clauses behaves like a subject. For example, like the nominative A of a verb like *lesa* 'read'(2.91), a dative subject of an embedded verb can be the subject of a raising verb such as *byrja* 'begin' (2.92).

(2.91) a. Ólafur   las   bókina.
           Olaf.Nom read book.Acc
           'Olaf read the book.'

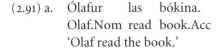

  b. Ólafur   byrjaði [∅   að lesa   bókina].
      boys.Dat began   A   to read book.Acc
      'Olaf began to read the book.'

(2.92) a. Ólafi   leiddist.
           Olaf.Dat bored
           'Olaf was bored.'

  b. Ólafi   byrjaði [að   ∅   leiðast].
      Olaf.Dat began   Comp S bore
      'Olaf began to get bored.'

Similarly, it is possible to have a dative subject as the pivot in a controlled complement clause (2.93a) or a conjunction-reduction structure (2.93b). As in English, the pivot in such constructions has to be the S/A dependent.

(2.93) a. Ég   vonaðist [til að ∅   verda hjálpað].
           1SgNom hoped   Comp S$_{DAT}$ was   helped
           'I hoped to be helped.'

  b. Ég   hafði mikið að gera] og [∅   var samt ekki hjálpað].
      1SgNom had   much to do   and S$_{DAT}$ was still not helped
      'I had much to do and was still not helped.'

As noted by Sigurðsson, even though German has certain superficially similar dative experiencer constructions, as illustrated by (2.94), the dative NP generally lacks syntactic subject properties, as illustrated—in brief—for complement control and conjunction reduction by the examples in (2.95).

(2.94) a. Mir   ist   kalt.
           1SgDat is   cold
           'I'm cold.'

  b. Mir   wurde geholfen.
      1SgDat was   helped
      'I was helped.'

(2.95) a.   *Ich   hoffte [Ø   geholfen zu werden].
            1SgNom hoped S$_{DAT}$ helped   to be
            'I hoped to be helped.'

      b.   *[Ich hatte viel   zu tun] und [Ø   wurde trotzdem nicht geholfen].
            I   had much to do   and S$_{DAT}$ was   still   not helped
            'I had much to do and was still not helped.'

Unlike in Icelandic, such dative NPs in German appear to be non-subjects, or, at most, quasi-subjects.

The experiencer dependent of certain psychological verbs in French is not a subject according to the dependent-marking, head-marking, and constituent-order conventions of the language. With respect to these conventions, it behaves like an indirect object (or dative oblique) as shown by the following examples (with essentially literal English glosses).

(2.96) a.   Pierre a téléphoné à Marie.
            Pierre telephoned to Marie. (i.e. 'called Marie')
      b.   Pierre lui a téléphoné.
            Pierre 3SgDat-telephoned.

(2.97) a.   Cette femme plait à Pierre.
            This woman pleases to Pierre. (i.e. 'is pleasing to Pierre')
      b.   Cette femme lui plait.
            This woman 3SgDat-pleases.

(2.98) a.   Elle manque à sa famille.
            She misses to her family. (i.e. 'Her family misses her.')
      b.   Elle lui manque.
            She 3SgDat-misses. (i.e. 'He/she misses her.')

Both the addressee NP of a verb such as *téléphoner* and the experiencer NP of verbs such as *plaire* 'please' and *manquer* 'miss' are marked with a preposition, are placed postverbally, and, when pronominal, are realized as a dative verbal affix/clitic (which the standard orthography shows as a preverbal word). The usual analysis is that dative/*à*-marked dependents such as these are indirect objects. They fail to behave like subjects with respect to such S-/A-restricted phenomena as conjunction reduction, raising, and complement control. For example, as in English, only the preverbal NP in a sentence such as (2.96a) can be an omitted element (i.e. pivot) in the second of two conjoined clauses, under the control of the S/A of the first clause, as shown by (2.99). Similarly in an inifinitival phrase embedded under a verb such as *vouloir* 'want,' the pivot, which is controlled by the subject of *vouloir*, can only be the S/A of the infinitival verb (2.101). With verbs in the *plaire* class, the stimulus NP can be a conjunction-reduction pivot or a controllee, but the dative experiencer cannot, as shown by (2.100) and (2.102).

(2.99) a.   [Pierre-$_S$ est entré dans un café] et [Ø-$_S$ a téléphoné à Marie].
            'Pierre went into a café and telephoned to Marie.'

b.   [Pierre-$_S$ est entré dans un café] et [Marie lui/*Ø a téléphoné].
            'Pierre went into a café and Marie 3SgDat/*Ø-telephoned.'

(2.100) a.   [Il-$_S$ est bien mignon] et [Ø-$_{NOM}$ plait à Corinne].
            'He is very cute and pleases to Corinne.'

b.   [Il-$_S$ a plusieurs amis] et [cela lui/*Ø plait].
            'He has many friends and that 3SgDat/*Ø-pleases.'

(2.101) a.   Pierre veut [Ø-$_S$ téléphoner à Marie].
            'Pierre wants to telephone to Marie.'

b.   *Pierre veut [Marie téléphoner Ø-$_{DAT}$].
            'Pierre wants Marie to telephone (to him).'

(2.102) a.   Pierre veut [Ø-$_{NOM}$ plaire à Marie].
            'Pierre wants to please to Marie.'

b.   *Pierre veut [Marie plaire Ø-$_{DAT}$].
            'Pierre wants Marie to please (him).'

The experiencer dependent of *plaire, manquer,* and other similar verbs in French is clearly not a dative/oblique subject in the Icelandic sense. It is, however, a quasi-subject, inasmuch as it has 'subject' properties with respect to control of missing subjects in certain kinds of adverbial phrases. As shown by the following examples (adapted from Legendre 1989*a*), the controller of 'before/after' infinitival phrases with a missing subject, which ordinarily must be an S/A, can also be the dative dependent of a verb in the *plaire* class.

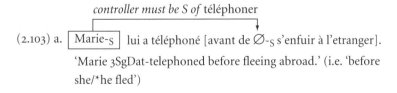

controller must be S of téléphoner

(2.103) a.   Marie-$_S$ lui a téléphoné [avant de Ø-$_S$ s'enfuir à l'etranger].
            'Marie 3SgDat-telephoned before fleeing abroad.' (i.e. 'before she/*he fled')

controller can be either Nominative or Dative dependent of plaire

b.   Que cette femme lui plaise [avant même de Ø-s lui avior parlé...]

'That this woman should 3SgDat-please before even 3SgDat-having spoken.' (i.e. 'That this woman should be pleasing to him before her having spoken to him' or 'before his having spoken to her').

Legendre also shows that the dative experiencer of verbs in the *plaire* class can be controllers for certain other kinds of participial or infinitival adverbial phrases, for which the constraint otherwise works in term of the notion 'subject'.

Similar kinds of limited syntactic subject properties (generally, ability to control adverbial phrases and reflexive pronouns) characterize the dative dependents of certain classes of verbs in languages such as Polish (Dziwirek 1994), Russian (Moore and Perlmutter 2000), and Italian (Perlmutter 1984). The extent to which these quasi-subjects are subject-like varies somewhat, however. In Italian, for example, the dative quasi-subject can not only be a controller for infinitival and participial adverbial phrases, but can also antecede certain reflexives and is preferably placed in the preverbal subject position (Belletti and Rizzi 1988), unlike in French. Choctaw (Davies 1986) is even closer to the Icelandic end of the quasi-subject spectrum. The dative quasi-subject in Choctaw triggers indirect object agreement on the verb and cannot be the pivot in a complement control construction (unlike in Icelandic, for example—see (2.93)). However, it is subject-like in that it has nominative dependent marking and can be a controller for the purposes of reflexives, switch-reference marking, and complement control.

2.3.2 *Quasi-objects and oblique objects*

Direct objects are sometimes marked in different ways, correlative with certain semantic distinctions. For example, in many languages overt morphological O marking can alternate with no marking, depending on relative salience in terms of either person/animacy or definiteness (Bossong 1991, Aissen 2003). By way of illustration, the Australian ergative language Pitjantjatjara uses the absolutive case marker -*nya* on O dependents if they are pronouns or proper names (2.104a) but not if they are common NPs (2.104b).

(2.104) a.   tjitji-ngku   Billy-nya/ngayu-nya   nya-ngu
              child-Erg   Billy-Abs/1Sg-Abs   see-Pst
              'The child saw Billy/me.'
        b.   Billy-lu   tjitji   nya-ngu
              Billy-Erg   child   see-Pst
              'Billy saw the child.'   (Aissen 2003)

There is a similar constraint in Romanian, which obligatorily case marks only animate-referring proper or pronominal NPs (Farkas 1978, Dobrovie-Sorin 1994) and certain Bantu languages, in which the obligatoriness of O head marking is contingent on whether the O is animate-referring or, in some cases, human-referring (Morimoto 2002). In other languages, such as Hebrew (Givón 1978) and Turkish (Enç 1991), only NPs whose referents are high in definiteness or specificity are overtly case-marked. Although these kinds of marking alternations have a semantic dimension, in general they do not indicate syntactic function distinctions.

In Spanish, human-referring NPs that are also specific are marked with the same preposition that is used for indirect objects (IOs) (e.g. Zagona 2002: ch. 1). The inanimate-referring O (*la casa* 'the house') in (2.105a) and (2.105b) is a bare NP, whereas the human-referring O in (2.105b) is marked with the preposition *a* 'to', like the IO in (2.105a).

(2.105) a. Marta le   vendió la   casa   *a*   una   mujer.
            Marta 3SgDat   sold   the   house to   a   woman
            'Marta sold the house to the woman.'

     b. Marta vio   la   casa / vio   *a*   una   mujer.
         Marta saw   the   house   saw   to   a   woman
         'Marta saw the house/saw a woman.'

The *a*-marked O is apparently a 'dative direct object' or oblique object, analogous to the Icelandic dative subject, rather than either an indirect object or a quasi-object, which is to say that it is morphologically marked like an indirect object/oblique while having all the syntactic privileges of an O.[23] O-dependents are distinguished from obliques and indirect objects by their ability to be the S of a passive clause (2.106) and the pivot in the *tough*-movement construction (2.107) or the *lo que* pseudocleft construction (2.108).

(2.106) a. La casa fue vendida/vista por Marta.
            'The house was sold/seen by Marta.'

     b. *La mujer fue vendida la casa.
         'The woman was sold the house.'

(2.107) a. Esas casas son difíciles de vender/ver.
            'These houses are difficult to sell/see.'

     b. *Esas mujeres son difíciles de (les) vender casas (a).
         'These women are difficult to (3PlDat) sell houses (to).'

(2.108) a. Lo que vendí/vi fue una casa.
            'What I sold/saw was a house.'

     b. *Lo que (le) vendí la casa fue a una mujer.
         'What I (3SgDat) sold the house was to a woman.'

Human-referring Os that are *a*-marked behave like their nonhuman-referring counterparts rather than like IOs with respect to these O-defining syntactic properties:

(2.109) a.   La mujer fue vista por muchas personas.
             'The woman was seen by many people.'
        b.   Los soldados a veces son difíciles de ver.
             'Soldiers are sometimes difficult to see.'
        c.   Lo que vi fue a una mujer.
             'What I saw was a woman.'

Brazilian Portuguese (Farrell 2004) provides a clearer example of a kind of quasi-object. Two of several classes of verbs designating psychological or emotional states or processes can be distinguished according to whether the stimulus-referring dependent is expressed as the O or as an oblique marked with *de* 'of, from', which is either a preposition or a prefixal marker on a determiner, as illustrated by the following examples (with more or less literal translations).

(2.110) a.   Eu amo/adoro/odeio aquela música.
             'I love/adore/hate that song.'
        b.   Eu cansei/enjoei daquela música.
             'I tired/sickened of-that song.'

The two kinds of non-subject dependents systematically differ with respect to the O-defining properties of the language. The bare NP type can be expressed as an accusative pronominal clitic (see Section 2.1.1), as shown by (2.111a), can be alternatively expressed as the subject of a passive clause (2.112a), can be the pivot in the *o que* pseudocleft construction (2.113a), the *tough*-movement construction (2.114a), and the reflexive/reciprocal *se* construction (2.115a) (see Section 1.3.2). The *de*-marked stimulus dependent of verbs such as *cansar* and *enjoar*, like other oblique dependents, has none of these O-defining properties, as shown by the (b)-examples in the following contrasting sentence pairs.

(2.111) a.   Minha mãe o amava.
             'My mother 3SgMasc-loved.'
        b.   *Minha mãe o cansou.
             'My mother 3SgMasc-tired.'

(2.112) a.   Aquela música foi adorada por todo mundo.
             'That song was adored by everyone.'
        b.   *Aquela música foi enjoada por todo mundo.
             'That song was sickened (of) by everyone.'

(2.113) a.   O que odiei foi a comida.
           'What I hated was the food.'
    b.   *O que cansei foi da comida.
           'What I tired was of-the food.'

(2.114) a.   Pessoas como essas são difíceis de amar.
           'People like those are hard to love.'
    b.   *Este lugar é difícil de cansar.
           'This place is hard to tire (of).'

(2.115) a.   Meus pais se amam muito.
           'My parents 3Rec-love a lot.'
    b.   *Meus pais se cansaram muito.
           'My parents 3Rec-tired a lot.'
           (i.e. *'got really tired of each other', but OK: 'got really tired'[24])

There is a third class of psychological verbs, including at least *gostar* 'like' and *precisar* 'need,'[25] whose stimulus dependent is obligatorily *de*-marked (at least when it is expressed in the default postverbal position) like the stimulus of *cansar* 'tire' and *enjoar* 'sicken', as illustrated by (2.116a). With this class of verbs, the *de*-marked dependent behaves like an oblique with respect to passivization (2.116b) and the accusative pronominal clitic (2.116c),[26] but like an O with respect to the other O-constrained phenomena (2.116d–f).

(2.116) a.   Eu gosto daquilo/*aquilo.
           'I like of-that/*that.'
    b.   *Aquela música foi gostada por todo mundo.
           'That music was liked by everyone.'
    c.   *Minha mãe o gostou.
           'My mother 3SgAcc-liked.'
    d.   O que gostei foi da comida.
           'What I liked was of-the food.'
    e.   Este lugar é difícil de não gostar.
           'This place is hard not to like.'
    f.   A gente se gosta muito.
           'We 3Rec-like a lot.' (i.e. 'We really like each other.')

To be more precise about the phenomena in question, only the passive and accusative clitic constraints are strictly O-specific constraints. The others do, however, distinguish between the categories O and oblique, and in most cases O, IO, and oblique. The pivot of the *o que* psedocleft construction, for example, can be any A/S/O dependent (e.g. *O que me irrita é a desonestidade* 'What irritates me is dishonesty'), but not an IO (*O que vendi isso foi a ele* 'What I sold

this was to him') or any oblique (*O que a meia desapareceu foi da gaveta* 'What
the socks disappeared was from the drawer'). The reflexive/reciprocal pivot is
restricted to the category O/IO (see Section 2.1.1). The *tough*-movement construction works on a split-intransitive basis, excluding A, IO, and oblique pivots,
but allowing both O pivots and sufficiently patient-like S pivots (e.g. *Essa
mancha vai ser difícil de sair* 'This stain is going to be hard to come out' vs.
Essa mulher vai ser difícil de gritar 'This woman is going to be hard to shout').
Thus, the categories of dependent types relevant to the constraints on the
phenomena in question are as shown in Table 2.4. The *de*-marked dependent
of verbs in the *gostar* class is a quasi-object, inasmuch as it is both O-like and
oblique-like in terms of its syntactic privileges and morphological properties.

Indonesian has a somewhat similar kind of quasi-object, with a large class
of verbs of cognition and emotion, including *sengan* 'like, happy', *sayang* 'love,
pity', *lupa* 'forget', and *takut* 'afraid' (Musgrave 2001, to appear). Unlike in
Brazilian Portuguese, the stimulus argument with these verbs can, in general,
be alternatively realized as a prepositionally-marked oblique, as shown by
(2.117a), a 'true' O with an applicative marker on the verb (2.117b), or a quasi-
object, which is unmarked (2.117c).

(2.117) a. Ali   sengan   dengan   rumah itu(*oblique, P-marked stimulus*)
           Ali   like/happy with   house   that
           'Ali likes the house.'

     b. Ali   sengan-i   rumah   itu   (*stimulus = applicative O*)
           Ali   like/happy-Appl   house   that
           'Ali likes the house.'

     c. Ali   sengan   rumah   itu   (*stimulus = quasi-O*)
           Ali   like/happy   house   that
           'Ali likes the house.'

As summarized in Table 2.5, the applicative O with verbs in the *sengan* class
has all the O or A/S/O properties of the language, including lack of a
prepositional marker and the potential to be construed with a 'floated'

TABLE 2.4. Grammatical properties of dependent types in Brazilian Portuguese

	S/A	S$_O$	O	Quasi-O	IO	Oblique
O que pseudocleft pivot	yes	yes	yes	yes	no	no
Tough-movement pivot	no	yes	yes	yes	no	no
Reciprocal *se* pivot	NA	NA	yes	yes	yes	no
Passive subject potential	NA	NA	yes	no	no	no
Accusative promominal clitic	no	no	yes	no	no	no
Not marked with preposition	yes	yes	yes	no	no	no

TABLE 25. Grammatical properties of stimulus non-subjects in Indonesian

	O/O$_{APPL}$	Quasi-O	Oblique
Controller of floated quatifier	yes	yes	no
Relativization potential	yes	yes	no
Not P-marked	yes	yes	no
Co-occurrence with transitive verbal prefix	yes	no	no
'Passive' subject potential	yes	no	no

quantifier, to be relativized, to co-occur with a transitive prefix on the verb, and to be realized as an S in a construction analogous to the English or Portuguese passive construcion. By contrast, the prepositionally-marked oblique realization of the same dependent has no O or A/S/O properties and the non-applicative 'quasi-O' has only three such properties.

The following examples illustrate the quantifier-float phenomenon, whereby the quantifier *semuanya* 'all' can appear in clause-final position, separated from the NP that it modifies.

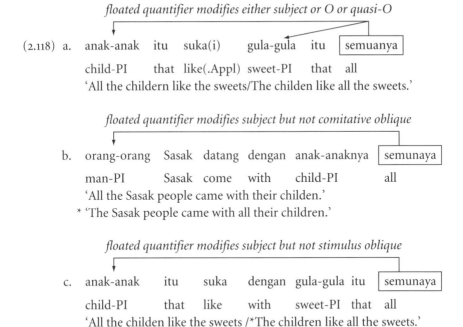

       floated quantifier modifies either subject or O or quasi-O

(2.118) a. anak-anak   itu   suka(i)   gula-gula   itu   semuanya

      child-PI   that   like(.Appl) sweet-PI   that   all

      'All the childern like the sweets/The childen like all the sweets.'

       floated quantifier modifies subject but not comitative oblique

  b. orang-orang   Sasak   datang   dengan   anak-anaknya   semunaya

     man-PI   Sasak   come   with   child-PI   all

     'All the Sasak people came with their childen.'

     * 'The Sasak people came with all their children.'

       floated quantifier modifies subject but not stimulus oblique

  c. anak-anak   itu   suka   dengan   gula-gula   itu   semunaya

     child-PI   that   like   with   sweet-PI   that   all

     'All the childen like the sweets /*The children like all the sweets.'

The distinction between quasi-objects and 'true' Os can be illustrated with the passive-like construction that in some ways resembles the so-called objective-voice construction of languages such as Tagalog (see Section 2.2.5), for which reason the voice prefix is glossed with *Obj* here. In an active-voice clause, such as (2.119a), the agent precedes the verb and the patient follows. In the objective voice, the patient precedes the verb and the agent follows, possibly—in some cases—marked with a preposition (2.119b).

(2.119) a. dia   baca   buku   itu
            3Sg   read   book   that
            'He/she read the book.'

        b. buku   itu   di-baca   (oleh) Ali
            book   that   Obj-read   by   Ali
            'The book was read by Ali.'

With the psychological verbs whose stimulus dependent alternates between oblique-marking and no marking, as illustrated for *takut* 'afraid' by (2.120a), the objective-voice construction can only be used if the applicative suffix appears on the verb, as shown by the contrast between (2.120b) and (2.120c). Thus, only the applicative O with verbs in this class can be 'promoted' to subject.

(2.120) a. saya   takut   (dengan)   lelaki   itu
            1Sg   afraid   with   man   that
            'I'm very afraid of that man.'

        b. *lelaki   itu   di-takut   saya
            man   that   Obj-afraid   1Sg
            'That man is feared by me.'

        c. lelaki   itu   di-takut-i   saya
            man   that   Obj-afraid-Appl   1Sg
            'That man is feared by me.'

Although there are many languages that either have idiosyncratically case-marked objects or systematic alternative options for case marking with certain verb classes, the extent to which the marking is indicative of quasi-objecthood is not always clear. Another kind of apparent quasi-object is the genitive-marked object in Polish (Dziwirek 1994) and Russian (Franks 1995), which appears as an alternative to or in place of an accusative NP in clauses that have been negated. In the Uralic language Ostyak (Nikolaeva 1999) the verb can either be marked for object agreement or not. The object in a clause with no verb agreement is a kind of quasi-object, inasmuch as it does not have all the syntactic properties and privileges of the agreement-triggering object. As with quasi-subjects, the inconsistent syntactic behaviour of these different kinds of objects poses a challenge to theories of grammatical relations, which are generally structured in such a way as to yield discrete rather than continuous categories.

3

Relational Grammar

Relational Grammar (RG) (Perlmutter 1983, Perlmutter and Rosen 1984, Blake 1990, Postal and Joseph 1990) is a theory of syntax that is built on the idea that grammatical relations such as subject, direct object, and indirect object are primitive (i.e. basic and indefinable) concepts in terms of which clause structure in all languages is organized. Its use of multiple levels of clause structure, whereby an NP with the patient role, for example, can be the direct object at an initial or 'logical' level and the subject at the final level, make it well-suited to describing the voice and relational-alternation constructions that are so pivotal to an understanding of the syntactic phenomena in most languages, as discussed in Section 2.2, as well as such ubiquitous phenomena as raising to subject, possessor raising, causativization, noun incorporation, quantifier float, and control of adverbial phrases and complement clauses, which are generally constrained in terms of relational categories such as subject and direct object. Coupled with its general user-friendliness, that is its relative lack of obscure and complex formalism, its cross-linguistic adaptability has made it particularly popular among field-workers, who have produced accessible and theoretically-informed descriptive work of enduring interest on a wide array of typologically and genetically diverse languages.

3.1 Basic design of the theory

Constituents are assumed to bear a relation within the phrase that contains them. In a simple transitive clause, for example, there are two NPs and a verb. The verb bears the relation of predicate (or P). The NPs bear the relations subject and direct object. Consistent with the typological research concerning a grammatical-relation hierarchy in the sense of Keenan and Comrie (1977; see Section 1.3.2), a set of core relations, known as 'term' relations, are assumed to be ranked relative to each other and to outrank all non-term relations. The numbers 1, 2, and 3 designate the term relations, that is subject, direct object, and indirect object, and indicate their ranking. The relations 1 and 2 constitute the class of 'nuclear terms'. The 2 and 3 relations constitute the class of object terms. More generally, the dependent (or non-P) relations are categorized and hierarchically-ranked as shown in Figure 3.1.

Although semantic roles such as agent and patient are not included in the inventory of grammatical relations, the individual oblique relations, such as loc(ative) and instr(umental), are, for all intents and purposes, simply semantic roles. They have the labels of standard semantic roles and constitute a set of similarly uncertain size. Moreover, unlike the chômeur relation and the term relations, they are purely semantically defined and cannot be revalued to. That is to say, although a dependent with the initial instrumental relation, for example, can revalue to 2 and therefore be a final 2, an initial 2 cannot be a final instrumental, as guaranteed by the Oblique Law in (3.26) below.

The non-oblique relations can, in principle, be borne by a dependent with any semantic role. However, it is generally assumed that at the initial level (or 'stratum'), there is a semantic basis for assigning the term relations as well as the oblique realtions. The prototypical agent, patient, and recipient dependents are initial 1, 2, and 3, respectively. Although this idea is codified in the Uniform Alignment Hypothesis (Perlmutter and Postal 1984), the precise details of how initial relations are determined from verb meanings within particular languages and across languages are given little attention and the meaningfulness and viability of any such universal principle are controversial (Rosen 1984).

The laws governing clause structure yield a set of possible construction types, defined by the nature of the revaluations, if any, that take place. Individual languages utilize possibly different subsets of the constructions made available by universal grammar. The passive construction, for example, is defined by a detransitivizing revaluation of 2 to 1.[1] The RG characterization of the passive construction in Halkomelem, for example, is illustrated in Figure 3.2, which shows the analysis of example (2.40b) from Section 2.2.1 (with the auxiliary omitted for the sake of simplicity). The formal representation of clause structure is a graph-theoretic object consisting of nodes that are linked by arcs labelled for grammatical relation and stratum. A phrase or word that is a constituent of a larger phrase, identified by a node labeled *a*, is said to 'head' an arc whose tail is *a*. In the diagram on the left in Figure 3.2, *tᶿə scéːɬtən* 'the salmon' heads two arcs with tail *a*. Thus, *tᶿə scéːɬtən* is a constituent of clause *a*. One of the arcs is labelled for the grammatical relation 2 and the coordinate c1, indicating that this NP is the initial 2 of the clause. The other arc is labelled for the grammatical relation 1 and the coordinate c2, indicating that this NP revalues to 1 and is, hence, the final 1 of the clause (since there are no arcs with coordinate c3). The other constituents of the

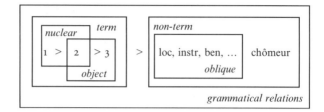

FIGURE 3.1. Typology of dependent (or 'nominal') grammatical relations

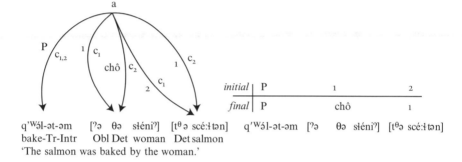

q'ʷə́l-ət-əm   [ʔə θə sɫéniʔ]   [tᶿə scé:ɫtən]   q'ʷə́l-ət-əm   [ʔə   θə sɫéniʔ]   [tᶿə scé:ɫtən]
bake-Tr-Intr   Obl Det woman   Det salmon
'The salmon was baked by the woman.'

FIGURE 3.2. RG analysis of a simple passive clause in Halkomelem

clause are the verb, which heads a P(redicate)-arc with coordinates c_1 and c_2 and is, thus, the initial and final P, and the oblique-marked *θə sɫéniʔ* 'the woman', which heads an initial-stratum 1-arc (coordinate c_1) and a final-stratum chô-arc. The key information about the grammatical relations and strata of the constituents of the clause is more perspicuously summarized in the tabular stratal diagram on the right in Figure 3.2.

The grammatical rules of the language, including rules having to do with constituent order, derivational and inflectional verbal morphology, case marking, and agreement, are formulated in terms of the relational and stratal information. This is a passive clause because there is a revaluation from 2 to 1 from a transitive stratum, that is a stratum with both a 1-arc and a 2-arc. Since there can be at most one dependent bearing a given term relation in a given stratum, the intial 1 revalues to chômeur. The combination of transitive and intransitive suffixes on the verb register the passive revaluation. The verb has zero agreement morphology because the final 1 is third person and the final stratum is intransitive. The NP *θə sɫéniʔ* is marked for oblique case with the oblique preposition because all non-term dependents are marked in this way.

Naturally, provided that no laws governing clause structure are violated, a clause can have multiple strata with various kinds of revaluations. The following Halkomelem example illustrates a clause type generally assumed to involve both advancement to 2 (in an applicative construction—see Section 2.2.4) and passive revaluation.

initial	P	3	1	2
	P	2	1	chô
final	P	1	chô	chô

(3.1) ʔi   ʔamʔ-əs-t-əm   tᶿə John ʔə-ƛ̓ʼ   Mary ʔə kʷθə šckíːks
       Aux give-Rec-Tr-Intr Det John Obl-Det Mary Obl Det vanilla
       'John is being given vanilla extract by Mary.'

The recipient applicative morpheme on the verb registers the revaluation of the initial 3 to 2, which induces demotion of the initial 2 to chômeur. The intermediate stratum being transitive enables the passive-voice advancement of the recipient dependent to 1. The verb, thus, bears the transitive and intransitive morphemes that register passive as well as the recipient applicative morphology. Since the agent and patient are both final non-terms, both are marked with the oblique preposition.

Some of the most basic (and largely uncontroversial) laws are as follows (see Perlmutter and Postal 1983 for more formal characterizations).

(3.2) a. *Stratal Uniqueness Law*
          A stratum can have at most one of each type of term arc.
     b. *Oblique Law*
          If a dependent bears an oblique relation *R*, it bears *R* in the initial stratum.
     c. *Final 1 Law*
          The final stratum of a clause has a 1-arc.
     d. *Motivated Chômage Law*
          A dependent may only bear the chômeur relation if it bears a relation *R* in some sratum (c_i) and another dependent bears *R* in the subsequent stratum (c_{i+1}).

The Stratal Uniqueness Law is meant to account for the fact that languages typically do not have two dependents in a clause with identical syntactic privileges and morphological marking properties. The Oblique Law, as noted above, prohibits the revaluing of any dependent to an oblique relation, the idea being that revaluations simply change syntactic privileges without substantially affecting meaning and 'instrumental', for example, is a relation that reflects an aspect of meaning. The Final 1 Law accounts for the fact that the sole argument of a single-argument verb is necessarily realized as the subject (*To do nothing won't help*), unless a 'dummy' pronoun functioning as subject is inserted (*It won't help to do nothing*). Chômage is the device that saves structures with revaluations from violating either the Stratal Uniqueness Law or the Oblique Law. If the 2 of a clause with an agent and a patient revalues to 1, the initial 1 must revalue. Since it cannot revalue to an oblique relation, it revalues to chômeur—a syntactic function that any dependent of a verb can, in principle, bear. The Motivated Chômage Law limits revaluation to chômeur to cases where some other revaluation induces it. In (3.1), for example, the agent and the patient are both final chômeurs. In both cases, their chômage is induced by a revlauation of the recipient (or initial 3).

3.2 Basic language types

It should be clear that the relations 1 and 2 correspond roughly to the concepts S/A and O discussed in Section 2.1. However, the relativization of all grammatical relations to strata makes it possible and necessary to be more precise about syntactic functions. An accusative language, for example, is one whose case marking and/or verb agreement (possibly as well as other syntactic phenomena) distinguish the final 1 and final 2 of clauses. Accusative languages are presumably the most common type because marking systems generally work in terms of final relations and 1 and 2 are the most basic relational notions. The notions 'ergative' and 'absolutive', by contrast, are more complex, since they are defined in terms of other notions:

(3.3) a.   *Ergative*
           x bears the ergative relation in stratum *s*, if *x* bears the 1 relation and
           s is transitive.
      b.   *Absolutive*
           x bears the absolutive relation in stratum *s*, if *x* bears the lowest-
           ranking nuclear term relation in *s*.

A morphologically ergative language is, thus, one in which case marking and/or agreement work in terms of the final ergative and final absolutive of clauses. For example, in the following monostratal transitive Halkomelem clause, the verb bears the suffix -*əs*, which indexes the final ergative (i.e. the final 1 of a finally transitive clause).

initial/final	P	2		1
(3.4) ni	qʼʷáqʷ-əθ-ám?š-əs			tᶿə John
	Aux club-Tr-1O-3A			Det John
	'John clubbed me.'			

Although *John* is also the final 1 of example (3.1), the verb of this clause does not bear the suffix -əs, because the final stratum of a passive clause is intransitive and the final 1 is, therefore, the final absolutive.

From an RG perspective it is unsurprising that so-called ergative languages often have some morphological marking and other syntactic phenomena that work on an accusative or some other non-ergative basis, since notions such as 'final 1' (= S/A) and 'final 2' (= O) are always available, even if more complex relational notions may be appealed to for certain purposes. In Halkomelem, for example, even though such syntactic phenomena as quantifier float and possessor extraction are constrained to work with the final absolutive, that is S/O (see Section 2.1.2), use of the first-person suffix on the verb in (3.4) works on an accusative basis, that is it only ever indexes the final 2 (= O). What remains most surprising about ergative languages from an RG perspective is that in languages whose syntax works primarily on an ergative basis, such as Dyirbal (see Section 2.1.2), the final absolutive of a clause is the one that is most privileged syntactically. Given a relational hierarchy on which 1 outranks 2, the ergative relation (which encompasses only 1s) should at least not be outranked by absolutive (which encompasses 2s).

Split-intransitive languages are characterized as having marking systems that are sensitive to initial as well as final relations. The basic idea is that such languages overtly display a universal basic distinction between two types of intransitive verbs (Perlmutter 1978, 1989). Patient-like dependents of initially intransitive verbs are initial 2s, whereas agent-like dependents of initially intransitive verbs are intial 1s. By way of illustration, consider the following examples of transitive and intransitive clauses in Choctaw discussed in Section 2.1.3.[2]

(3.5) a.   chi-bashli-li-tok   is-sa-bashli-tok
           2sgO-cut-1sgA-past   2sgA-1sgO-cut-past
           'I cut you.'   'You cut me.'

                    A-marking   O-marking

      b.   hilha-li-tok   sa-hohchafoh
           dance-1sgA-past   1sgO-be hungry
           'I danced.'   'I'm hungry.'

The two types of intransitive clause are assumed to have the following relational structures:

initial/final	P	1

(3.6) a.   hilha-li-tok
           (*unergative clause*)

initial	2	P
final	1	P

      b.   sa-hohchafoh
           (*unaccusative clause*)

Given this analysis, verbs such as 'be hungry' show O marking for the dependent because it is a direct object at the initial level. The rules for head-marking on verbs can be formulated as follows:

(3.7)   *Head marking in Choctaw*
    a.   O marking is used for dependents that bear the 2 relation (in any stratum) and a final nuclear term relation.
    b.   A marking is used for dependents that bear the initial and final 1 relation.

Since languages may have morphosyntactic rules keyed in various ways to the distinction beween intransitive verbs with an initial 2 (unaccusatives) and intransitive verbs with an initial 1 (unergatives), there is no reason to expect so-called split-intransitive languages to have a fundamentally different syntax than other languages. All languages are assumed to have two main classes of intransitive verbs. Split-intransitive or active languages are simply languages that key some aspect of their main grammatical-relation marking mechanisms (usually head marking) to the distinction. The fact that the syntax of some languages, such as Acehnese (see Section 2.1.3), appears to use no other distinction between core grammatical-relations than initial/final 1 vs. initial 2 is certainly not ruled out as a logical possibility; but it is (appropriately) rather unexpected.

Summarizing, in RG all languages are assumed to have the same basic clause structure and the same grammatical relations. Morphosyntactic phenomena, however, can work in terms of categories that can be defined in different ways, taking into account stratal and relational information. The three main kinds of languages in terms of grammatical-relation systems define their two main relational categories as shown in Table 3.1.

3.3 Some case studies

3.3.1 *Dative quasi-subjects*

One of the main advantages of RG is that the revaluation mechanism makes it possible to account for the fact that dependents of a clause sometimes behave only partially like a subject or object, indirect object, etc. The quasi-subject phenomenon, in particular, has provided one of the main motivations for multistratal representations of grammatical relations (Perlmutter 1982). Consider, for example, the hybrid category $S/A/Obl_a$ (i.e. the category consisting of S/A and oblique agents), which is needed to characterize the raising-to-object

TABLE 3.1. RG definitions of main syntactic categories in three language types

Accusative		Ergative		Split-intransitive	
S/A =	O =	A =	S/O =	A/S$_a$ =	O/S$_o$ =
Final 1	Final 2	Final 1 of finally transitive clause	Lowest-ranking final nuclear term	Initial and final 1	Initial 2 and final nuclear term

pivots in Halkomelem (see Section 2.2.1), for example. Since oblique agents are always initial 1s that have been demoted to chômeur and the S/A category is that of final 1s and there are no other kinds of dependents that head a 1-arc in Halkomelem, raising-to-object pivots are a natural class: dependents that head a 1-arc (in some stratum). In languages such as French, Italian, Polish, and Choctaw, which have classes of indirect objects with only certain subject properties, there is also a straightforward analysis. The quasi-subject indirect object is an initial 1 that has been demoted to 3, as shown in the following stratal diagram for the *plaire* 'please' clause in a French sentence with two possible controllers of an adverbial phrase.

(3.8)   *controller can be either Nominative or Dative dependent of plaire*

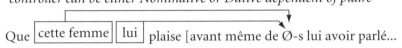

Que cette femme lui plaise [avant même de Ø-s lui avoir parlé...

'That this woman should 3SgDat-please before even 3SgDat-having spoken.' (i.e. 'That this woman should be pleasing to him before her having spoken to him' or 'before his having spoken to her')

initial	2	1	P
final	2	3	P
	1	3	P
	cette femme	lui	plaire

The controller has to (minimally) be a subject (i.e. head a 1-arc in some stratum). It can be *cette femme*, because this is the final 1 and has all or most subject privileges; but it can also be *lui*, which is both a final term and an initial 1. *Lui* is a quasi-subject, that is only manifests a restricted range of subject privileges, because most syntactic phenomena in French are keyed to final relations.

3.3.2 *Philippine voice alternations*

The complex grammar of Philippine languages is amenable to a straightforward treatment if subject revaluations of the 1 to 3 kind, which yields quasi-subjects, are allowed. Recall from Section 2.2.5 that grammatical phenomena are, by and large, sensitive to four main grammatical-relation categories. The most important is that of what is called here the ➤ (or *ang*-marked) dependent, which can have virtually any semantic role, contingent on the choice of voice-marking morphology on the verb. Most grammatical phenomena are contrained to work with only the ➤ dependent. Another category consists of both the ➤ dependent and the non-➤ or 'demoted' agent. Only dependents in this category can be controllees in participial complements or controllers of participial adjuncts. Instrument-referring NPs and non-➤ agents and patients constitute the category of genitive-marked dependents. Finally the category consisting of PPs and locative case-marked NPs, including goals and recipients, is distinguished by the ability of its members to undergo adjunct fronting. The situation concerning the syntactic phenomena related to these categories is summarized in Figure 2.2.

The key assumptions for a successful analysis are as follows:

- The ➤ dependent is always the final 1, implying that the multiple voices indicate different kinds of 1s or advancements to 1, as in Bell's (1983) analysis of Cebuano, for example.
- Recipients and other locative NPs are simply obliques, like PPs, rather than initial/final 3s.
- Initial 1s displaced by advancements to 1 demote to 3.
- Instrumental NPs are initial/final 3s (if they do not advance to 1).
- Patients are initial 2s (that can advance to 1 but otherwise don't revalue).

Given this set of assumptions, most syntactic phenomena, including, for example, relativization, quantifier float, number agreement, and conjunction reduction, work in terms of the final 1 category (S/A). These phenomena therefore work as in many languages, particularly the most common accusative type, which Tagalog would be on this analysis. The controller of a participial adjunct and the controllee in a participial adjunct must be either the ➤ dependent or a demoted agent in a non-active voice (i.e. S/A/Agent). On the proposed analysis, this category is defined as dependents that bear the 1 relation in any stratum (whether initial or final). Genitive marking is used for final objects, that is 2s or 3s, including deomoted agents. Adjunct fronting, which doesn't work with the ➤ dependent and genitive-marked dependents, is restricted to final non-terms.

There is really only one non-standard assumption in this version of the classic RG analysis, which is that initial 3-hood can vary considerably across languages, insofar as instrumental NPs are claimed to be initial 3s in Tagalog and recipients, for example, are not.[3] Since there appears to be no viable universal semantic characterization of the category 'initial 3', in any case, let alone an empirical basis for the claim that all languages even utilize the 3 relation (see Section 1.3.2), this seems to be an unproblematic assumption.[4]

By way of example of how Tagalog is seen as working under this analysis, consider the proposed analyis of a complex clause with an advancement to 1 (from an oblique relation) in the main clause and control of a participial complement in which an advancement from 2 to 1 has occurred, that is (2.82b), repeated here as (3.9), with a literal (non-idiomatic) gloss that reflects the analysis.

(3.9)

initial	P	1	Loc
final	P	3	1

iniwanan   ko   siya=ng

leave.Imperf.Loc 1SgGen ➤ 3Sg=Comp

[sinususulat   Ø   ang=liham]

write.Imperf.Obj Gen ➤=letter

initial	P	1	2
final	P	3	1

'I left him writing the letter.'
Literally: 'He was left (to) me the letter being written.'

The controller is the final 1 of the main clause. The controllee is the initial 1/final 3 of the participial complement. The main clause verb is in the locative voice, signalling the advancement to 1 from a (generalized) locative oblique. The initial 1 (or agent) is marked genitive because it is a final object (or final term other than 1). In the participial complement the verb is in the objective voice due to the advancement to 1 of the intial 2 (or patient); even though it is a final 3, the agent is eligible to be a controllee by virtue of its initial 1-hood. Thus, both the quasi-subject properties of the 'demoted' agent and its superficial non-subject term properties are straightforwardly accounted for.

3.3.3 *A/O-reversal in Jarawara*

The syntactic inverse voice phenomenon of the kind described for Jarawara in Section 2.2.3 is also explicable in terms of simple revaluations. The idea is that, in the inverse voice, the initial 2 advances to 1 and, rather than being demoted to chômeur, as it would be in the cross-linguistically more common passive construction, the initial 1 is demoted to 2, as shown in the following analysis of examples (2.66), repeated here as (3.10).

initial/final	1	2	P		*Direct voice*
(3.10) a.	Mioto	Watati	awa-ka		
	Mioto(Masc)	Watati(Fem)	see-DeclMasc		
	'Mioto saw Watati.'				

initial	2	1	P		
final	1	2	P		*Inverse voice*
b.	Watati	Mioto	hi-wa	hi-ke	
	Watati(Fem)	Mioto(Masc)	Inv-see	Inv-DeclFem	
	'Mioto saw Watati.' (or, 'Watati was seen by Mioto.')				

The basic facts are that in the inverse-voice construction the patient (=initial 2) has virtually all of the syntactic properties and privileges that the agent (= initial/final 1) has in the direct-voice construction (with respect to constituent order, verb/mood gender agreement, conjunction reduction, etc.) and the demoted agent in the inverse voice, nevertheless, has the properties of the final 2 of a transitive clause. The reversal analysis accounts for the object-like properties of the agent in the inverse-voice construction, while also accounting for the subjecthood of the patient. Beyond this, the final 2 is a quasi-object and the final 1 is a quasi-subject in the inverse voice, insofar as the former behaves like a 1 and the latter behaves like a 2 with respect to one phenomenon: preverbal pronominal positions. In essence, the order is patient-referring pronoun first, agent-referring pronoun second, independently of voice. One need only say that the preverbal pronominal placement constraint, unlike the other morphosyntactic phenomena in the language, are sensitive only to *initial* syntactic relations.

3.3.4 *Unaccusativity and the alignment problem*

Relational Grammar is probably most well known for the pioneering work of Perlmutter (1978, 1989) and others (e.g. Rosen 1984, 1988, Harris 1982) on what would become known as the UNACCUSATIVE HYPOTHESIS,[5] that is the hypothesis that the subject of some intransitive verbs is an initial 2 rather than an initial 1, which plays a critical role in the RG approach to split-intransitive languages, as noted in Section 3.2. It has long been clear that many languages have subclasses of verbs, generally definable in semantic terms, and that there is a semantic dimension to even the common distinction between two super-categories of intransitive verbs that is used in many languages. As argued persuasively in Rosen (1984), there are good reasons for abandoning the original idea that there might be a universal semantic basis for the distinction between unaccusative intransitive verbs (those with an initial 2) and unergative intransitive verbs (those with an initial 1). Typological work on split-intransitive languages (e.g. Mithun 1991, Dixon 1994: ch. 4) also makes clear that the unaccusative/unergative distinction is not semantically predictable across languages, since these kinds of languages use different semantic features to draw the distinction. The question for the proponents of the unaccusative hypothesis then is how the decision is made language-internally as to which verbs take initial 2s and which take initial 1s. Given that lexical semantic features appear to be clearly relevant, the idea would have to be that languages differ with respect to which lexical semantic features matter. In some languages, for example, only the single dependents of stative verbs are initial 2s, whereas in other languages the single dependents of telic (i.e. change of state) verbs are initial 2s, and so forth. For some languages, the choice may even be partially idiosyncratic.

However, since the rationale for assigning different initial grammatical relations to the dependents of different classes of verbs is that these two types of dependents behave differently, one might argue that the distinctive behaviours are explicable directly in terms of the semantic features that would have to be said to motivate the unaccusative/unergative distinction in the first place, obviating the need for an initial syntactic-function difference. This tack is taken in a number of studies (e.g. Centineo 1986, Van Valin 1990, McClure 1990, Zaenen 1993, Kishimoto 1996, Yang 1996, Aranovich 2000). The key problem is that of unaccusative mismatches. Suppose, for example, there are two classes of intransitive verbs in a given language: one indexes the S with characteristic O-marking and the other with A-marking and the difference hinges on whether or not the dependent is construed as controlling the action. One could either say that the choice of head marking depends on the semantic factor or that the semantic factor determines whether the dependent is an initial 1 or 2 and the head marking depends on the initial grammatical relation. If there is only one syntactic phenomenon at stake or all phenomena at stake work on precisely the same basis, either analysis seems at least viable. If, however, there are multiple phenomena at stake and at least some are keyed to different semantic features of verbs, then the motivation for claiming an unaccusative/unergative distinction appears to evaporate. The choice of which of the distinct phenomena reveals the basis for the unaccusative/unergative distinction would be essentially arbitrary. Moreover, at least some phenomena would have to be explained directly in semanatic terms and, indeed, all apparently *could*. The syntactic unaccusative hypothesis would seem, therefore, to be superfluous at best.

Making the problem more concrete, consider a contrast between Acehnese, described in Section 2.1.3, and English. In Acehnese, for example, pronominal proclitics are used for subjects of transitive verbs and of intransitive verbs denoting controlled actions (= members of the descriptive category A/S_a), whereas pronominal enclitics are used for direct objects and subjects of intransitive verbs denoting non-controlled actions (= members of the descriptive category O/S_o). The only other syntactic phenomena that appear to draw a distinction among A/S/O dependents work on the same basis. That is to say, possessor raising is possible for O/S_o dependents only and the pivot of the so-called control construction with verbs like 'want' must be an A/S_a dependent. One could say, essentially, that only core dependents whose referents are interpreted as being in control of the action designated by the predicate can be pivots in the 'want' construction or pronominal proclitics, whereas pronominal encliticization and possessor raising are constrained to work with core dependents whose referents are not so interpreted.[6] On the other hand, one could say that 'control' is the basis for the unaccusative vs. unergative distinction in this language, that is that in-control dependents are initial 1s and other core dependents are initial 2s. The constraints on the phenomena in question could then be formulated in terms of intitial grammatical relations, that is only initial 2s can undergo possessor raising and determine pronominal enclitics, for example. The only motivation, however, for engaging the unaccusative hypothesis would be that it limits the role of semantics in grammar. One might claim, for example, that the meanings of verbs are only relevant for determining initial grammatical relations.

In English, in contrast to Acehnese, most of the phenomena that might be claimed to motivate unaccusativity work on somewhat different bases.[7] For example, only a subset of intransitive verbs can form participial adjectives, which can otherwise only be formed from verbs that can have a patient/direct object, that is transitive verbs (Bresnan 1982*b*, Rappaport and Levin 1988, Farrell 1994*a*: 125–8, 1994*b*):

(3.11) a.   a recently *arisen* national security problem   (*intransitive verb*)

      b.   a *lapsed* candidacy   (*intransitive verb*)

      c.   a *fallen* angel   (*intransitive verb*)

      d.   a *rebuilt* engine   (*transitive verb*)

      e.   a recently *announced* result   (*transitive verb*)

      f.   *a recently *laughed* person   (*intransitive verb*)

      g.   *a *shone* star   (*intransitive verb*)

At the same time, only a subset of intransitive verbs, including many that form participial adjectives, can appear with an expletive *there* subject:

(3.12) a.   There *arose* a controversy over the use of this test.(*intransitive verb*)
  b.   There *lapsed* three years before his return. (*intransitive verb*)
  b.   There *fell* from the sky an angel wrapped in light.(*intransitive verb*)
  c.   *There *laughed* a child. (*intransitive verb*)
  d.   *There *announced* the results a celebrity. (*transitive verb*)
  e.   *There *rebuilt* some engines a local mechanic. (*transitive verb*)

The problem is that the two classes of intransitive verbs identified by these phenomena only partially overlap. Although the full story is undoubtedly more complex, *there* insertion seems to be largely restricted to occurring in sentences with intransitive verbs in which existence or appearance is somehow at stake, including the state of existence (*exist*), coming into existence or appearing (*fall from the sky*), or going out of existence (*lapse*). Participial-adjective formation on the other hand seems to be restricted to telic intransitive verbs with a patient dependent, that is those that denote a change of state or location for a participant in an event. The two phenomena, thus, work with different verbs in many cases and in different ways with many of the same verbs. *Fall* for example, does not felicitously occur with an expletive *there* subject in a context where the denoted falling does not have an appearance or disappearance meaning (*There fell a wrench out of my tool belt*) even though this meaning of *fall* is compatible with participial adjective formation (*I got down on my knees to look for the fallen wrench*). Moreover, certain verbs that allow *there* insertion do not allow participial adjective formation and vice-versa:

(3.13) *telic and atelic intransitive verbs with existence/appearance at stake*
  a.   There *shone* down on me the full rays of a bright October moon.
  b.   *The *shone* rays of the bright October moon left me dazzled.
  b.   There *came* a time when nothing worked anymore.
  c.   *The *come* time turned out to be very different.
  d.   There *exist* very good reasons for doing it that way.
  e.   *The *existed* reasons are the same.

(3.14) *telic intransitive verbs with no existence/appearance at stake*
  a.   She didn't want to touch the *fainted* soldier.
  b.   *There suddenly *fainted* a soldier.
  c.   We walked across the *frozen* lake.
  d.   *There recently *froze* a lake on the other side of the county.

In short, one could claim that the collective set of intransitive verbs that either work with *there* insertion or that form participial adjectives constitutes the class of unaccusative verbs, that is verbs that have an initial 2 and not an initial 1. In that case, however, the initial 2 status of the dependent of each class of verbs would not be sufficient to explain the contrasting membership of the two sub-classes and to account for the constraints on participial-adjective formation and *there* insertion. Additional semantic factors such as telicity and existence or appearance would need to be appealed to. But even if it were assumed that all intransitive verbs simply have an initial/final 1 the semantic factors that are relevant to an understanding of the phenomena appear to suffice to define the sub-classes and to account for the constraints. One could, on the other hand, claim, somewhat arbitrarily, that only one of the sub-classes is unaccusative. For example, it might be claimed that only the patient of a telic intransitive verb can be an initial 2. The constraint on participial-adjective formation could then be stated in terms of initial 2-hood. However, this account ultimately just masks what is a semantic constraint on participial adjective formation, inasmuch as no general explanatory benefit accrues from the claim that the class of verbs in question has an initial 2. Moreover, since initial 2-hood cannot be appealed to for the constraint on *there* insertion, it is still necessary to make use of semantic factors to characterize a grammatical constraint. There is, thus, no clear motivation for the unaccusative hypothesis internal to English.

Language-internal 'unaccusative' mismatches of the kind found in English appear to be quite common, as in Dutch (Zaenen 1993), French (Legendre 1989*b*), (Levin and Rappaport Hovav 1995), Japanese (Kishimoto 1996), and Spanish (Rex 2001).[8] As noted in Section 2.1.3, the O-marking for intransitive predicates that appears to announce unaccusativity in Kamaiurá yields an unaccusative mismatch: stativity is criterial for O marking on intransitive verbs, whereas agentivity (or participant control) is criteral for O marking on nominalized verbs. The problem is exacerbated by the fact that there are equally clear cross-linguistic mismatches with respect to the semantic basis for split intransitivity (see especially Mithun 1991). In the absence of a substantive theory of how initial 2-hood is determined either universally or in particular languages, which RG has not developed, it is difficult to see how it might be claimed that the general phenomenon of intranstitive verb classes is illuminated in an interesting way by the idea that some intransitive verbs have subjects that are 'underlying' direct objects.

The larger problem, of course, is that the general basis for determining the initial relations of the dependents of verbs in general remains uncertain. There obviously would have to be both at least some universal semantic constraints of the kind envisioned but not spelled out by the Universal Alignment Hypothesis (Perlmutter and Postal 1984) and language-specific semantic constraints. It may well be that an explicit theory of the interface between lexical semantics and grammatical relations would indeed yield a viable version of the unaccusative hypothesis. However, articulating such a theory remains an unmet challenge for RG.

3.3.5 *Icelandic dative subjects*

Dative/oblique subject constructions in which the apparent final subject only fails to behave like a subject with respect to case marking and verb agreement constitute another kind of challenge for RG. Consider, for example, the fact that there is a relatively large class of psychological verbs in Icelandic that can have either the stimulus or experiencer as the apparent final subject, as illustrated by *henta* 'please' in the following examples from Barðdal (2001), discussed in Section 1.2.

(3.15) a. Ég veit að þetta mun henta mér.
       I   know that this.Nom will.3Sg please 1SgDat
       'I know that this will be pleasing to me.'

    b. Ég veit að mér mun henta þetta.
       I   know that 1SgDat will.3Sg please this.Nom
       'I know that I'll be pleased with this.'

It might be tempting to utilize some version of the standard RG 'inversion' analysis, as illustrated in Section 3.3.1 for French. The problem, however, is that the Icelandic constructions have quite different properties than the dative experiencer constructions of French. According to Barðdal (2001) the nominative stimulus in the construction illustrated by (3.15a) has all the subject-defining properties of the language (conjunction reduction pivot, initial position in main declarative and subordinate clauses, raising pivot, controller of infinitival clauses, reflexive controller, auxiliary inversion pivot, etc.) and the dative experiencer has none. In the construction illustrated by (3.15b), on the other hand, the dative experiencer alone has all the subject-defining properties, except that it is in the dative case and does not determine verb agreement, which is restricted to work with the nominative dependent.

Based on the assumptions that the sentences are paraphrases and that initial grammatical relations are determined semantically in a consistent way across paraphrases (and across languages), one possible RG revaluation analysis would have inversion (1–3 demotion) occurring in both (3.15a) and (3.15b). The difference between the two would be that (3.15b) is an 'impersonal' inversion construction, in which the stimulus is demoted to final chômeur by a phonologically null expletive pronoun (*pro*), as shown in the following stratal diagrams:

initial	2	P	1	(*Inversion*)
	2	P	3	
final	1	P	3	

(3.16) a.
þetta mun henta mér
this.Nom will.3Sg please 1SgDat
'This will be pleasing to me.'

initial	1	P	2	(*Impersonal inversion*)
	3	P	2	
	3	P	1	
final	1 3	P	chô	

b.   *pro* mér   mun   henta   þetta
1SgDat   will.3Sg   please   this.Nom
'I'll be pleased with this.'

Under this analysis, all the subject-defining phenomena as well as case morphology and verb agreement could be said to be determined by the final relations, with the proviso that a dependent that is retired to chômeur by an expletive pronoun bears the case of this pronoun and determines verb agreement via a 'brother-in-law' relation with the final 1 (Aissen 1988). The fact that the dative experiencer in (3.16a) has no subject properties could be attributed to the fact that it is a final 3. Although there would be no evidence supporting its initial 1-hood in this construction, there would also be no counterevidence, since final relations would be what matters for syntactic phenomena. One problem is that the subject-defining properties of the language could not be said to be properties of final 1s, since in (3.16b) it is the final 3 that has these properties. What one would have to say instead is that what are generally considered to be the properties of 'true' or final subjects, are, rather, the properties of the non-expletive highest-ranking final term.[9] This approach is problematic in that it depends on positing an otherwise unmotivated phonologically null expletive pronoun and requires recognizing a novel (apparently Icelandic-specific) grammatical-relation category, that is non-expletive highest-ranking final term. In essence, it is necessary to take the position that although the null expletive pronoun counts as being a dependent of the clause for the purposes of meeting the demands of certain putative laws of clause structure,[10] it must be said not to count for purposes of determining the highest-ranking final grammatical relation.

If one gives up the usual RG assumption that dative experiencers are necessarily initial 1s, a simpler analysis emerges, as illustrated by the following stratal diagrams:

initial/final	1		P	3

(3.17) a.

	þetta	mun	henta	mér
	this.Nom	will	please	1SgDat

'This will be pleasing to me.'

initial	3		P	1
final	1		P	2

b.

	mér	mun	henta	þetta
	1SgDat	will	please	this.Nom

'I'll be pleased with this.'

The idea is that the preverbal nominative stimulus construction is monostratal, as shown in (3.17a), whereas the preverbal dative experiencer construction involves 3–1 advancement, with the demoted initial 1 remaining a final term. This analysis dispenses with the phonologically null expletive pronoun and allows the subject-sensitive syntactic phenomena (conjunction reduction, raising, constituent order, etc.) to be restricted to the final 1. What makes Icelandic unusual is mainly that case marking and agreement may be determined by initial rather than final relations. That is to say, dative case marking is used for initial 3s and nominative case marking and verb agreement are keyed to the initial 1.

The problem with this analysis is that it is unclear how one might also account for the standard passive construction (with prototypical agent and patient dependents), in which the demoted 1 (or agent) is marked by the preposition *af* 'by' rather than being marked nominative and the promoted 2 (or patient) is marked nominative rather than accusative (Zaenen *et al.* 1985, Van Valin 1991, Minger 2002):

initial/final	1		P	2		

(3.18) a.

	Lögreglan	tok	Siggu	fast
	Police.Nom	took.3Pl	Siggu.Acc	fast

'The police arrested Sigga.'

initial	2		P		1
final	1		P		chô

b.

	Sigga	var	tekin	föst	af	lögreglunni
	Sigga.Nom	was.3Sg	taken	fast	by	police.Dat

'Sigga was arrested by the police.'

Since it is apparently not the case that initial relations systematically determine case marking, why they should apparently be relevant in the case of alternations that occur with certain classes of verbs, such as psychological verbs of the *henta* type, for example, remains a mystery.

3.4 Other relational theories

RG evolved from an attempt to build an alternative to classic Transformational Grammar (see Chapter 5) in which syntactic functions such as subject, direct object, and indirect object are central rather than epiphonemal. Although phrase-structure representations of sentences built around lexical cateories such as noun, verb, and preposition were abandoned, the 'transformation' idea, which involved primarily changing the position within a sentence of noun phrases (NPs) and other constituents, was retained in the form of revaluations. Many of the phenomena that are of central concern to transformational grammarians (passive, raising, complement control, causativization, etc.) are relatively easy to reconceptualize in terms of operations on grammatical relations. Passive, for example, can be thought of as involving promotion of the direct object to subject rather than movement of a VP-internal NP to a VP-external position.

3.4.1 *Lexical-Functional Grammar*

Lexical-Functional Grammar (LFG) (Bresnan 1982*a*, 2000, Falk 2001) also developed as an alternative to classic Transformational Grammar. Like RG, LFG grants syntactic functions (called 'grammatical functions') a central role and has developed for them an elaborate representational system independent of phrase-structure trees. Unlike RG, however, LFG maintains phrase-structure representations of constituent structure and linear precedence, while abandoning the idea of transformations as such. For each sentence, there is assumed to be a single 'functional' structure (without revaluations) and a single phrase-structure representation (without movements or other transformations). Passive, for example, is conceived of as a purely morhpo-lexical operation: a passivized verb has a different functional structure and a different associated phrase structure than those of the base verb.

Focusing just on the assignment of grammatical functions to clausal constituents, and putting aside the rather elaborate formal representation in terms of functional structures as well as constituent structures, grammatical relations are characterized essentially as follows. First, the lexical semantics of words (for which no standard LFG-specific representational schema exists, although Jackendoff's (e.g. 1990) model is often assumed) yield semantic roles (or 'theta-roles') of the familiar kind for predicates. The argument structure of a predicate consists of a list of the arguments from the conceptual structure assigned an intrinsic grammatical-function feature and ordered according to the position of their associated semantic role on a hierarchy of the following kind (based on Falk 2001: 104).

(3.19)   *Thematic hierarchy*
         Agent > Beneficiary/Patient > Instrument > Theme > Path/Location

All arguments are mapped to a grammatical function, of which there are four: subject, object, object$_\theta$ (aka 2nd object), and oblique$_\theta$, where the theta notation on *object* and *oblique* is a variable ranging over semantic roles. Thus, it is possible to have oblique$_{loc}$, oblique$_{instr}$, etc. The mapping of semantic roles to grammatical functions for a typical three-place active-voice verb such as *put* as used in *I put my socks in the drawer* is as follows.

(3.20)   *Mapping from argument structure to functional structure*

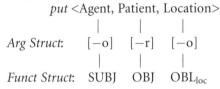

$$put \text{ <Agent, Patient, Location>}$$

Arg Struct: $[-o]$ $[-r]$ $[-o]$

Funct Struct: SUBJ   OBJ   OBL$_{loc}$

The intrinsic grammatical function classifications of the arguments follows default specifications, that can sometimes be overridden. The patient or theme (see Section 1.3.4 on the difference) is associated with the semantically unrestricted function feature $[-r]$, for which reason it can in principle be either subject or object. All other arguments are $[-o]$ by default, that is unable to be object. The mapping algorithm is as follows.

(3.21)   *Argument to functional structure mapping algorithm*
  a.   A $[-o]$ argument maps to SUBJ if it is the highest-ranking argument on the thematic hierarchy.
  b.   The $[-r]$ argument maps to subject if possible and otherwise to OBJ.
  c.   Any $[+o]$ argument is mapped to OBJ$_\theta$.
  d.   Any remaining arguments are mapped to OBL$_\theta$.
  e.   There can only be at most one SUBJ and one OBJ.

In the case of (3.20), the patient cannot map to subject because there can be only one subject and the agent, being $[-o]$ and the thematically highest-ranking argument must map to subject. Therefore the patient maps to object.

The patient of *put* can map to subject only if the agent is taken out of the picture. The effect of passivization is to do just that. The thematically highest-ranking argument is suppressed for mapping purposes (and therefore left implicit or expressed as an adjunct):

(3.22)   passive *put* <Agent, Patient, Location>

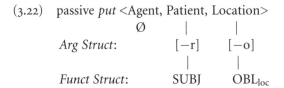

The double-object construction, and applicative constructions more generally, allow for alternatives to the patient = [−r] default. The idea is that the recipient (or goal) argument of verbs such as *give* is construed as a beneficiary when not realized as a PP and is therefore intrinsically classified as a [−r] argument, for which reason the theme is classified as [+o]:

(3.23)   *give* <Agent, Beneficiary, Theme>

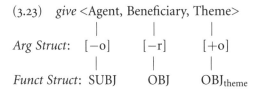

Naturally, the beneficiary/recipient is mapped to subject in a passive construction built on double-object *give* (*The boy was given a bath*), as it is the only [−r] argument.

One nice result of the feature-based definitions of grammatical functions (i.e. [−o, − r] = SUBJ; [+ o, − r] = OBJ$_\theta$; [+ o, + r] = OBJ$_\theta$; [−o, + r] = OBL$_\theta$) is that LFG has a built-in mechanism for dealing with quasi-object phenomena in languages (at least to some extent). The O2 in the English double-object construction, for example, is object-like by virtue of its [+o] status but doesn't have all the properties of an object, since it is like an oblique in being [+r]. It cannot be the subject of a passive sentence because a [−r] intrinsic classification would be necessary.[11] Consider, also, the quasi-objects of verbs in the *gostar* 'like' class in Brazilian Portuguese discussed in Section 2.3.2. The stimulus dependent of these verbs is marked with a preposition, unlike direct objects, and fails to behave like an object with respect to passivization and accusative pronominal cliticization. However, it behaves like a direct object with respect to reflexivization, pseudoclefting, and *tough* movement. Assuming (as in the Role and Reference Grammar schema discussed in Section 4.1.1) that the experiencer role, being beneficiary-like, is higher than theme on the thematic hierarchy and that what I have been calling 'stimulus' is encompassed in a generalized theme category, the grammatical function assignment for verbs such as *gostar* can be characterized as in (3.24). *Gostar* is different from similar psych verbs that take a direct object theme in that its theme argument is lexically stipulated to be intrinsically $[+o]$ rather than $[-r]$, for which reason it maps to object$_\theta$.

(3.24)   *gostar* <Exp, Theme>

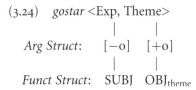

Arg Struct: $[-o]$ $[+o]$

Funct Struct: SUBJ   OBJ$_{\text{theme}}$

It follows without stipulation that verbs such as *gostar* cannot undergo passivization, since suppression of the experiencer argument leaves no possibility for a subject (i.e. the $[+o]$ theme argument cannot map to subject, which is necessarily $[-o]$). One need only assume that accusative pronouns must have the object function (i.e. must be $[+o, -r]$, whereas pseudoclefting, reflexivization, and *tough* movement work for any $[+o]$ argument, that is either object or object$_\theta$).

It is somewhat less clear how LFG might deal with the more complex problem of quasi-subject phenomena, since there is no subject$_\theta$ function, for example. It is, however, possible for constraints on grammatical phenomena to be formulated in terms of argument structure rather than simply functional structure. Dative arguments typically show subject properties only in constructions in which they are associated with the highest-ranking semantic role. For example, French verbs in the class of *plaire* 'please/like' (see Sections 2.3.1 and 3.3.1) are stative verbs with experiencer and theme arguments (as with *gostar* in Brazilian Portuguese). The difference between the two languages is simply that in French the experiencer argument has a special lexical specification that causes it to be mapped to oblique, for which reason the $[-r]$ theme is mapped to subject, as shown in (3.25).

(3.25)   *plaire* <Exp,   Theme>

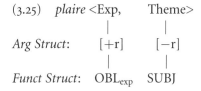

Arg Struct: $[+r]$ $[-r]$

Funct Struct: OBL$_{\text{exp}}$ SUBJ

The quasi-subject behaviour of the experiencer argument can be attributed to the fact that the controller of adverbial phrases must simply be the highest ranking agrument on some grammatical-relation hierarchy (i.e. either the thematic hierarchy or the function hierarchy, which puts subject first).

3.4.2 *Arc Pair Grammar*

Arc Pair Grammar (APG) (Johnson and Postal 1980, Postal 1986, 1989) is a kind of evolutionary alternative to RG. In essence, APG focuses on the formalism of relational networks (with labelled arcs) as a device for representing linguistic structure, while maintaining most of the basic RG assumptions about clause structure and grammatical relations. Various new relations are posited, so as to deal with such things as coordination, anaphora, the internal relational structure of words with inflectional morphemes, and such constituents as PPs, which RG, in practice, simply treats as nondistinct representationally from other so-called 'nominal' dependents of clauses. Primitive relations between arcs (particularly, 'sponsor' and 'erase'[12]) are also explicitly recognized and represented, in such a way as to allow for new or alternative conceptualizations of relational 'laws' and various kinds of grammatical phenomena. Additionally, a larger set of term relations is posited (e.g. Postal 1990), including 4, 5, and 6, largely in order to deal with quasi-object and other quasi-term phenomena in languages, without resorting to demotion to oblique relations. The daunting formalism, which requires abandoning simple stratal diagrams in favour of relational networks that include many more arcs than those of classic RG as well as various kinds of arrows connecting arcs (for the sponsor and erase relations, for example), seems to have made APG less appealing than RG to descriptively-oriented theoreticians and fieldworkers. With the notable exception of Aissen's (1987) study of Tzotzil, APG has not been widely used to produce comprehensive grammatical descriptions of languages in the same way that RG has.

4

Role and Reference Grammar

Role and Reference Grammar (RRG) (Foley and Van Valin 1984, Van Valin and La Polla 1997, Van Valin 1993, to appear) provides an interesting contrast to Relational Grammar precisely because it focuses considerable attention on the issue that RG needs to address most but doesn't, that is the details of a presumed relationship between verb meaning and grammatical relations. Furthermore, while drawing a clear line between semantic roles, which are ascribed considerable importance, and syntactic functions, the latter are held to be defined and used in language-specific and even construction-specific ways that are subject to considerable variation and the former are ascribed a relatively central role in accounting for grammatical phenomena. Whereas RG attempts to provide a framework for analysing the syntactic component of grammar, which is assumed to be autonomous in the sense of Chomsky (1957), RRG maintains that syntax cannot be properly understood without an integrated account of the semantic and pragmatic functions of language. The design of RRG from its inception has been informed by a concern for accounting for the grammatical properties of typologically and genetically diverse languages, considered on their own terms. It has been utilized in grammatical descriptions of a wide variety of languages and its central ideas have been widely appealed to in theory-neutral typological and descriptive work.

4.1 Basic design of the theory

4.1.1 *Lexical decomposition and semantic roles*

The meanings of lexical items such as verbs and adjectives and the clauses containing them are explicitly represented in RRG using a lexical-semantic decomposition model akin in certain respects to those developed in or for Localist Case Theory (Anderson 1971, and see Section 1.3.4), the Natural Semantic Metalanguage framework (Wierzbicka 1996),[1] and Generative Grammar in various forms (McCawley 1971, Gruber 1965, Jackendoff 1972, 1990, Pinker 1989). The idea is that lexical items can be decomposed into logical structures (LSs) consisting primarily of combinations of primitive predicates (e.g. **do′**, **see′**, **be-at′**, **dead′**), predicate modifiers such as CAUSE, BECOME, NOT and &, and arguments, which are typically lexical variables that are instantiated by NPs at the sentence level—but may also take the form of specific predicates. The relationship between predicates and arguments is indicated in the traditional predicate-calculus format used in formal semantics: an LS of the form **predicate′** (x, y) indicates a predicate with two arguments ordered in a significant way, that is (first, second), such that **feel′** (x, y), for example, means *x feels y*. By way of illustration, the lexical LSs of the adjective *broken*, the verb *break* in its accomplishment and causative senses, the verb *eat*, and the verb *take*, are as follows (with examples sentences and translations of the LSs from the metalanguage into more or less idiomatic English—for the more complicated cases).

(4.1) a.   LS of *broken*: **broken′** (x)
      Example: The window is broken.
   b.   LS of accomplishment *break*: BECOME **broken′** (x)
      Example: The window broke.
   c.   LS of causative *break*: [**do′** (x, Ø)] CAUSE [BECOME **broken′** (y)]
      Translation: *x* does something (unspecified = Ø) that causes *y* to become broken.
      Example: The boy broke the window.
   d.   LS of *eat*: **do′** (x, [**eat′** (x, y)])
      Example: The children are eating pizza.
   e.   LS of *take*: [**do′** (x, Ø)] CAUSE [BECOME NOT **have′** (y, z) & BECOME **have′** (x, z)]
      Translation: *x* does something that causes (i) *y* not to have *z* and then (ii) *x* to have *z*.
      Example: The boy took the money from his mother.

The theory of LSs is articulated in such a way as to give meanings in a format that can be applied across languages and to yield distinctions concerning Aktionsart (types of action) in the sense of Vendler (1967) and semantic roles (or cases/thematic relations) in the sense of Gruber (1965) and Fillmore (1968). Stative verbs/adjectives have the simplest kind of LS, that is **predicate′** (x), as in the case of *broken* (4.1a), or **predicate′** (x,y), as in the case of *like* (**like′** (x, y)).[2] Activity verbs are formally indicated in the metalanguage by the generalized activity predicate **do′**, as with *eat* in (4.1d) or the single-argument verb *laugh* (**do′** (x, [**laugh′** (x)])). Accomplishment verbs are defined by the addition of the BECOME modifier to a state LS, as in the case of *break* in (4.1b) or *learn* (BECOME **know′** (x, y)). Causative verbs are defined by the inclusion of the CAUSE modifier, as in the case of *take* in (4.1e).

In principle, any two LSs can be related by CAUSE. For example, *scare*, as in *Earthquakes scare me*, involves an unspecified activity that causes a feeling state ([**do'** (x, Ø)] CAUSE [**feel'** (y, **afraid'**)]). Although there are certain other modifiers that can be included in LSs and other patterns that yield further Aktionsart distinctions, the basic idea of the metalanguage and how it can be used to define verb classes should be clear.

At the most fine-grained level of analysis, a large variety of semantic roles can be recognized in terms of relations between basic kinds of predicates and their arguments, as shown in Table 4.1 (adapted from Van Valin and La Polla 1997: 115). In general, the semantic role of an NP can be identified from the lexical decomposition, since NPs either instantiate a variable argument of a basic state or basic activity predicate or of such a predicate embedded within a more complex LS. Thus, *the window* in *The boy broke the window* has the role of patient because it expresses the only argument of the predicate **broken'** (x), which happens to be modified by BECOME in a sub-LS of a complex causative LS, as shown in (4.1c).

In essence, by combining information about basic predicate type (activity vs. state), argument status (only vs. first vs. second), and other semantic factors (e.g. motion vs. creation vs. consumption vs. sound emission, etc.), numerous semantic roles can be distinguished. However, these semantic roles can effectively be collapsed into a smaller set of distributionally *contrastive* roles, as in (4.2), where one of the possible semantic roles can be chosen as a mnemonic category label (or prototype) for each class of noncontrastive roles.

(4.2) a. **pred'** (x)
           single argument of state predicate = PATIENT, entity
       b. **pred'** (x, y)
           second argument of **pred'** = THEME, stimulus, content, possessed, target, consumed, creation, implement, etc.
       c. **pred'** (x, y)
           first argument of **pred'** = LOCATION, perceiver, possessor, cognizer, emoter, etc.
       d. **do'** (x, y)
           first argument of **do'** = EFFECTOR, l-emitter, s-emitter, creator, consumer, user, etc.

In addition to these basic classes of roles, there are a few other more specific roles that need to be defined, because they demonstrably play a role in the grammars of languages. For example, the role of agent, conceived of as a volitional, purposeful instigator of an action is distinguished from that of

TABLE 4.1. Some possible semantic roles in relation to verb types and LSs

Type of verb	Example LS	Semantic roles
State verbs		
state or condition	**broken'** (x)	x = PATIENT
existence	**exist'** (x)	x = ENTITY
pure location	**be-loc'** (x, y)	x = LOCATION; y = THEME
perception	**hear'** (x, y)	x = PERCEIVER; y = STIMULUS
cognition	**know'** (x, y)	x = COGNIZER; y = CONTENT
possession	**have'** (x, y)	x = POSSESSOR; y =POSSESSED
emotion	**love'** (x, y)	x = EMOTER; y = TARGET
inner experience	**feel'** (x, y)	x = EXPERIENCER; y = SENSATION
Activity verbs		
unspecified action	**do'** (x, Ø)	x = EFFECTOR
motion	**do'** (x, [**walk'** (x)])	x = MOVER
light emission	**do'** (x, [**shine'** (x)])	x = L-EMITTER
sound emission	**do'** (x, [**babble'** (x)])	x = S-EMITTER
creation	**do'** (x, [**make'** (x, y)])	x = CREATOR; y = CREATION
consumption	**do'** (x, [**eat'** (x, (y))])	x = CONSUMER; y = CONSUMED
use	**do'** (x, [**use'** (x, (y))])	x = USER; y = IMPLEMENT

effector by the element DO in LSs. Thus, the verb *murder*, for example, whose effector must be interpreted as wilful and purposeful would have the lexical representation DO (x, [**do'** (x, Ø)] CAUSE [BECOME **dead'** (y)]) (i.e. *x* acts wilfully and purposefully in doing something that causes *y* to become dead). The verb *kill* does not require that its subject be construed as an agent (in the relevant sense), as evidenced by the possibility of *The poison killed the rats*. Thus, *kill* does not have a lexically represented DO in its LS, although, as with many verbs, its effector can be interpreted as an agent in particular contexts of use.

The traditional roles of recipient, source, and goal are basically special versions of the first argument of **pred'** (x, y), that is variants of what can be considered a location-type role, as can be seen from the LSs for *put*, *give*, *remove*, and *receive*:

(4.3) a. *put*: [**do'** (x, Ø)] CAUSE [BECOME **be-loc'** (y, z)]
         The man (effector) put the beer (theme) in the refrigerator (location).
     b. *give*: [**do'** (x, Ø)] CAUSE [BECOME **have'** (y, z)]
         The man (effector) gave the letter (possessed) to the boss (possessor).

c. *remove*: [**do**' (x, Ø)] CAUSE [BECOME NOT **be**-LOC' (y, z)]
    The man (effector) removed the beer (theme) from the refigerator (location).
d. *receive*: BECOME **have**' (x, y) & NOT **have**' (z, y)
    The man (possessor) received a ticket (possessed) from the policeman (possessor).

A recipient, that is a typically animate participant that comes to have something, is the possessor (= first) argument of BECOME **have**' (y, z), as with the object of *to* in (4.3b) and the subject in (4.3d). A goal, that is a typically inanimate entity to which something moves, is the location (= first) argument of BECOME **be**-LOC' (y, z), as with the object of *in* in (4.3a). A source is the location or possessor (= first argument) of BECOME NOT **have**' (y, z), as in (4.3d), or BECOME NOT **be**-LOC' (y, z), as in (4.3d). Other traditional roles that arguably play a role in grammatical phenomena, such as instrument, speaker, and addressee, can be defined in similar ways, although these require further elaborations of LSs (Van Valin and La Polla 1997: Ch. 3).

4.1.2 *Macroroles*

The most important semantic roles from the perspective of grammatical phenomena in languages are the so-called macroroles, actor and undergoer. Analogues of these roles, which have been pivotal in RRG since its inception (e.g. Foley and van Valin 1984), include the two arguments on the action tier in the lexical decomposition schema of Jackendoff (1990), the proto-agent and proto-patient of Dowty (1991), and the agent and theme of Delancey (1991). Although these also correspond more or less to the initial subject and direct object, respectively, of RG, they differ in being considered semantic roles. In some sense, at least for the subject and object relations, RRG has an explicit account of the semantic constraints on initial relations envisioned by the Universal Alignment Hypothesis of RG (see Section 3.3.4). However, in recognizing the semantic factors at play in the determination of actor and undergoer roles and in characterizing syntactic functions as being fundamentally different, the RRG conception of grammatical relations differs significantly from that of RG. Moreover, the RRG assignment of the undergoer macrorole, in particular, doesn't always correspond to standard RG assumptions about what are initial direct objects in English and other languages.

Several factors play a role in determining which arguments of a verb or other lexical item are assigned which macroroles. The first is a hierarchy of markedness for actor and undergoer assignment, which ranks semantic roles with respect to their relative distance from agent and patient, as shown in

Figure 4.1. The general principle is that the markedness of actor macrorole assignment increases in correlation with distance from agent on the hierarchy, whereas the markedness of undergoer macrorole assignment increases in correlation with distance from the patient role. If a verb has one semantic argument and one macrorole to assign, there are only two basic scenarios, which makes the choice between actor and undergoer predictable. The single argument will be the patient (or entity) argument of a state predicate, as with *die* (BECOME **dead'** (x)) or *exist* (**exist'** (x)), in which case it is an undergoer, by virtue of the maximal closeness to the prototype for undergoer. Otherwise, a single-argument verb has an activity LS, as with *laugh* (**do'** (x), [**laugh'** (x)]), in which case it is assigned the actor macrorole, by virtue of the closeness to the prototype for actor (and, of course, the distance from the prototype for undergoer). The principle can be formulated as follows:

(4.4) *Default macrorole assignment for verbs with one macrorole*
    a. If the verb has an activity predicate in its LS, the macrorole is actor.
    b. Otherwise, the macrorole is undergoer.

If a verb has exactly two (distinct) semantic arguments that are both assigned macroroles, it is also predictable from the hierarchy which one will be actor and which one will be undergoer. For example, *hear* has two semantic arguments, that is perceiver and stimulus (*x* and *y* respectively in the LS **hear'** (x, y)). The perceiver is the actor, since it is a less marked choice for actor than the stimulus is. Similarly, in the case of causative *break* (4.1c), the effector is actor and the patient is undergoer, since the effector is a less marked actor than the patient and the patient is a less marked undergoer.

A second factor bearing on the assignment of macroroles is M(acrorole) transitivity, which is strongly influenced by but doesn't necessarily correlate

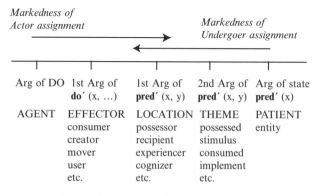

FIGURE 4.1. Actor–undergoer hierarchy and semantic roles

perfectly with number of LS arguments. Although the number of macroroles a verb may assign cannot exceed the number of its LS arguments, its arguments need not all be aligned with macroroles. The verb *run*, for example, can have both mover and goal arguments, as in the case of *The boy ran to the store*, the LS of which is **do**′ (boy, [**run**′ (boy)]) & BECOME **be-LOC**′ (store, boy). The mover (effector-type) argument is the actor, since the first argument of **do**′ is always assigned the actor macrorole.[3] However, the goal argument, which is expressed as the oblique PP *to the store*, is not assigned a macrorole. Verbs with a goal argument and an effector/theme argument are typically M-intransitive in English, since English is a satellite-framed language in the sense of Talmy (2000), that is a language in which the goal or path argument of verbs of motion is typically overtly expressed outside the verb in a PP, or 'satellite'. The general schema for macrorole expression across languages is that macroroles are assigned maximally and macrorole arguments are 'direct', that is NPs rather than PPs in a language like English and NPs assigned one of the primary cases in a typical case-marking language. Thus, by default, a verb with two LS arguments assigns two macroroles to (bare) NPs. However, certain classes of verbs, as with English verbs of directed motion, and even individual verbs can have special M-transitivity features that lead to different patterns of argument expression. Moreover, the passive-voice construction, to which we return in Section 4.2.1, also involves a mismatch between between macroroles and direct core arguments.

The default for verbs with only a state predicate is that M-transitivity is determined by number of LS arguments. *Love* and *hate*, for example, have only a two-argument state verb in their LSs (**love**′ (x, y) and **hate**′ (x, y)) and therefore have actor and undergoer macroroles, assigned to the first and second arguments respectively. However, a verb such as *belong* must be lexically marked in a way that its quasi-synonym *have* does not, that is it must be specified to take only one macrorole (MR1):

(4.5) a. *have*: **have**′ (x, y)
      The neighbour has a new car.
      (actor = possessor; undergoer = possessed)
   b. *belong*: **have**′ (x, y) [MR1]
      This car belongs to the neighbour.
      (undergoer = possessed)

Since there is no activity verb in its LS, the single macrorole of *belong* is necessarily undergoer, in conformance with (4.4b). The possessed argument is the one assigned the macrorole, since it is the least marked undergoer, or most patient-like, as shown on the actor–undergoer hierarchy. The possessor of *belong* is expressed as an 'oblique' core argument, marked with *to,* which is the default preposition for a non-macrorole first argument of a state predicate.

Finally, more marked macrorole choices can be made. Particularly in the case of 3-argument verbs, languages and verb classes within languages can differ with respect to how the undergoer macrorole is assigned. In Brazilian Portuguese, for example, the verb *dar* 'give', like other similar verbs, only allows the least-marked choice for the undergoer (i.e. the second argument of BECOME **have′** (x, y)), whereas in Halkomelem, the recipient (or first argument of BECOME **have′** (x, y)) is necessarily the undergoer:[4]

(4.6)   'give': [**do′** (x, Ø)] CAUSE [BECOME **have′** (y, z)]

   a.   [O homem]$_x$ deu [um presente]$_z$ para [a mãe dele]$_y$
        'The man gave a present to his mother.'   *Brazilian Portuguese*
        x = actor/effector; z = undergoer/possessed; y = oblique recipient

   b.   ni   ʔám-əs-t-əs$_x$ [kʷθə   sqʷəmáyʔ]$_y$ ʔə   [kʷθə   sθʼámʔ]$_z$
        Aux give-Recip-Tr-3 Det   dog   Obl Det   bone
        'He gave the dog the bone.'   *Halkomelem*
        x = actor/effector; y = undergoer/recipient; z = oblique possessed

In English, on the other hand, such verbs must be said to allow the undergoer macrorole to be assigned to either the recipient (*I gave the dog a bone*) or the theme-type argument (*I gave a bone to the dog*), for which reason sentences with macrorole assignments analogous to both (4.6a) and (4.6b) are possible expressions of the same LS. The English double-object construction differs from the Halkomelem recipient-O construction only in that it has the theme-type argument expressed as a 'direct' non-macrorole core argument.

In some cases, the general rules can be overridden with specific verbs. The verb *allow* in English, for example, only makes available the marked linking of undergoer (*This country allows us many privileges* vs. **This country allows many privileges to us*), for which reason it must be lexically specified that the U(ndergoer) role is necessarily associated with a particular argument:

(4.7) *allow*: [**do′** (x, Ø)] NOT CAUSE [NOT **have′** (y, z)] [U = y]
       [This country]$_x$ allows us$_y$[many privileges]$_z$.
       x = actor/effector; y = undergoer/possessor; z = non-macrorole core argument

Although there is a clear connection between the traditional notion of direct object and undergoer, these notions only partially overlap. Clearly, primary O privileges are generally associated with the undergoer of a 2-macrorole clause. An undergoer, however, can also be associated with subject privileges—both in intransitive clauses, as noted above, and in passive clauses, to be discussed in Section 4.2.1.

4.1.3 *Clause structure and syntactic functions*

As in Transformational Grammar, the constituents of clauses are classified by the lexical category of their head (NP vs. PP, etc.) and are organized in hierachical structures that indicate their constituency, their linear order, and the nature of the relations between them. The verb and its arguments constitute the 'core' of the clause, organized around the nucleus, which is typically a verb. Adjuncts, such as adverbial phrases and PPs that indicate locative and temporal settings are outside the core, in the 'periphery' of the clause. The main distinctions drawn for arguments are macrorole vs. non-macrorole, actor vs. undergoer, and direct vs. oblique. Since, at most, two arguments can be linked to macroroles, one of the arguments of a verb with three arguments will be a non-macrorole argument, as in the case of the example from Kamaiurá in Figure 4.2.

Kamaiurá distinguishes the macrorole arguments from other arguments (to some extent) with both dependent marking (postpositions) and head marking (agreement) and constituent order. The default constituent order is: macrorole argument(s) pre-nucleus; non-macrorole argument(s) post-nucleus. Only macrorole arguments are also direct; non-macrorole arguments are systematically marked with a postposition and only these cannot be indexed by agreement morphology on the verb. As noted in Section 2.1.3 only one of the macrorole arguments is typically indexed on the verb; but which one is indexed depends primarily on person (1st > 2nd > 3rd).[5] Only in case the person ranking of the two macrorole arguments is the same, does the actor take precedence over the undergoer. Thus, in RRG the actor and undergoer semantic roles may be appealed to directly in the formulation of grammatical constraints. In the case of verb agreement in Kamaiurá, they are essentially surrogates for the traditional subject and direct object syntactic functions. Instead of saying subject > object for agreement with 3rd person dependents in a transitive clause (as one would in RG); one can say actor > undergoer. There are, however, other cases in which the notions are not interchangeable.

The concept 'non-macrorole argument' corresponds roughly to the traditional concept 'oblique argument', although a distinction is also drawn between direct non-macrorole arguments (e.g. dative and certain accusative case-marked NPs or 'bare' NPs) and other non-macrorole arguments. Only the latter are considered oblique.[6] Unlike in RG and in traditional grammar, there is no clear equivalent of the indirect object syntactic function in RRG.

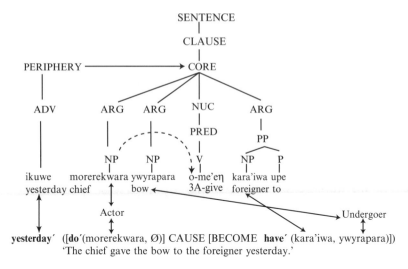

yesterday′ ([**do**′(morerekwara, Ø)] CAUSE [BECOME **have**′ (kara'iwa, ywyrapara)])
'The chief gave the bow to the foreigner yesterday.'

FIGURE 4.2. A sentence with a 3-argument verb and an adjunct in Kamaiurá

The analysis of a 3-argument clause with a source argument in Kamaiurá (or any other language) would not differ significantly from that of the analysis shown in Figure 4.2. The source argument would simply be a non-macrorole argument expressed as a PP with the 'from' postposition. Hence, an oblique vs. indirect object distinction is not drawn. This works well for Kamaiurá, since as noted in Section 1.3.2, the only difference between recipient arguments and source arguments seems to be the choice of postposition (*upe* 'to' vs. *wi* 'from'), which can be attributed, in part, to the relevance of LS details for postposition selection: *wi* for source (= first argument of BECOME NOT **have**′/**be-LOC**′ (x,y)) and *upe*, presumably, as default—or 'elsewhere' choice— for a non-macrorole first argument of any **pred**′ (x, y), given that it is used for various semantic roles, including beneficiary, animate goal, addressee, and actor of passive verb—see example (2.40a). For a language such as Brazilian Portuguese which distinguishes so-called indirect objects from other oblique arguments less by choice of preposition than by the possibility of being expressed as a dative pronominal clitic or being a reflexive/reciprocal pivot (see Section 1.3.2), it is not entirely clear how the privileged class of argument types might be specified.[7]

RRG also takes a nontraditional approach to the notion 'subject'. In essence, phenomena such as reflexivization, relativization, conjunction reduction, verb agreement, raising, etc. are viewed as being possibly restricted to working with subclasses of arguments that in many (indeed most) languages cannot be strictly semantically characterized. These subclasses can be defined in different ways, both across languages and on a construction-specific basis within a given language. Two kinds of elements are recognized with respect to syntactic phenomena: pivots and controllers. A controller determines the form or interpretation of some other constituent of a clause; a pivot is a grammatically privileged argument type that is not a controller, such as an argument that is omitted in a particular construction and whose intepretation is controlled by some other constituent. Consider, for example, the phenomenon of conjunction reduction in Dyirbal (see Sections 2.1.2 and 2.2.2). As the following example (= (2.11)) illustrates, the O (or undergoer) of the first clause, which is overtly expressed, is understood as having the same referential value as the S (in this case, the actor) of the second clause, which is not overtly expressed.

(4.8)

[ŋuma   yabu-ŋgu   bura-n]   [∅ banaga-nʸu]
father.Abs mother-Erg see-Nonfut   S return-Nonfut
'Mother saw father and he/*she returned.'

The undergoer of the first clause is the controller of conjunction reduction and the actor of the second is the pivot. In Dyirbal, both controller and pivot in this construction are restricted to macrorole arguments. However, there is a further restriction, as only one of the two macrorole arguments in a clause with two can ever be controller or pivot. Which of the two is predictable—but not entirely semantically predictable. It is necessary to take into account both clause type and the actor vs. undergoer distinction. In an M-intransitive, clause the single macrorole argument (either actor or undergoer) can be a controller or pivot for conjunction reduction. These privileges extend only to the undergoer in an active-voice clause, as illustrated by (4.8) for controller, and the actor in an antipassive clause, as illustrated by the following example (= (2.47)), again for controller.

(4.9)

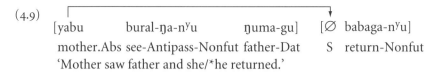

[yabu   bural-ŋa-nʸu   ŋuma-gu]   [∅ babaga-nʸu]
mother.Abs see-Antipass-Nonfut father-Dat   S return-Nonfut
'Mother saw father and she/*he returned.'

'Pivot' and 'controller' are quite different from 'subject', because they are phenomenon-specific relations. The controller of conjunction reduction, for example, may be restricted to one type of argument, whereas a relative clause pivot may be restricted to quite another. Although one can talk about the conjunction-reduction pivot in Dyirbal, it makes no sense to talk about the pivot in Dyirbal. However, since the same kind of voice-contingent neutralization of semantic roles is involved in the choice of pivot and controller for conjunction reduction and in the choice of controllers and pivots in various other grammatical phenomena in Dyirbal, it is possible to generalize over the construction-specific pivots and controllers. For each clause type, it is possible and useful to identify a default privileged syntactic argument (PSA), which corresponds more closely to the traditional subject notion, albeit relativized to specific languages. By way of example, the undergoer can be said to be the default PSA in an active clause in Dyirbal, whereas the actor is the default PSA in an antipassive clause, as shown in Figure 4.3. In an antipassive clause, the undergoer macrorole is not assigned. The LS argument that would be the undergoer in the active clause is realized as a non-macrorole direct core arument, which is assigned the default dative case. The generalization concerning the default PSA across construction types in Dyirbal is that it is the lowest-ranking macrorole argument (where actor outranks undergoer). In an antipassive or other M-intransitive clause, there is only one macrorole argument, which therefore is the lowest-ranking, whether it is undergoer or actor; in an M-transitive clause, the undergoer is always the lowest-ranking macrorole argument.

The PSA is characterized as a default, since the pivots and controllers that the notion PSA generalizes over are phenomenon-specific. Since absolutive case is assigned to the default PSA, the undergoer is marked absolutive in (4.8) and the actor is marked absolutive in (4.9). It is also the default PSA that is necessarily the pivot and controller in conjunction reduction. However, as

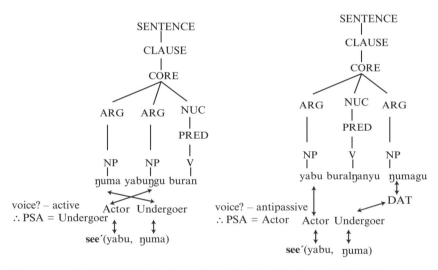

FIGURE 4.3. Default PSA choice in active and antipassive clauses in Dyirbal

noted in Section 2.1.2, pronominal case assignment, which works on an accusative basis, treats the actor in both active and antipassive clauses in the same way: nominative case is assigned to the macrorole argument (either actor or undergoer) of M-intransitive clauses and to the actor in M-transtitive clauses. Thus, nominative case assignment works in terms of a phenomenon-specific PSA: the highest-ranking macrorole argument.

Not only can the choice of default PSA differ across languages—an issue addressed further in Section 4.2—but so can whether there even is a default PSA. In Acehnese, for example, the grammatical phenomena of the language are either essentially open to all core arguments, as in the case of the raising construction (Van Valin and La Polla 1997: 259), or are, from an RRG perspective, only semantically restricted. Possessor raising, with incorporation of the head noun, is restricted to the O or S_o, as shown by the following examples, repeated from Section 2.1.3, with the relevant details of the RRG analysis.

(4.10) a.   seunang   [até   lôn]$_x$
             happy   liver   1Sg
             'I'm happy.' (Literally, 'My liver (is) happy.')
             happy' (x); (x = patient & undergoer)

    b.   lôn   seunang-até   *Possessor-raising host is undergoer*
             1Sg   happy-liver
             'I'm happy.' (Literally, 'I'm liver-happy.')

(4.11) a.   ka   lô n$_x$-tët   [rumoh gopnyan]$_y$
             Asp   1SgA-burn   house 3Sg
             'I burned his/her house.'
             [**do'** (x, Ø)] CAUSE [BECOME **burned'** (y)]
             (y = patient & undergoer)

    b.   gopnyan   ka   lôn=tët-rumoh *Possessor-raising host is undergoer*
             3Sg   Asp   1SgA=burn-house
             'I burned his/her house.' (Literally, 'Him/her, I house-burned.')

(4.12)   *gopnyan   ka   aneuk-woe   *Possessor-raising host is actor*
          3Sg   Asp   child-return
          'His/her child returned.'
          LS of *woe*: **do'** (x, Ø) & BECOME **be-back'** (x)
          (x = effector/patient & actor)

Possessor raising can be said to be restricted to the undergoer argument, which is to say the traditional O of transitive clauses and the undergoer S of intransitive clauses. As noted in Section 2.1.3, argument-indexing pronominal forms are constrained by the A/S$_a$ vs. O/S$_o$ distinction and control of infinitival complements of verbs such as 'want' is constrained to work with A/S$_a$ pivots. Inasmuch as the O is always undergoer, the A is always actor and the S$_o$ vs. S$_a$ distinction appears to be reducible to actor S vs. undergoer S (Van Valin and La Polla 1997), the only distinction among arguments that needs to be drawn for grammatical purposes is actor vs. undergoer. Since this is viewed as a semantic distinction in RRG, no phenomena work in terms of a privileged *syntactic* argument. Thus, from an RRG perspective, there are no syntactic functions in Acehnese.[8]

4.2 Basic language types

Role and Reference Grammar's characterization of the traditional subject relation as a phenomenon-specific privileged argument type whose definiton can vary within and across languages yields a multi-faceted typology of languages. The default privileged argument for a language can be semantically defined (actor only, for example) or partially syntactically defined (actor or S, for example). Moreover, since different grammatical phenomena can work in terms of differently defined pivots and/or controllers, languages can have one kind of privileged argument for head marking and dependent marking and another for such syntactic phenomena as relativization and control of reflexives, or one kind for head marking, another kind for dependent marking, and several different kinds for other syntactic phenomena. Before turning to the question of how the traditional typology of grammatical-relation systems (see Secton 3.2) is characterized in RRG, it is useful to have a better understanding of how the main voice constructions are analysed.

4.2.1 *Voice constructions across languages*

The antipassive construction in Dyribal (see Figure 4.3) illustrates one of the basic kinds of voice construction. There are two effects: the default PSA is a different macrorole argument than in the active construction, that is actor rather than undergoer, and the argument that would be the undergoer in the active construction has a different coding and status: it is a non-macrorole dative core argument rather than an undergoer with absolutive case. Prototypical voice constructions, such as passive and antipassive, are characterized in terms of which of these two kinds of functions it has:

(4.13) a. *PSA modulation*:
           The default PSA is an argument of a different kind than in the active voice.

b.   *Argument modulation*:
One of the active-voice macrorole arguments has a noncanonical realization.

The antipassive construction in Dyirbal involves both PSA modulation and argument modulation.

A syntactically ergative language can have both passive and antipassive constructions; but only the antipassive involves PSA modulation. In Inuit, for example, the undergoer in an antipassive construction is in instrumental case, as is the actor in a passive construction, as illustrated by the following examples adapted from Woodbury (1977),[9] with an RRG analysis.

(4.14) a.   Gimmi$_x$-p   miiraq$_y$ kii-vaa   *Active clause*
dog-ERG   child.Abs   bite-Ind.Tr.3SgA3gO
'The dog bit the child.'
default PSA: Undergoer; *Macrorole arguments*: Actor and undergoer are direct core arguments (DCAs) (= default)

b.   Gimmi$_x$ miiraq$_y$-mik   kii-a-voq   *Antipassive clause*
dog.Abs   child-Instr   bite-Antipass-Ind.Intr.3SgS
'The dog bit a child.'
default PSA: Actor; *Macrorole arguments*: Actor only

c.   Miiraq$_y$ gimmi$_x$-mik   kit-tsip-puq   *Passive clause*
child.Abs   dog-Instr   bite-Pass-Ind.Intr.3SgS
'The child was bitten by a dog.'
default PSA: Undergoer; *Macrorole arguments*: Undergoer is a DCA and actor is an adjunct
Invariant aspects of these three clauses:
LS of *kii* 'bite': **do'** (x, [**bite'** (x, y])
x = actor; if there is an undergoer, y = undergoer

As in Dyirbal, the antipassive construction has the actor marked absolutive and functioning as the default PSA, whereas the default undergoer is realized as a non-macrorole oblique argument assigned instrumental case. There is, thus, both PSA modulation, that is the PSA is the actor rather than the undergoer, and argument modulation, that is the undergoer macrorole is suppressed and the argument that has this macrorole in the active voice is noncanonically coded as an oblique argument with instrumental case. The actor in the passive construction is analysed as an adjunct, that is a non-core macrorole argument with instrumental case marking. There is, however, no PSA modulation in the passive construction as the undergoer is the default PSA, just as in the active construction.

Unlike in Inuit, in English the passive construction involves both PSA modulation and argument modulation, as illustrated in Figure 4.4. In a passive clause, the actor is realized as an adjunct (or is omitted) rather than a canonical direct core argument and the undergoer rather than the actor is the default PSA.[10] This difference in the effect of passivization correlates with the difference between ergativity and accusativity. Active clauses in an ergative language have an undergoer default PSA, whereas they have an actor default PSA in an accusative language. For English the generalization about the default PSA is that it is the highest-ranking core macrorole argument, that is the only macrorole argument (actor or undergoer) in an M-intranstive clause, the actor in an active M-transitive clause, and the undergoer in a passive clause, in which the actor is not a core argument.

All of the cases discussed thus far involve argument modulation, with or without PSA modulation. It is also possible to have PSA modulation without argument modulation. The Jarawara inverse-voice construction discussed in Sections 2.2.3 and 3.3.3 provides an example from an accusative language. The key fact is that the PSA (for conjunction reduction, verb agreement, and consitituent order, among other things) is the actor in an M-transitive active clause. In the inverse voice, the PSA for the same syntactic phenomena is the undergoer. The actor, however, remains a direct core argument, occurring in the same position as the undergoer in an active clause, and does not receive noncanonical coding. Thus, the analysis of the following sentences ($= (2.59)$), would be as shown in Figure 4.5.[11]

(4.15) a. Mioto   Watati   awa-ka   *Direct voice*
           Mioto(Masc)   Watati(Fem)   see-DeclMasc
           'Mioto saw Watati.'

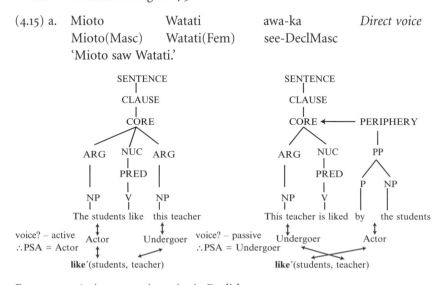

FIGURE 4.4. Active vs. passive voice in English

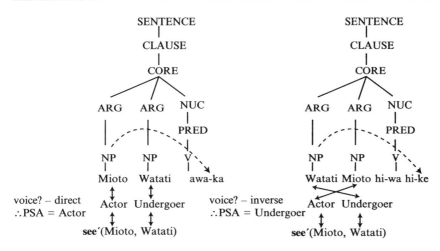

FIGURE 4.5. Direct vs. inverse voice in Jarawara

b. Watati   Mioto   hi-wa   hi-ke   *Inverse voice*
    Watati(Fem)   Mioto(Masc)   Inv-see Inv-DeclFem
    'Mioto saw Watati.' (or, 'Watati was seen by Mioto.')

For Jarawara, as for English and Dyirbal, the semantic roles actor and undergoer are assigned in the same way and the choice of default PSA is keyed to
voice. In RRG terms, there is no reversal of grammatical relations in Jarawara,
since actor and undergoer are semantic roles, which cannot be reversed. The
inverse voice (really just a version of passive voice) simply involves allowing
the undergoer to be the PSA, without any correlative argument modulation.
Some of the key grammatical constraints for Jarawara can be formulated as
follows (DCA = direct core argument).

(4.16) a. The preferred constituent order is default-PSA DCA V.
       b. The conjunction-reduction pivot is the default PSA.
       c. The default PSA controls verb/mood gender agreement.

The default PSA for Jarawara is not simply the highest-ranking core macrorole argument, as in English and most accusative languages, as the undergoer
in an inverse-voice clause is the PSA in spite of the fact that the actor is also a
direct core argument and actor outranks undergoer. Thus, a definition of the
default PSA is necessarily voice-contingent in Jarawara.

    In a syntactically ergative language, a construction with only PSA modu-
lation would have the actor as default PSA and an undergoer macrorole
associated with a direct core argument that is indistinguishable in terms of

marking and syntactic privileges from an undergoer in an active M-transitive clause. The Austronesian language Sama is claimed to have precisely this kind of antipassive construction in Van Valin and La Polla (1997: ch. 7) and Van Valin (to appear: ch. 4).

4.2.2 *Ergativity, accusativity, and split intransitivity*

In a syntactically ergative language, such as Dyirbal or Inuit, the default PSA is the undergoer of M-transitive active clauses (and passive clauses if these occur) and the single macrorole argument of M-intransitive clauses. The basic generalization is that the default PSA is the lowest-ranking macrorole argument, where actor > undergoer. If there is an an antipassive construction, the actor is the default PSA in this construction, whether or not the undergoer macrorole is suppressed (although it typically is). In a syntactically accusative language, such as English or Jarawara, the default PSA is the highest-ranking core macrorole, that is the actor in M-transitive clauses and the only macrorole argument in M-intransitive clauses. If there is a passive (or inverse-voice) construction the undergoer or some other argument is the default PSA, whether the actor is still realized as a core argument (as in Jarawara) or not (as in most languages). If such a language has an antipassive construction, it is not a PSA-modulation construction, as it would only involve noncanonical status and coding for the argument that would be undergoer in an active clause.[12] A syntactically split-intransitive language, such as Acehnese, has only a semantic preferred argument: actor for certain constructions and phenomena and undergoer for others. A pure language of this type does not have a PSA-modulation voice, since it does not have a PSA. Thus, the three most distinct types of languages in terms of how grammatical relations are treated can be characterized as in Table 4.2.

Naturally, at least certain of the coding properties (head marking or dependent marking) work on the basis of the same distinctions in languages of these three types. Thus, Dyirbal, for example, marks only the actor in an active M-transitive clause with ergative case. However, as noted above, since syntactic functions are phenomenon-specific, it is fully expected that particular phenomena in any given language might work in terms of either particular semantic roles (agent, for example), semantic macroroles (actor, for example), or syntactic functions defined in various ways (highest-ranking macrorole argument, for example).

More generally, by allowing construction-specific pivots and controllers to be defined in various ways rather than assuming that grammatical phenomena work in terms of a fixed set of primitive syntactic functions, RRG accounts for

TABLE 4.2. Language type and main grammatical-relation categories in RRG

Language type	Traditional	RRG Active voice	(PSA-modulation voice)[a]
Accusative	S/A	Highest-ranking core macrorole argument	(Non-actor argument)
	O	Undergoer	
Ergative	S/O	Lowest-ranking macrorole argument	(Actor)
	A	Actor	
Split-intransitive	A/S_a	Actor	
	O/S_o	Undergoer	

[a] The PSA-modulation voice column is in parentheses because only in languages such as Jarawara and Sama in which there is PSA modulation without argument modulation do the traditional S/A or S/O grammatical-relation categories require a more complicated characterization.

the fact that languages tend not to be strictly limited to ideal ergative, accusative, or split-intransitive systems, either with respcect to agreement and case or with respect to other syntactic phenomena. At the same time, the prevalence of accusative languages and the tendency for most languages to have some phenomena restricted to an S-/A-type category of arguments is explicable, insofar as one of the key functional motivations for grammatical-relation constraints is to privilege the cognitively most salient argument. It is well known that animacy and agency play an important role in various facets of differential privileging in grammatical organization (Silverstein 1976, Delancey 1981, Aissen 1999*b*). In a transitive clause, the more agent-like argument is more likely to be animate-referring, which yields a preference for privileging the actor. In an intransitive clause, the animacy/agency preference is less important, since there usually is only one argument available to be privileged. Hence, an S-/A-type category is a natural candidate for privileged syntactic status. Since accusative languages have an S-/A-type category as the default PSA, it is not surprising that these are more common than ergative languages. However, given the explanatory centrality of the actor and undergoer roles in RRG, it is somewhat surprising that few languages seem to have pivots and controllers systematically defined in the most basic terms, that is simply in terms of the actor vs. undergoer distinction. It would seem that languages like Acehnese ought to be much more common than they are.

4.3 Some case studies

By virtue of the fact that the actor macrorole is not necessarily the same as the default PSA and syntactic phenomena can be keyed to either semantic roles, such as actor, or argument classes defined in various ways, RRG provides a means of explaining many of the phenomena that motivate multistratal representations of grammatical relations in Relational Grammar. The notion 'initial subject', for example corresponds essentially to the actor macrorole. The notion 'first subject' corresponds essentially to 'highest-ranking macrorole argument'. Even though RRG doesn't recognize object syntactic functions as such, the notions 'direct core argument' and 'undergoer' can be used, in conjunction with voice and transitivity distinctions, to define language-specific categories corresponding to direct object, 2nd object (or 2 chômeur), and the like, as well as to generalize over various combinations of such categories.

4.3.1 *Preverbal pronominal slots in Jarawara*

Consider the following direct- and inverse-voice clauses in Jarawara (= (2.64)) with an RRG analysis).

(4.17) a. aba_y mee_y $otaa_x$ kaba-haro $otaa_x$ ama-ke
fish(Masc) 3Nsg 1NsgExcl eat-TnsFem 1NsgExcl extent-DeclFem
'We were eating fish.'
do' $(x, [eat' (x, y)])$; $x =$ Actor; $y =$ Undergoer
Direct voice; default PSA: Actor

   b. aba_y mee_y $otaa_x$ kaba-haro mee_y ama-ke
fish(Masc) 3Nsg 1NsgExcl eat-TnsFem 3Nsg   extent-DeclFem
'We were eating fish.' (or, 'Fish was being eaten by us.')
do' $(x, [eat' (x, y)])$; $x =$ Actor; $y =$ Undergoer
Inverse voice; default PSA: Undergoer

Since the actor is realized as a 1st person pronoun, leaving only the undergoer to be realized as a full NP and since gender agreement in clauses with both preverbal pronominal slots filled is the default feminine, the only indication of voice in these two sentences is the pronoun preceding the secondary verb *ama*. The constraint is that this pronoun is necessarily a manifestation of the default PSA, that is the actor in (4.17a) and the undergoer in (4.17b). Although most morphosyntactic phenomena that distinguish among macrorole arguments are keyed to the default PSA vs. DCA distinction (see (4.16)), which varies with voice, the order of the preverbal pronominals (*mee* and *otaa* in these examples) is determined instead by the actor vs. undergoer distinction, independently of voice. That is to say, the first slot is for the actor and the second for the undergoer.

4.3.2 *Passive and switch reference in Seri*

In the accusative language Seri (see Section 2.2.1), a different-subject (DS) marker is used to indicate that the 'subject' of two related clauses (main and adjunct, for example) is different. If both of the clauses in question are in the active voice, the default PSA (= highest-ranking macrorole argument), which also determines 'subject' agreement, for example, is what counts for switch reference. For a clause in passive voice, however, the default PSA (= undergoer) does not count for purposes of switch reference. Instead, the actor, which is not overtly realized, is what counts, as can be seen from the following examples:

(4.18) a. [[mi-naił kom m-po-kiːxk   (*ta)-x] ʔataːp
           2Pos-skin the 2SgSubj-Irr-wet DS-Aux mucus
           ko-m-si-aː   ʔa=ʔa]
           3Obl-2SgSubj-Irr-be Aux=Decl
           'If you wet your skin, you will be with mucus.' (i.e. 'get a cold')
           Embedded clause: [do′ (2Sg, Ø)] CAUSE [BECOME **wet′** (mi-naił)]
           Active voice; default PSA = 2Sg (Actor)
           Main clause: **be-LOC′** (ʔataːp, 2Sg) [MR1]
           Active voice; default PSA = 2Sg (Undergoer)

    b. [m-yo-aːʔ-kašni   [kokašni šo m-t-aʔo   ma]]
        2SgSubj-Dist-Pass-bite   snake   a   2SgSubj-Real-see DS
        'You were bitten, after you had seen a snake.'
        Main clause: **do′** (Ø, [**bite′** (Ø, 2Sg)])
        Passive voice; default PSA = 2Sg (Undergoer)
        Embedded clause: **see′** (2Sg, kokašni)
        Active voice; default PSA = 2Sg (Actor)

DS marking is not keyed to the default PSA, since the DS marker must appear in (4.18b) in spite of the fact that the default PSA is the same in both clauses. It is also not keyed to the actor macrorole, since the DS marker does not appear in (4.18a) because the actor PSA of the embedded clause is the same as the undergoer PSA of the main clause. The RRG analysis of passive clauses as M-transitive provides an explanation. In both passive and active clauses, the actor is what counts for switch reference, not the PSA. Only in M-intransitive clauses is the distinction between actor and undergoer neutralized for switch reference; what counts is the only macrorole argument. The generalization is that DS marking occurs if and only if the highest-ranking macrorole argument of the two clauses is different.[13] Whether or not the macrorole arguments are part of the core is irrelevant, since the actor macrorole is not even realized syntactically in (4.18b), as indicated by the Ø argument in the effector-role slots in the LS.

4.3.3 *Dative subjects and quasi-subjects*

The phenomenon of dative subjects in a language such as Icelandic can be accounted for again by distinguishing the default PSA from the privileged argument for certain specific phenomena. Consider, to begin with, the RRG analysis of M-transitive active and passive clauses with prototypical actor and undergoer:

(4.19) a. Lögreglan   tok   Siggu   fast.
           Police.Nom   took.3Pl   Siggu.Acc   fast
           'The police arrested Sigga.'
       b. Sigga   var   tekin   föst   af   lögreglunni.
           Sigga.Nom   was.3Sg   taken   fast   by   police.Dat
           'Sigga was arrested by the police.'

In (4.19a) the actor is marked with nominative case, determines verb agreement, appears in preverbal position, and is the PSA for conjunction reduction, raising, control, reflexive antecedence, etc. (hence, the default PSA for this construction). The undergoer, on the other hand, is marked with accusative case and does not have PSA behaviour. In (4.19b), which is a PSA-modulation and argument-modulation passive construction, the actor is realized as an adjunct marked with the prepositon *af* and the undergoer is marked with nominative case, determines verb agreement, and is the PSA for essentially the same range of phenomena as the actor is in the active construction. Thus, Icelandic appears to have a typical accusative grammar, including a passive PSA-modulation construction and rules for case and agreement of the following form (based on Van Valin 1991).

(4.20) a. *Nominative and accusative case assignment*
           The highest-ranking core macrorole argument (where actor > undergoer) is assigned nominative case; the other macrorole argument, if there is one, is assigned accusative case.
       b. *Verb agreement*
           The finite verb agrees with the highest-ranking core macrorole argument, if there is one; otherwise it is in a non-agreeing 3Sg form.

Certain verbs which in English have a typical actor–undergoer syntactic frame have the lower-ranking argument marked dative rather than accusative, as in the case of *hjálpa* 'help', which can be analysed as M-intransitive by lexical stiupulation:

(4.21) Ég$_x$ hjálpaði   honum$_y$. **do**$'$ (x, [**help**$'$ (x, y)] [MR1]; x = actor)
        1SgNom   helped.1Sg   3SgMascDat
        'I helped him.'

Since *hjálpa* has an activity predicate in its LS, the single macrorole is actor. The other argument is realized as a direct core argument and marked with dative case, which is the default case for non-macrorole core arguments. Such verbs can be passivized, in which case there is both argument modulation (the actor is omitted or realized as a non-core adjunct) and PSA modulation (the non-macrorole DCA is realized as the PSA).

(4.22) Mér   var   hjálpað (af   honum).
       1SgDat   was   helped by   3SgMascDat
       'I was helped (by him).'

Since there is no core macrorole argument, there is no nominative case assigned and the verb is in a non-agreeing (default 3Sg) form. The preverbal dative argument is, however, the PSA with respect to the usual 'subject'-sensitive phenomena (see Section 3.3.5). Thus, the possibility of dative subjects arises for two reasons. First, certain verbs with two or more arguments in their LS are nevertheless M-intransitive, which opens up the possibility of a dative-marked core argument. Second, although nominative case and verb agreement are keyed to the highest-ranking core macrorole argument, the default PSA is not limited in the same way. In the passive construction, a core argument can be the PSA, whether it is a macrorole argument or not.

Consider now the class of alternating psychological verbs discussed in Sections 1.2 and 3.3.5, illustrated by *henta* 'please/like' in (4.23), which have either a dative or nominative PSA for the usual subject-sensitive phenomena, correlated with preverbal constituent order, as shown by the conjunction reduction examples from Barðdal (2001) in (4.24).

(4.23) a.   Ég veit   að   þetta$_y$ mun   henta   mér$_x$.
            I know   that   this.Nom   will.3Sg   please   1SgDat
            'I know that this will be pleasing to me.'
       b.   Ég veit   að   mér$_x$ mun   henta   þetta$_y$.
            I know   that   1SgDat   will.3Sg   please   this.Nom
            'I know that I'll be pleased with this.'

(4.24) a.   [þetta fyrirkomulag er ágœtt] og [__ mun líka henta
            mér ágœtlega].
            'This arrangement (Nom) is fine and will also please me (Dat) fine.'
       b.   [Ég er ánœgð] og [__ mun örugglega henta þetta ágœtlega].
            'I (Nom) am happy and will surely be pleased with this (Nom).'

(4.25) *henta*: like' (x, y) [MR 1]; y = undergoer

Given an analysis of the LS of *henta* as shown in (4.25) with a stipulation of M-intransitivity,[14] it follows that the single macrorole is undergoer and that it is (by default) associated with the second, or theme-type argument, in conformance with the actor–undergoer hierarchy (Figure 4.1). It also follows from the general case-marking and verb-agreement rules that the undergoer is nominative and determines verb agreement. The other argument is a non-macrorole core argument assigned the default dative case. The question is why either argument can be the PSA for conjunction reduction and the various other subject-sensitive phenomena. Building on an idea from Van Valin (1991), who proposes that the possibility of alternative PSAs in ditransitive passive clauses is due to the possibility of satisfying either the general principle in (4.26a) or a preference for an undergoer PSA in the passive construction, the following potentially conflicting universal principles may be said to be active in different ways in different languages.[15]

(4.26)   *PSA selection principles*
    a.   The highest-ranking core argument with respect to the actor end of the actor–undergoer hierarchy is the preferred PSA.
    b.   A macrorole core argument is the preferred PSA.

Principle (4.26b) is simply a more general way of stating the undergoer PSA preference in passive clauses, since the undergoer is the only core macrorole in a passive construction. In English, for example, (4.26a) and (4.26b) are both active principles. In an M-transitive clause with two macrorole arguments both (4.26a) and (4.26b) are satisfied only by making the actor the PSA. In any clause with only one macrorole core argument, (4.26b) takes precedence, guaranteeing that the undergoer is the only (or at least the least-marked) PSA choice in a passive clause and that an oblique core argument never trumps the undergoer for PSA selection in an active M-intransitive clause (thus, *This belongs to me* and not **To me belongs this*). Where Icelandic differs from English is that in cases where it is only possible to satisfy either (4.26a) or (4.26b), neither systematically takes precedence. Example (4.23a) has the only macrorole argument as PSA, in conformance with (4.26b). On the other hand, (4.23b) has the highest-ranking core argument as PSA, in conformance with (4.26a). This ambivalence with respect to the relative dominance of PSA selection principles is also manifested in passives of ditransitive verbs such as 'give' and 'show', as illustrated by the following examples (from Zaenen *et al.* 1985 via Van Valin 1991)

(4.27) a.   Bílarnir   voru   sýndir   henni.
             cars.Nom were   shown   3SgFemDat
             'The cars were shown to her.'
      b.   Henni   voru   sýndir   bílarnir.
             3SgFemDat were   shown   cars.Nom
             'She was shown the cars.'

In the passive voice, verbs such as *sýna* 'show' have two direct core arguments. The undergoer, which invariably controls verb agreement and is marked nominative because it is the only core macrorole argument, can be selected as the default PSA, in conformance with (4.26b), in which case it is clause-initial and has all the correlative typical PSA behavioural properties. The dative core argument can alternatively be selected as the default PSA, in conformance with (4.26a), since as a locative-type argument it is higher on the actor end of the actor–undergoer hierarchy than the theme-type undergoer.

RRG provides an apparently viable and interesting approach to so-called dative subjects in Icelandic. However, dative 'quasi-subjects' of the kind found more commonly in languages provide a different kind of challenge, since these show subject privileges with respect to certain phenomena, without, however being the default PSA. Consider, for example, how the *plaire* class of French psych verbs, exemplified by the following example, might be analysed.

(4.28)   Cette femme$_y$lui$_x$ plait.
         This woman 3SgDat-pleases, i.e. 'This woman is peasing to him/her.'
         like' (x, y) [MR1]; y = undergoer

As with Icelandic *henta*, *plaire* can be analysed as an M-intransitive verb with only a state predicate in its LS. The single macrorole is undergoer and is assigned to the second argument. The first argument is realized as an oblique core argument, wich is marked with the preposition *à* 'to' or, when pronominal, expressed as a dative clitic. The verb necessarily agrees with the undergoer, that is *cette femme* in (4.28), because it is the highest-ranking core macrorole argument. Indeed, as the default PSA in all French constructions is the highest-ranking core macrorole argument, only the undergoer in this construction is the pivot or controller for most syntactic phenomena. Put differently, for most syntactic phenomena, PSA selection principle (4.26b) takes precedence over (4.26a) when the two are in conflict. This has the effect of limiting the PSA to a core macrorole argument. The problem is that when it comes to control of certain kinds of adverbial phrases, either argument of verbs in the *plaire* class can function as the controller (see (2.103b) and the discussion in Section 2.3.1). The fact that PSA selection can be not only construction-specific but phenomenon-specific as well provides a potential explanation. For control of adverbial phrases it is necessary to say that the PSA is *not* the default PSA. Rather, either (4.26a) or (4.26b) can be satisfied, with neither taking precedence with respect to PSA selection *for this phenomenon*. In essence, Icelandic differs from French only in that the default PSA in Icelandic (i.e. the privileged argument for most syntactic phenomena) can be determined either by (4.26a) or by (4.26b), whereas only with respect to a particular phenomenon does French allow this kind of PSA alternation.

4.3.4 *Applicative objects vs. quasi-objects in Indonesian*

As noted in Section 2.3.2, Indonesian has a class of verbs of psychological and emotional experience that have three different active-voice frames for the theme-type argument (i.e. the target or stimulus of the psychological or emotional state), which is not the PSA. It can be realized as a bare NP with a verb that bears applicative morphology, in which case it has all the privileges of a prototypical O, which is to say that it can co-occur with a transitive verbal prefix, be the PSA in a passive (i.e. PSA-modulation voice) construction, be the controller of a floated quantifier, and be the pivot in a relative clause. It can also be realized as a bare NP with a non-applicative form of the verb, in which case it has only two O-defining properties (other than being a bare NP), that is it can control a floated quantifier and be a relative-clause pivot. Finally, it can be realized in a PP, in which case it has none of the O-defining properties. Given that applicative morphology generally indicates a specific choice of undergoer or the addition of an undergoer argument (e.g. Roberts 1995), it seems clear that the applicative case should be analysed as being M-transitive, as illustrated by the following example.

(4.29) Ali_x sengan-i   [rumah $itu]_y$
         Ali   like/happy-Appl   house   that
         'Ali likes the house.'
         LS of *sengani*: **like'** (x, y); x = actor, y = undergoer

If a verb in this class does not bear applicative morphology, it is M-intransitive by default. Since these are stative verbs, the single macrorole is undergoer by general principle (see (4.4)). One pattern that occurs in many languages with such M-intransitive psych verbs is that the undergoer macrorole is associated with the lowest-ranking argument on the actor–undergoer hierarchy, leaving the other argument to be realized as either a dative-marked direct core argument or an oblique argument, as in the case of English *The team matters to me* (**matter'** (1Sg, team)) or *plaire* in French and *henta* in Icelandic (Section 4.3.3). Under the second option, which also has the undergoer functioning as PSA by virtue of being the only macrorole argument, the more marked undergoer linking occurs, leaving the theme-type argument to be realized as a direct non-macrorole argument or an oblique argument, as with English psych adjectives such as *pleased* in *I'm pleased with the outcome* (**pleased'** (1Sg, outcome)). Indonesian appears to systematically opt for the latter kind of linking, while allowing either an oblique or a direct-core realization of the theme-type argument:

(4.30) a. Ali$_x$ sengan   dengan   [rumah itu]$_y$
           Ali   like/happy   with   house that
           'Ali likes the house.'
           LS of *sengan*: **like'** (x, y); x = undergoer; y = oblique
       b. Ali$_x$ sengan   [rumah itu]$_y$
           Ali   like/happy   house that
           'Ali likes the house.'
           LS of *sengan*: **like'** (x, y); x = undergoer; y = DCA

Now, the three different realizations of the theme-type argument account for the differences and similarities between the constructions, given the following constraints on the syntactic phenomena in question.

(4.31)   *Phenomena restricted to M-transitive clauses and/or undergoer*
       a. The default PSA in the passive voice is the undergoer.
       b. A transitive prefix appears only on M-transitive verbs.
           Phenomena restricted to direct core arguments
       c. Only a DCA can be a relativization pivot.
       d. A floated quantifier controller must be a DCA.

Thus, the O-like behavioural properties of the bare postverbal NPs in sentences like (4.30b) and (4.29) can be attributed to their status as direct core arguments.[16] The fact that only the (4.29) paraphrase allows transitive marking or passive voice can be attributed to the fact that only in the applicative case is the theme-type argument an undergoer (yielding an M-transitive clause). Sentences like (4.30a) show no O properties since the theme-type argument is neither an undergoer nor a DCA.

4.3.5 *Quasi-objects in Brazilian Portuguese*

The quasi-object properties of the theme-type argument of the small class of verbs with *gostar* 'like' as prototype in Brazilian Portuguese (see Section 2.3.2) are less amenable to a straightforward RRG analysis. As in the case of psych verbs in Indonesian, *gostar* is a two-argument stative verb. Since its theme-type argument is marked with the preposition *de* 'of, from', it appears to be an oblique non-macrorole argument, as with the *de*-marked argument of a verb such as *cansar* 'tire' and unlike the bare NP argument of such semantically similar verbs as *adorar* 'adore':[17]

(4.32) a. Eu   gostei   de   tudo   isso.
          I   liked   of   all   that
          'I liked all of that.'
          like' (x, y) [MR1]; x = undergoer, y = oblique complement

    b. Eu   cansei   de   tudo   isso.
          I   tired   of   all   that
          'I got tired of all of that.'
          BECOME **tired'** (x, y) [MR1]; x = undergoer, y = oblique complement

    c. Eu   adorei   tudo   isso.
          I   adored   all   that
          'I adored all of that.' (i.e. 'really liked')
          adore' (x, y); x = actor, y = undergoer

The problem is that unlike the *de*-marked oblique argument of *cansar* and oblique arguments in general, the apparently oblique argument of *gostar* is O-like (or undergoer-like) in its ability to be a pivot in the reciprocal/reflexive *se* construction, the pseudocleft construction, and the *tough*-movement construction, although it is oblique-like in being marked by a preposition and in its inability to be a passive-clause 'subject' or an accusative pronominal clitic (see Table 2.4 and the associated examples and discussion).

One possible approach would be to claim that the *de*-marked argument of *gostar* is actually a non-macrorole DCA in spite of the fact that it is *de*-marked and even though the *de*-marked argument of *cansar*, for example, would have to be analysed as an oblique argument. One might claim for example that the theme-type argument of *gostar* is really an ablative case-marked NP, that the theme-type argument of *cansar* is a PP with an ablative preposition, and that ablative case-marked NPs are direct arguments. The idea then would be that passive-subject and accusative-clitic potential is limited to undergoers, whereas the other apparently O-sensitive phenomena are allowed to work with DCAs, which would include undergoers as well as the *de*-marked arguments of *gostar*-type verbs. In other words, essentially the same approach to quasi-object phenomena taken for Indonesian could be extended to Brazilian Portuguese.

This kind of analysis is problematic, to begin with, in that it is at odds with the standard RRG assumption that 'direct' is a meaningful designation, i.e. only bare NPs (as in Indonesian) and NPs case-marked with a core case, such as nominative, accusative, or dative in a language with case marking, are direct arguments. A bigger problem is that the *de*-marked argument of *gostar* shows evidence of being a PP of the same kind as the *de*-marked argument of verbs such as *cansar*. There is a general constraint on across-the-board topicalization illustrated by the following examples.

(4.33) a.   Aquele carro, eu queria muito mas não comprei.
            'That car, I really wanted __ but didn't buy __.'
       b.   Naquela loja, eu vi muita coisa interessante mas não comprei nada.
            In that store, I saw a lot of interesting things __ but didn't buy anything __.
       c.   *Naquela loja, eu gostava muito mas não comprei nada.
            In that store, I really liked __ but didn't buy anything __.
       d.   *Daquela música, eu adorava mas cansei.
            Of that song, I adored __ but got tired __.

The sentence-initial topicalized phrase in (4.33a) functions as a direct core argument (undergoer) of the verbs of both the conjoined clauses. Similarly, the topicalized PP functions as an adjunct in both of the conjoined clauses in (4.33b). Example (4.33c) is ungrammatical because, although the topicalized PP can be interpreted as an adjunct of the second clause, it cannot be interpreted as the 'missing' theme-type argument of *gostar* in the first clause. Example (4.33d) is ungrammatical because a *de*-marked topicalized phrase can be interpreted as the PP argument of *cansar* in the second clause but not as the direct core argument of *adorar* 'adore'. By the same token, the topicalized bare NP in (4.33d) can function as an argument of *adorar* but not as the PP complement of *cansar*. In short, an NP cannot count as the PP argument of a conjunct and a PP cannot count as the NP argument of a conjunct in an across-the-board topicalization construction. Now, a topicalized PP with the preposition *de* as its nucleus can function as the argument of both a *cansar* clause and a *gostar* clause, as illustrated by the following example, suggesting that the *de*-marked argument of *gostar* has the same status as the *de*-marked argument of *cansar*, which is presumably an oblique object of a preposition.

(4.34) a.   Daquela música, eu gostava muito mas cansei.
            'Of that song, I really liked __ but got tired __.'

Another approach, which doesn't require drawing a dubious distinction between oblique and direct PPs, would be to analyse the theme-type argument of verbs in the *gostar* class as an oblique/PP argument with the undergoer macrorole. That is to say, instead of lexically stipulating that *gostar* is M-intransitive with its first argument as undergoer, it could be assumed to be M-transitive (which is the default for 2-argument stative verbs). Its first argument would have the actor macrorole and its second the undergoer role, in the same way as *adorar* (4.32c) or other stative psych verbs, such as *amar* 'love', *odiar* 'hate', and *entender* 'understand'. It would simply need to be stiplulated that the second argument is realized in a PP with *de* as nucleus, in spite of having the undergoer macrorole. By way of illustration of how this analysis would account for the facts, consider the *tough* movement construction, whose pivot can generally be an undergoer, whether it functions as a non-PSA direct core argument (4.35a) or as the PSA of an M-intransitive accomplishment verb such as *sair* 'come out' (4.35b) or the PSA of a passive clause (4.35c). It cannot, however, be an actor of an M-intransitive activity verb such as *gritar* 'shout' (4.35e), or a non-macrorole oblique argument (4.35f–g).

(4.35) a.   Pessoas como essas são difíceis de amar/odiar/entender.
             'People like those are hard to love/hate/understand.'
       b.   Essa mancha vai ser difícil de sair.
             'This stain is going to be hard to come out.'
       c.   Carros como esses são difíceis de serem encontrados.
             'Cars like these are difficult to be encountered.'
       d.   Este lugar é difícil de não gostar.
             'This place is difficult not to like.'
       e.   *Pessoas como essas são difíceis de gritar.
             'People like these are hard to shout.'
       f.   *Este lugar é difícil de cansar.
             'This place is difficult to get tired (of).'
       g.   *Pessoas como essas são difíceis de dizer isso.
             'People like these are hard to say this (to).'

The constraint appears to be simply that the *tough* movement pivot must be linked to the undergoer macrorole. The possibility of (4.35d) then follows from the analysis of *gostar* as a verb with an exceptional linking of the undergoer macrorole with an oblique argument. Similarly, the oblique argument of *gostar* can be the pivot in the *o que* pseudocleft construction because being a macrorole argument is criterial, and it can be the pivot in the reflexive/reciprocal *se* construction because being an undergoer is sufficient. The fact that it cannot be the default PSA in the passive construction or an accusative pronominal clitic, as illustrated by the following examples, can be attributed to the fact that only an undergoer that is a direct core argument can be realized as a passive-voice PSA or an accusative clitic.

(4.36) a.   *Eu a gostei.
             'I 3FemSg-liked.'
       b.   *Essa música foi gostada por todo mundo.
             'This song was liked by everyone.'

One potentially big problem with this second approach to an explanation for the quasi-object phenomenon in Brazilian Portuguese is that it challenges the fundamental RRG assumption that the undergoer macrorole *must* be associated with a direct core argument (e.g. Van Valin and La Polla 1997: 147). This brings out an interesting difference between the actor and undergoer macroroles. The criteria for determining the presence of the actor macrorole are semantic. For example, a verb with an activity predicate in its LS always has an actor macrorole (linked to the effector-type argument), whether it is realized as a direct core argument (the default) or as an oblique argument or adjunct, as in passive clauses. With the undergoer macrorole, on the other hand, there is both a semantic constraint and a syntactic one:

(4.37)   *The undergoer role must be associated with*
   a.   an argument that is lower than the effector-type argument with respect to the actor end of the actor–undergoer hierarchy, and
   b.   a direct core argument.

To the extent that there is a good reason for (4.37b), which isn't entirely clear, this second suggested analysis of Brazilian Portuguese quasi-objects poses a problem.

4.4 Other functional theories

RRG is an example of what has come to be known as the functional approach to grammar. In fact, the line between so-called functional and formal approaches is blurred by the rigorous formalization of RRG on the one hand and the increasing incorporation of aspects of conceptual semantic structure and discoure-pragmatic roles into such formal theories as Lexical-Functional Grammar (see Section 3.4.1) and the Minimalist Program of Transformational Grammar (see Chapter 5). In any case, from the perspective of grammatical relations, functional approaches begin with a model of the lexical (conceptual) semantics of predicates and attempt to account for grammatical phenomena as much as possible in terms of the semantic roles implicated in such a model and other aspects of lexical semantic structure. Syntactic functions such as the traditional subject, object, and indirect object relations are either themselves given a (quasi-)semantic characterization or are used sparingly and defined on language-specific and/or construction-specific bases. Among such theories are (Localist) Case Grammar and Lexicase Grammar, discussed in Sections 1.2 and 1.3.4, Systemic-Functional Grammar (Halliday 1973, 1985), Functional-Typological Syntax (Givón 1984, 1997), Construction Grammar (Goldberg 1995), and Radical Construction Grammar (Croft 2001). By way of illustration, the remainder of this section provides brief overviews of the approaches to grammatical relations of two such theories: Functional Grammar and Cognitive Grammar.

4.4.1 *Functional Grammar*

Functional Grammar (FG) (Dik 1978, 1980, 1997, Siewierska 1991) shares with RRG the general functionalist perspective on grammar and, thus, a concern for explicating grammatical phenomena in terms of related semantic, pragmatic, and discourse factors. Moreover, FG uses a similar layered clause structure, with the verb and its arguments forming the core of a structure with outer layers for adjuncts and question and focus operators and the like. Semantic roles, called 'semantic functions', also play a critical role in grammatical organization. They are conceived of as grammatically relevant semantic inferences from the intersection of primitive properties of predicates and their arguments. Predicates are classified according to the kind of state of affairs that they designate (e.g. state, position, accomplishment, activity, change, dynamic process) following a definitional schema that is reminiscent of the Vendler/Dowty schema underlying the LSs of RRG, although different in various respects. Semantic functions are defined as kinds of entities involved in certain ways in states of affairs of different kinds. For example, the following semantic functions are among those recognized (Dik 1997: 118–20).

(4.38) Agent
the entity controlling an activity or accomplishment
John (Agent) read a book.

Positioner
the entity controlling a position
John (Positioner) keeps his money in a shoe box.

Force
the non-controlling entity that instigates a process
The earthquake (Force) moved the rock.

Processed
the entity that undergoes a process
The rock (Processed) moved.
the entity primarily involved in a state
The rock (Zero) was near the tree.

ProcExp
the entity that experiences an experienced process
John (ProcExp) realized that it was raining.

ZeroExp
the entity that experiences an experienced state
John (ZeroExp) was happy.

Goal
the entity affected or effected by the operation of some controller or force
John kissed Mary (Goal).

Recipient	the entity into whose possession something is trans-ferred
	John gave the book to Mary (Recipient).
Direction	the entity into whose possession something is trans-ferred
	John drove the car to Chicago (Direction).

Semantic functions are ordered into contrastive generalized categories in a way that is reminiscent of the macroroles of RRG, although there are three of them and the correspondence of even the closest two is not perfect. The idea is that there can be as many as three arguments of a predicate and when there are two or more they are ranked A1 > A2 > A3, following an algorithm such as the following (Dik 1997: 120).[18]

(4.39)
(1)	(2a)	(2b)
Agent	Goal(Exp)	Recipient(Exp)
Postitioner		Location
Force		Direction
Processed(Exp)		Source
Zero(Exp)		

1. In all predicate frames, A1 has one of the functions in (1).
2. In two-place predicate frames, A2 has one of the functions in (2a–b).
3. In three-place predicate frames A2 has the function in (2a) and A3 has one of the functions in (2b).

In some languages, grammatical constraints are understood as working directly in terms of either specific semantic functions or the generalized semantic role categories A1, A2, and A3. For example, since Choctaw has no passive construction that allows an argument of type (2a–b) to be 'promoted' to subject, nominative case (see Section 2.1.3) would be said to be assigned to the A1. Halkomelem, on the other hand, restricts the reflexivization pivot to the goal (i.e. what is generally called 'patient' or 'theme') (see Section 2.2.4).

The only syntactic functions posited are subject and object, which are assumed to reflect different perspectives on the same predicate frame. The subject is taken to define the primary perspective for the state of affairs designated by a given predicate frame. The object defines the secondary perspective. The subject function only occurs in languages that have a passive construction, or something equivalent. What the passive construction does is allow a state of affairs to be depicted from the primary perspective of some entity other than the A1 in a predicate frame. Similarly, the syntactic function object only occurs in languages that have an applicative (or 'dative shift') construction, which allows a state of affairs to be depicted from the secondary perspective of some entity other than the A2 in a predicate frame. Thus, the following English sentences have their NPs associated with semantic 'macro-roles and syntactic functions in the way illustrated.

	A1(*subject*)		A2(*object*)	A3
(4.40) a.	Martha	gave	the book	to Sam.
	A1(*subject*)		A3(*object*)	A2
b.	Martha	gave	Sam	the book.
	A3(*subject*)		A2	A1
c.	Sam	was given	the book	by Martha

The subject and object notions correspond closely to the final subject and object of Relational Grammar (at least for semantically transitive clauses in English, which are the only kind in which either the subject or object function are assigned in FG). There is no real analogue of the traditional indirect object notion, since the A3 category includes location, direction (= goal of RRG and other theories), and source, for example. The notion 'A3 object', however, corresponds to indirect object (in English at least) for those who take the term *indirect object* to refer only to the O1 in the double-object construction (see Section 1.3.2). The quasi-object properties of the second NP in sentences such as (4.40b) can be attributed to its status as a non-object A2.

4.4.2 *Cognitive Grammar*

Cognitive Grammar (CG) (Langacker 1987, 1991, 1999) uses what can be characterized as a billiard-ball model of event conceptualization. The basic idea is that we conceive of the typical events designated by verbs as involving entities that act upon each other in a force-dynamic manner causing move-ment or some analogous change of state to occur. From the complex concepts evoked by sentences such as *The boy killed the insect* or *The man removed the branches from the lawn* the same basic kind of image schema of action is at play, as illustrated in Figure 4.6. A participant or entity does something to another entity (i.e. there is a targeted force-dynamic action) and because of this the targeted entiy undergoes a change of state or location. What differs crucially with *kill* vs. *remove*, for example, is the precise nature of the effect of the targeted action: motion of the affected entity out of some place with *remove* vs. a change from alive to dead for the affected entity in the case of *kill*. At a schematic level of conceptualization, however, the basic action chain is the same: an action results in a change (i.e. movement relative to places or states) for the participant targeted by the actor.

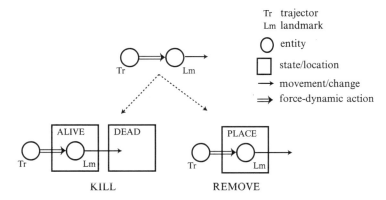

FIGURE 4.6.   Cognitive Grammar action-chain schema and verb meanings

An important further aspect of the conceptualization of events is perspective in the Functional Grammar sense discussed above or figure-ground organization in the sense of Talmy (2000). One of the participants in a multiple-participant event is necessarily more salient than the others, because the event is conceptualized primarily from the perspective of this participant. The same state of affairs is often amenable to alternative conceptualizations in which only the choice of primary participant, for which the term *trajector* is used, varies. For example, *The painting is above the table* designates the same objective state of affairs as *The table is beneath the painting*. The choice reflects different perspectives: the entity whose location is at stake (a trajector) relative to some other entity (a landmark) is allowed to vary. The clause-level trajector, the default value of which is the head of an action chain, is grammatically privileged (i.e. has the traditional 'subject' behaviours and properties) because of its conceptual prominence. A final key aspect of event conceptualization, which can have an effect on grammatical phenomena and grammatical relations, is profiling. Only certain aspects of an overall conceptual image schema may be in relief in a particular sentence frame. For example, in the case of *The window broke*, the overall concept 'x did something to y and because of this y became broken' is activated at some level (just as it is in the case of *The boy broke the window*). However, only the 'y became broken' part of the concept is profiled. Since only a participant that is part of a profiled action chain can be the trajector, the undergoer of the change in the event designated by *The window broke* is conceived of as the trajector, as shown in Figure 4.7.

The CG equivalents of the RRG semantic macroroles are 'head of an action chain' (= actor) and 'tail of an action chain' (= undergoer). In the case of transitive *break*, the subject is the head of the action chain and the object is the

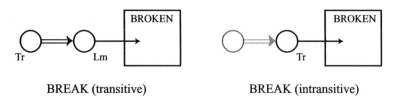

BREAK (transitive)   BREAK (intransitive)

FIGURE 4.7. Profiling and trajector choice with transitive and intransitive *break*

tail. In the case of intransitive *break,* the subject is the tail of an action chain (albeit a non-profiled one). The traditional subject notion corresponds to the clause-level trajector in CG, which is systematically related to but not fully determined by position in action chains, as the choice of trajector is construction-specific and language-specific to some extent. The most active profiled participant in an event image schema (the head of a profiled multiple-participant action chain, for example) is the default trajector in most languages. Passive and inverse voice constructions involve alternative conceptualizations in which a non-default participant is the trajector. Syntactically ergative languages have the passive sort of conceptualization of events as the default: the tail of a multiple-participant action chain, that is the undergoer of the main action, is the default trajector. Although the trajector in the conceptual structure of a clause is the dependent that is traditionally analysed as the subject, this is a conceptually (i.e. semantically) defined role in CG. The trajector is the entity that is most prominent in the conception of a state of affairs, by virtue of a very general process of figure-ground conceptualization that is manifested in other cognitive domains.

The CG approach to grammatical relations is particularly effective in explaining the crosslinguistic variablility and diachronic instability of grammatical relations with verbs of cognitive, perceptual, and emotional experience, and the related quasi-subject behaviour of dative experiencers in various languages. It is clear that an emotional experience such as that designated by the verbs *like* and *please* in English does not involve a force-dynamic action in the same way as transitive verbs such as *remove* or *kill.* However, from the perspective of grammatical relations the distinction is not significant: both *like* and *kill* are transitive and their A and O NPs have similar properties and grammatical privileges. Although there may be no physically manifested action with *like* and *please,* we conceive of the feelings as involving one or more actions in the domain of ception, that is the domain of perceiving, feeling, and cognizing (Talmy 1996), which can be represented in action chain image schemas with a single-lined dotted arrow. To begin with, the feeling itself is conceived of as a mental action focused on some entity that is analogous to the affected entity in a physical action. Moreover, the stimulus, which is conceived of as giving rise to the feeing, 'acts' on the experiencer, causing, in some sense, the feeling. Inasmuch as either participant can, in principle, be construed as the primary actor, action profiling and trajector choice can go in either direction, yielding the difference between (stative) *please* and *like*, as shown in Figure 4.8. In the case of *like*, only the mental action of the sentient participant targeting the stimulus is profiled, with the result that the experiencer of the emotion is chosen as trajector, as it is the head of a profiled action chain. The stimulus landmark is the tail of a profiled action chain, which behaves analogously to the tail of a profiled force-dynamic action chain with respect to grammatical properties and behaviour. The stimulus and experiencer have inverse properties in the case of *please*, since only the conceived action of the stimulus is profiled.

The highly abstract nature of the domain of ception and the partial fictivity of the conceived actions involved facilitate alternative construals of the primary direction of what is an inherently symmetrical action situation. As noted in Croft (1993), a natural consequence of this state of affairs is that there is both considerable crosslinguistic variation in grammatical relations with verbs of cognitive and emotional experience as well as the potential for diachronic instability. The dative experiencer construction, for example, illustrated by French *plaire* (4.41a) (see Section 2.3.1) and the Old English etymological source of *like* (4.41b) (Allen 1986), can have the analysis shown in Figure 4.9.

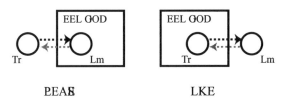

FIGURE 4.8. Profiling and trajector choice with English *please* and *like*

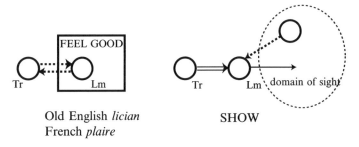

Old English *lician*
French *plaire*

SHOW

FIGURE 4.9. Profiling and trajector choice with dative constructions

(4.41) a.   Cette femme plait à Pierre.
            This woman pleases to Pierre. (i.e. 'is pleasing to Pierre')
       b.   Ge   noldon   gode   lician.
            you.NomPl   wouldn't.PlSubj God.Dat   like
            'God wouldn't like you.' or 'You wouldn't be pleasing to God.'

The dative/oblique marking of the experiencer can be attributed to profiling of both conceived actions in the emotional experience. Because of its profiled secondary action, the experiencer is marked in the same way as the 'indirect object' dependent of verbs such as *show* (e.g. *I showed the pictures to him*) which also is a sentient participant in a secondary receptive action. The experiencer argument of the verb *plaire* in French, which has the same conceptual schema as Old English *lician*, does not trigger subject–verb agreement or behave like a subject with respect to most phenomena because it lacks trajector status. However, its cognitive prominence due to its animacy and sentience and its heading an action chain motivate its subject-like behaviour with respect to adverbial control.

According to Allen, Old English *lician*, like Icelandic *henta* (see Sections 1.2 and 4.3.3), allowed an alternative conceptualization in which the experiencer had trajector status without, however, losing its dative marking. Thus, the same alternation with respect to choice of trajector that occurs with *henta* and other psych verbs in Icelandic was apparently possible in Old English as well. The only difference in the image-schematic conceptualization for the dative subject construction in Icelandic and Old English would be that the experiencer would be the trajector, for which reason it would have typical subject privileges. The nominative case marking of the stimulus in this alternative construction, although not a necessary consequence, would be conceptually motivated by the profiling of the action chain headed by the stimulus. Over time in English, accusative case marking for the stimulus and nominative case marking for the experiencer became possible, presumably by analogical pressure from the prototypical transitive action-chain scenario, and the nominative–accusative frame, with the associated asymmetrical action profiling shown for *like* in Figure 4.8 eventually became the only possibility.

5

Transformational Grammar

From the classical models (Chomsky 1957, 1965) through Government-Binding (GB) theory (Chomsky 1981, 1986) and the more recent Minimalist program (Chomsky 1995), (Generative-)Transformational Grammar (TG) has concerned itself primarily with an understanding of constituent structure and the implications of constituent structure for grammatical phenomena, including case marking, agreement, and other phenomena in which grammatical relations such as subject and object are implicated. The main idea is that representations of sentence structure primarily show the syntactic categories of elements (i.e. noun, verb, adjective, noun phrase, verb phrase, etc.), relations of constituency and containment (i.e. in what way elements, including words and phrases, are contained within larger phrases), and the linear order of constituents. Unlike in Relational Grammar, Role and Reference Grammar, and most other theories, both syntactic functions and semantic roles can and often do have a defining configurational instantiation. Unlike in other theories in which constituent structure plays a central role, such as Head-Driven Phrase-Structure Grammar (Pollard and Sag 1994), mismatches between linear order and grammatical relation and/or grammatical-relation sharing, splitting, or ambiguity can be attributed, at least in part, to transformations, that is movements of constituents within structures. Having been the most widely used theory of syntax for some time, it has been employed in analyses of countless phenomena in many languages and consequently has remained in considerable flux. Thus any detailed characterization of the theory's approach to grammatical relations is necessarily era- and movement-contingent to some extent.

5.1 Basic design of theory

5.1.1 *Classical TG*

The key idea of constituent-structure analyses of sentences is that phrases are built from words and other lexical and grammatical items which give them their categorical status and determine, to a large extent, what other elements must or may be contained in the same phrase (or clause). In the so-called

Aspects model of classical TG (Chomsky 1965), also known as 'standard theory', sentences are constructed following language-specific phrase-structure rules, which specify the possible kinds of phrases, their possible immediate constituents, and the linear order of all elements. Words drawn from the lexicon can be placed freely into structures generated by the phrase-structure rules, provided that the lexically-specified combinatorial constraints of the words themselves (so-called subcategorization rules and selectional restrictions) are not violated. Thus, for example, the verb *please* is lexically specified to occur with a following animate-referring NP in the same VP as it, the verb *put* is lexically specified to occur with both a following NP and a PP in the same VP as it, and so forth. Language-specific transformational rules, some of which are optional and others of which are obligatory, allow sentence structures constructed by the base component of the grammar (phrase-structure rules plus lexicon), known as a DEEP STRUCTURE, to be modified in various ways, to yield a SURFACE STRUCTURE.

By way of example, the phrase-structure rules shown in (5.1) together with the lexical specifications of the verb *put* and other relevant words, sanction a deep structure such as shown in Figure 5.1. An obligatory transformational rule of 'affix hopping' moves all verbal inflectional affixes to the right of the verbal element on which they appear. Thus, the deep structure of a tensed clause will always be changed in some way to produce a surface structure.[1] Moreover, because there is an optional passive transformation, which may apply prior to affix hopping, a single deep structure can have alternative surface structures associated with it. The meanings of related passive and active clauses are the same, for all intents and purposes, because they share the same deep structure, which is where meaning is encoded.

(5.1)   *Abbreviated set of phrase-structure rules*
   a.   S → NP Aux VP
        A clause, S, consists of a N(oun) P(hrase) followed by an Aux and a V(erb) P(hrase).
   b.   VP → V (NP) (PP)
        A VP consists of a V followed by an optional NP and an optional P(repositional) P(hrase).
   c.   NP → Det (AdjP) N (PP)
        An NP consists of a determiner followed by an N which optionally has a preceding Adjective phrase and/or a following PP.
   d.   PP → P NP
        A PP consists of a P(reposition) followed by an NP.

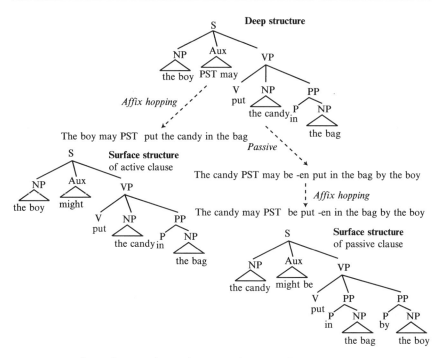

FIGURE 5.1. Classical TG analysis of active and passive clauses

e. Aux → Tense (Modal) (*have* + *-en*) (*be* + *-ing*)
    An Aux constituent consists of a Tense element followed optionally by
    one or more verbal auxiliary elements and any associated affixes.

Concepts such as subject, object, patient, actor, etc. are given no formal
status in the representational system. Nevertheless, as noted by Chomsky
(1965), it is possible to define certain traditional grammatical relations in
configurational terms, that is in terms of position in a canonical sentence
structure, as shown in (5.2). Moreover, notions such as actor (or 'logical'
subject) and patient (or 'logical' object) can be defined by taking into account
the distinction between deep and surface structure. Thus, for example, the
logical subject of a passive sentence is the NP immediately dominated by S at
deep structure and the surface subject is the logical object or patient, which is
the NP immediately dominated by VP at deep structure.

(5.2) *Definitions of syntactic functions*
    a. Subject = NP immediately dominated by S
    b. Object = NP immediately dominated by VP
    c. Oblique = NP immediately dominated by PP

5.1.2 *The GB approach*

The GB model of TG was developed with a view to eliminating language-specific rules in favour of universal constraints with a limited range of interlanguage variation. With respect to grammatical relations, it introduces more elaborate ways of dealing with semantic roles and offers some new ways of defining syntactic functions, while maintaining the idea that traditional subject and object functions are primarily defined in configurational terms.

Consider the GB-style analysis of a basic kind of active clause shown in Figure 5.2.[2] Following the constraints of so-called X-bar theory (Jackendoff 1977, Chomsky 1986: ch. 2), which is a universally valid set of constraints on phrase structures, phrases such as VP and possibly subphrases such as V′ are built around heads that determine their category. The clause is headed by inflectional elements (I = inflection), which ultimately are manifested on an auxiliary or main verb by a transformational process not shown here.[3] Three basic kinds of non-head constituents are recognized: specifiers, which occur in the position immediately dominated by an *X*P (or maximal projection of any category *X*), such as the clausal subject; complements, which occur in the minimal (or lowest) *X*′ containing the head; and adjuncts (= non-arguments of the head) which are adjoined to a phrasal category (typically an *X*′, as in the case of the temporal adverbial *on Thursday*). Beyond this classification, complements can be either direct, as in the case of *the pictures* in the active clause or indirect as in the case of *my mother*, which occurs in a (virtual) PP.

The primary definition of subject is 'the NP in the specifier position of IP' and the primary definition of object is 'NP sister of the verb' (where two phrases are sisters if they share the node immediately above them in the tree). Thus, *my brother* is the subject and *the pictures* is an object in the active clause in Figure 5.2. There are, however, other ways of defining grammatical relations. For example, it is assumed that all NPs must be assigned asbtract case, which may or may not be manifested morphologically. If I contains a finite tense it assigns 'structural' nominative case to its specifier position, where a structural case is one of the cases indicating a primary grammatical relation and which is assigned in a structure-specific way. Thus, 'subject' can also be defined as the nominative-marked NP. Because structural case is assigned to positions, case marking and position generally yield the same definitions of grammatical relations. However, there are cases where they diverge. For example, in an infinitival clause such as *for me to lie* in *It would be crazy for me to lie* the subject, *me*, which occupies the specifier of IP position in its clause, is marked accusative by the preceding *for*. Generally, prepositions, like verbs, assign accusative (or some other) case to their complement. Thus,

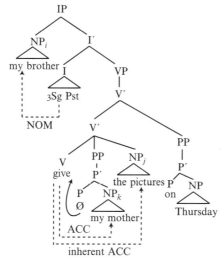

Argument structure of *give*: <agent^i, [patient^j, recipient^k]>

FIGURE 5.2. GB-style analysis of an English double-object clause

Thursday gets case from *on* in *My brother gave my mother the pictures on Thursday.* Verbs have a structural accusative case to assign, as well (possibly) as 'inherent' or semantically-restricted cases such as dative, ablative, instrumental, accusative, etc. In the case of the double-object construction, the recipient is expressed in a PP with a null or abstract preposition which incorporates into the verb (Baker 1988*b*). Such prepositions, which would be overt incorporated applicative morphemes in languages such as Kinyarwanda and Halkomelem (see Section 2.2.4), are unable to assign case to their object. The structural accusative case of the verb is therefore assigned to the recipient NP, accounting for its primary object status, including its adjacency to the verb. Thus, 'the NP that receives structural accusative case' is another definition of object. The recipient could also be defined as an indirect object, that is an object (in terms of case and behaviour) that is underlyingly in a PP. The second object in the double-object construction is assigned an inherent accusative case, accounting for its quasi-object properties (see Section 2.3). Naturally, in clauses without a recipient or in which the recipient (or other non-patient argument) is case-marked by a preposition, the patient is the object both by virtue of being an NP compement of the V and by virtue of being assigned the verb's structural accusative case.

The argument structure (i.e. semantic/syntactic valence) of a verb (e.g. Marantz 1984, Zubizarreta 1987, Grimshaw 1990), which can be derived from a decomposition of verb meaning or conceptual structure similar to the 'logical structure' of RRG (e.g. Jackendoff 1990), specifies how many semantic roles (or 'theta roles') it has and in what way they must be related to NPs in the syntactic structure. Although the theta-role labels are not critical, labels of a generic kind are used here for ease of exposition. Square brackets are used to indicate one critical distinction: internal vs. external theta role. Theta roles within square brackets must be aligned with NPs that are internal to the minimal V′ projection of the V. Italicization is used to indicate an argument that is realized as an indirect (or oblique) complement. The first theta role, which is outside the square brackets must be aligned with a constituent that is external to the minimal V′ projection of the V—the default case being the specifier position of IP. Thus, theta-role assignment yields potentially distinct notions of grammatical relations (construed broadly). The external argument corresponds to the actor of RRG and the initial (or 'logical') subject of RG. The direct internal argument corresponds to the initial (or 'logical') direct object of RG.

5.1.3 *The Minimalist approach*

The Minimalist approach within TG has a somewhat different basic conception of grammatical relations, as it implements a new technical mechanism for handling case and agreement (i.e. the case and agreement features of NPs are said to be 'checked' with matching features on heads) and introduces a more elaborate clausal architecture that has certain substantive ramifications. The defining idea of TG, that is that constituents can move within the clause structure, continues to play a key role. An NP, for example, may move from one position to another, in which case it leaves behind a coindexed trace. In effect, an NP and its traces conjointly occupy more than one position and, thus, have the grammatical properties associated with each of the positions. There are four main new ideas with respect to grammatical relations. First, following Kuroda (1988) and Koopman and Sportiche (1991), the so-called external theta role is assumed to be associated with a specifier position within the verb phrase. Thus, the position of the 'logical' subject is dissociated from the canonical clausal subject position (i.e. specifier of IP), allowing, in effect, different potential manifestations of subjects. Second, following ideas from Larson (1988), Hale and Keyser (1993), and others, the traditional VP is given a much more elaborate structure, with more possibilities for distinguishing grammatical relations, both in terms of positions and in terms of case relationships. Third, a more elaborate structure is also posited for the extra-VP part of the clause, yielding more positions for NPs to move to. Fourth, in addition to allowing structural case features of NPs to be checked in a canonical way (i.e. the NP moves to a specifier position to check its case with a head), NPs can check their case features by moving (or having their features move) virtually or covertly. This is accomplished by having a level of representation known as logical form (LF),[4] which is an abstract representation of the syntactic/semantic structure of a sentence which need not match the phonologically-produced linear order. In effect, grammatical relations in the form of case may be partly dissociated from overt structural position.

By way of example, consider the Minimalist-style analysis of the simple English clause shown in Figure 5.3, which adopts Baker's (1997) analysis of semantic-role positions coupled with the so-called 'bare phrase structure' and multiple-specifier framework (e.g. Chomsky 1995, Ura 2000, 2001). Intermediate levels in the phrases are dispensed with where not needed explicitly to introduce arguments or adjuncts and otherwise need not be labelled, as they are predictably X'. The basic schema, however, is that a head (X) can combine with a complement and one or more specifiers and/or adjuncts to form a phrase XP. Although semantic roles can be seen as being projected from an argument-structure representation (and an underlying conceptual structure) as in GB, a common alternative view is that such additional levels of representation are superfluous, given that semantic roles are instantiated configurationally in a uniform way within and across languages (Hale and Keyser 1993, Baker 1997).[5] In essence, the syntactic structure is itself a (more or less schematic) representation of verb meaning, such that at least the general semantic role types of the referents of NPs can be read off the structure.[6] The VP can be split into at least two levels: an outer vP and an inner VP. The v receives an interpretation like 'cause' when it has a 'transitive' VP complement and the NP originating in its specifier position is interpreted as referring to an agent(-like) participant. The inner VP can have both specifier and complement arguments. The referent of the NP that originates in the specifier of VP position is interpreted as having a patient-type role (prototypically, its referent undergoes motion or change) and the PP in the complement position has a goal or other locative-type role (prototypically, its referent specifies the state, location, or participant to or from which movement or change occurs).[7]

The base structure, with NPs in their semantic-role positions, can be modified by movement processes in several ways. The V, for example, moves overtly from its base position to join with the higher v and in some languages and under certain conditions to the I node (often analysed as simply T, for tense). The need to check case and/or other grammatical features (collectively 'nominal features') is one of the primary motivations for NP movement. A nominative case feature, for example, is located in the head of IP and a structural accusative case feature is located in the head of v. The head of IP can also have agreement features (person/number, for example) and a

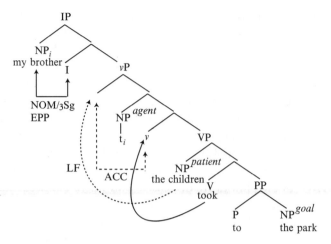

FIGURE 5.3. Minimalist-style analysis of a basic transitive English clause

so-called EPP feature, both of which can in effect force the presence of an NP in the specifier position of IP, independently of or conjointly with the case feature.[8] The EPP feature is a remnant of the GB Extended Projection Principle (Chomsky 1981), according to which all clauses must have a subject (an analogue of the Final 1 Law of Relational Grammar). Being closest, the agent moves to the specifier of IP position to check the case, person/number (agreement), and EPP features of the head. Movement to check features cannot be covert (i.e. at LF—indicated by the dashed line in the diagram) if one or more of the features of the head is specified as being 'strong', as in the case of the EPP feature in English, which forces the NP destined to be the traditional subject to move to a specifier position of IP. Since the accusative case feature and any other nominal features of *v* are 'weak' in English, overt movement of the patient to the specifier of *v*P does not occur. Instead, the accusative case feature is checked by covert or LF movement—technically only the features of the NP move to *v* (Chomsky 1995, Ura 2000).

One reason for saying that the *v* contains nominal features (including accusative case) that attract an NP is that some languages allow objects to appear in positions that suggest fronting to a pre-*v* position. In Icelandic, which is a language in which tensed verbs move to I overtly, an object can precede a subject that has not been moved out of its base position, as illustrated by the following examples (Ura 2000: 52).

(5.3) það   borðuðu   [*v*P ostinn*i*   margar   mýs [VP t*i*]]
        there   ate   the cheese   many   mice
        'Many mice ate the cheese.'

The Icelandic object shift phenomenon can be accounted for by assuming that the nominal features hypothesized for *v* must be checked and may (in some languages) be checked by an NP that has overtly moved to a second specifier position of *v*P. The claim that this kind of overt object movement cannot take place in English is motivated by the contrast between the following examples, in conjunction with the assumption that the verb is necessarily in the *v* position overtly.

(5.4) a.   My brother might [$_{vp}$ send the children to the park].
      b.   *My brother might [$_{vp}$ the children send to the park].

Nevertheless, because the basic template of clause structure is assumed to be essentially invariant across languages, the idea that there is a feature-checking relationship between *v* and the object is maintained. One notion of direct object is 'NP in a nominal feature-checking relationship (but not a semantic-role relationship) with *v*.'[9]

In short, the basic structure of transitive clauses (in accusative languages) is as shown in Figure 5.4, with V movement ignored. There are, however, several provisos. First, languages may differ with respect to matters of linear order (e.g. head before or after complement and specifier to the left or right of the head). Second, languages may differ with respect to whether NPs may, must, or cannot move overtly to check features with the appropriate heads. Third, languages can vary with respect to whether obliques, such as a goal or source complement, are realized as a PP, as in English, or as an NP (possibly inherently case-marked). The traditional subject and object grammatical relations are ephiphonemal. The theory yields a set of natural classes or categories of NP types, based on structural positions and feature-checking relationships. Syntactic phenomena often work differentially across and within languages in terms of these notions. For the sake of theory comparison, another way of looking at the situation is that there are various potential definitions of the traditional subject and object notions, as shown in (5.5).

(5.5)   *Potential definitions of subject and object*
      a.   Logical subject = base specifier of *v*P
      b.   Subject = checker of nominal features (case, agreement, etc.) of I
      c.   Subject = specifier of IP
      d.   Logical object = NP in the highest base position in VP[10]
      e.   Object = checker of nominal features of *v*

5.2   Typological variation

5.2.1 *Ergativity*

Largely in response to fundamental typological distinctions among languages with respect to grammatical relations, TG (especially in its Minimalist

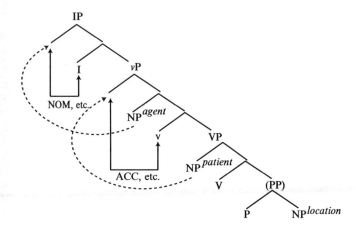

FIGURE 5.4. Minimalist schema for transitive clause in accusative languages

manifestation) makes available a range of options with respect to possible manipulations of what can be conceived of as a basic universal clause structure. Given the framework outlined above, an ergative language can be characterized as one with only a couple of deviations from the accusative schema, from which most of the other differences essentially follow. In a syntactically ergative language such as Dyirbal (see Section 2.1.2), the S/O category (i.e. the object/patient or subject of an intransitive) is the most syntactically privileged. The patient in a transitive clause, thus outranks the agent in terms of grammatical prominence. To the extent that grammatical prominence means a checking relationship with I via the specifier of IP position, it is necessary to get the patient to move out of the *v*P. This can be accomplished by attributing to ergative languages the ability to case-check the agent in its base position. In essence, the only structural case of *v* is called ergative and is necessarily checked with the base specifier, unlike in the default scenario in accusative languages. The agent still moves (or can move) to the specifier position of IP, where it can check the EPP feature of I. However, the structural case feature of I ($=$ absolutive) cannot be checked by the agent, which has an ergative case that has been checked with *v*. Consequently, the patient (which cannot check a case feature with *v* anyway) must move to a second, higher specifier of IP position to check the absolutive case feature and any remaining nominal features of I. In a nutshell, the basic schema for an ergative transitive clause is as shown in Figure 5.5 (abstracting away from V movement, overt vs. covert movement, and language-specific linear order differences).[11]

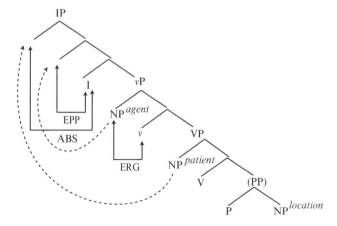

FIGURE 5.5. Minimalist schema for transitive clauses in ergative languages

In order to explain case marking with intransitive verbs in ergative languages, it is necessary to take into account the two main types of intransitive verbs, for which a form of the Unaccusative Hypothesis (see Section 3.3.4) is adopted. With unergative verbs, the *v*P part of the VP shell is present and the agent dependent originates in the specifier position of the *v*P. Although the inner VP may contain an oblique argument, it does not have a patient argument. With unaccusative verbs, since there is no agent there is no *v* and therefore no *v*P. The patient argument originates within the VP, in the same position as the patient in a transitive clause. In the case of unaccusatives, the VP-internal NP must check the absolute case of I, as that is the only way for it to have its case feature checked and the only way for the nominal features of I to be checked. In the case of unergatives, there are only two possible scenarios: the agent NP checks an ergative case feature of *v* and I has no case feature (that needs to be checked) or the *v* has no case feature and the agent NP checks the absolute case feature of I. In either case, the agent NP may still move to the specifier of IP position (to check the EPP feature of I, if it is strong). Only in the latter case, however, does the language have a true ergative case marking system. In the former, the language would have a split-intransitive case marking system, since there would be a split among intransitive verbs. Thus, the relative rarity of the ergative pattern can be attributed, in part, to the unlikelihood of a language both allowing the *v* to enter into a case-checking relation with its base specifier (which might be characterized as a marked option) and allowing the *v* to not have an ergative case in intransitive clauses. The feature-checking and NP movment scenario for intransitive clauses in an ergative language are illustrated in Figure 5.6.

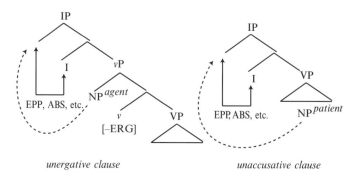

unergative clause   *unaccusative clause*

FIGURE 5.6. Minimalist schema for intransitive clauses in ergative languages

For languages such as Dyirbal (Section 2.1.2), in which the absolutive NP
is the syntactically most privileged dependent (controller of conjunction
reduction, relativization pivot, controller of purposive clauses, etc.), the
highest-ranking grammatical relation can be defined either as the absolutive
case-checker or as the highest specifier of IP. Whatever subject-like (or 'quasi-
subject') properties the ergative NP may have can be attributed either to its
status as the EPP-feature checker or as a specifier of IP.[12] Inuit (Eskimo-Aleut)
is generally considered to be another example of a syntactically ergative
language (Woodbury 1977, Bittner 1987, Bittner and Hale 1996*a*, 1996*b*),
because the absolutive NP, for example, is the agreement controller in infinitival clauses (in which only one NP triggers agreement), the controller of the
missing NP in subordinate adjunct clause constructions, and the relativization pivot, as illustrated by (5.6) (from Bittner and Hale 1996*b*).

(5.6) a. [arna-p   [_   ani-sima-su-p]]   angut
         woman-Erg$_i$ *Abs pivot$_i$*   go.out-Perf-Relat.Intr-Erg   man
         taku-v-a-a
         see-Ind-Tr-3SgA.3SgO
         'The woman who had gone out saw the man.'
     b. [arna-t   [_   miiqqa-p   isiginnaa-ga-i]]
         woman.Abs-Pl$_j$ *Abs pivot$_j$*   child-Erg   watch-Relat.Tr-3Sg$_i$.Pl
         mirsur-p-u-t
         sew-Ind-Intr-3PlS
         'The women the child is watching are sewing.'

Nevertheless, the reflexivization controller is the S/A dependent (i.e. the
absolutive NP of an intransitive clause but the ergative NP of a transitive
clause) as indicated by (5.7) (from Ura 2000: 190).

(5.7) a. *Junna*   *immi*-nut   tatigi-v-u-q
          Junaa.Abs   self.Dat   trust-Ind-Intr-3SgS
          'Junna trusts in self.'
     b. *Junna*-p   Kaali   *immi*-nik   uqaluttuup-p-a-a
          Junna-Erg   Kali.Abs   self-Instr   tell-Ind-Tr-3SgA3SgO
          'Junna_i told Kali_j about self_{i/*j}.'

Thus, the reflexive controller must be the lowest specifier of IP, whereas for other subject phenomena the highest specifier of IP is implicated.[13]

Morphologically ergative languages whose syntax is primarily accusative, such as Warlpiri and Basque (see Section 2.1.2), are accounted for by assuming that, in such languages, the patient NP does not move overtly to the specifier of IP position (because the absolute case feature of I is 'weak'). Thus, a variant of the schema shown in Figure 5.5 has only the ergative NP in a specifier of IP position. The absolute NP checks the absolute case of I by moving (its features) only covertly to I. With respect to 'subject'-sensitive phenomena, the ergative NP wins out over the absolute in such languages (yielding, in effect, syntactic accusativity) because an NP in a specifier of IP position outranks an NP that only checks a nominal-feature of I at LF. Naturally, the kinds of split-ergative coding properties (case vs. agreement, for example) and split-ergative syntactic behaviour that many languages show create a myriad of complexities that can be difficult to explain. However, by providing a myriad of possible syntactic-function definitions (e.g. LF I-feature checker vs. overt I-feature checker, higher specifier of IP vs. lower specifier of IP, case checker vs. person/number checker vs. EPP checker, etc.), the Minimalist approach provides a means of navigating through at least some of this complexity, while maintaining the view that there is a cross-linguistically invariant configurational manifestation of basic generalized semantic roles (agent in specifier of *v*P position, for example) and some kind of more or less invariant hierarchy of syntactic function privilege (higher specifier of IP > lower specifier of IP > LF checker of I features, etc.).

5.2.2 *Split intransitivity*

A split-intransitive head-marking or dependent-marking language is one in which the agent (or most agent-like) dependent is marked in the same way and the patient (or most patient-like) dependent is marked in a different way, independently of the transitivity of the verb. From a TG/Minimalist perspective, this can occur if the case-marking and agreement properties of either the agent-referring NP or the patient-referring NP (or both) are determined on the basis of base position, given the kind of unaccusative/unergative distinction among intransitive clauses shown in Figure 5.6. Thus, under one scenario, the ergative case of the *v* in an unergative clause is not suppressed and is checked by the agent NP which then moves to the specifier position of IP to check the EPP feature of I (and any other nominal features of I, other than absolutive, which must either be suppressed or, as suggested by Ura, allowed to go unchecked). This would technically be a split-intransitive ergative language, such as Georgian, for example, is claimed to be in Bittner and Hale (1996*a*).

Although it is unclear that this basic analysis could not be extended in some form to all split-intransitive languages, since a distinction between ergative and accusative split-intransitive languages may be largely terminological, as noted by Dixon (1994: 78), there is also a way of getting accusative split intransitivity. It might be assumed that the agent always moves to the specifier of IP position to check all nominal features of I (including a nominative case feature). The patient, on the other hand, is case-licensed internal to the VP, perhaps because V can have an accusative case feature, analogous to the ergative case feature of *v* in ergative languages. This kind of analysis (certain details aside) is posited for Acehnese and Eastern Pomo (a Hokan language of Northern California) in Bittner and Hale (1996*a*). Eastern Pomo provides a nice example, inasmuch as it is a dependent-marking language in which the case of the patient is overtly marked and the agentive case is zero (which is, crosslinguistically, typical of nominative rather than ergative), as shown by the following examples from Bittner and Hale.

(5.8) a.	míip	míip-al	sáaka	*transitive*
	he.Nom	him-Acc	killed	
	'He killed him.'			
b.	míip-al	xáa	baakúma	*unaccusative*
	him-Acc	in.the.water	fell	
	'He fell in the water (accidentally).'			
c.	míip	káluhuya		*unergative*
	he.Nom	went.home		
	'He went home.'			

It is preferable to analyse the nominative NPs as subjects and the accusative NPs as non-subjects (even in intransitive clasues like (5.8b)), insofar as the nominative NPs of either transitive or unergative clauses count for purposes of same-subject marking in subordination structures, whereas the accusative NP of an unaccusative clause cannot yield same-subject marking with respect to a nominative NP in a related clause, as shown by the following examples (SS = same-subject marking; DS = different-subject marking):[14]

(5.9) a. [háa   káluhu-y],   siimáa _   mérqakiihi
          I.Nom_i   went.home-SS   Ø(Nom)_i   went.to.bed
          'I went home, and then I went to bed.'

     b.   [háa   qákki-qan]   wi   qaalál   táala
          I.Nom_i   took.a.bath-DS   me.Acc_i sick   became
          'I took a bath, so I got sick.'

Thus, the most straightforward analysis of transitive and intransitive clauses in Eastern Pomo is as schematized in Figure 5.7, ignoring V movement and any feature checking other than for case and EPP. It is, of course, necessary to assume that I can have its nominative case suppressed or unchecked in unaccusative clauses, as must be assumed for absolutive case in unergative clauses on the ergative split-intransitive analysis discussed above.[15] For languages (such as Kamaiurá and Choctaw, discussed in Section 2.1.3) in which the patient NP of unaccusative clauses has clear subject-like properties, including (preferred) clause-initial positioning, it could be assumed that this NP moves overtly to the specifier of IP position. Needless to say, since this approach to split intransitivity is built around the Unaccusative Hypothesis and the problematic assumption that universal grammar somehow yields the unaccusative vs. unergative distinction automatically, it faces the same challenges as the Relational Grammar approach discussed in Section 3.3.4.

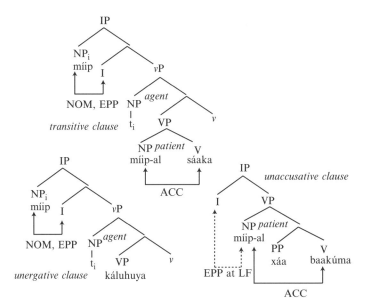

FIGURE 5.7. Three clause types in Eastern Pomo

5.3 Some case studies

5.3.1 *Multiple subjects and quasi-subject phenomena*

Given that there can be multiple specifiers of a phrase, including either *v*P or IP, and multiple (overt or covert) checkers of nominal features of I, certain kinds of quasi-subject phenomena in languages can be attributed to the secondary subjecthood of an NP. This is routinely the case for syntactically ergative languages, as noted above, since these can have the ergative case-marked NP in a lower specifier of IP position and the absolutive case-marked NP in a higher specifier of IP position, for example. There is no reason why this basic kind of structure could not occur in syntactically accusative languages as well, albeit only as a consequence of voice.

One obvious candidate for a multiple-subject analysis is the Seri passive construction, discussed in Section 2.2.1. The interesting fact about Seri is that although the patient in the passive construction has most of the 'subject' coding and behavioural properties, for the purposes of subject-sensitive switch-reference marking only the implicit agent in the passive construction counts as a subject. The following sentence, for example, shows that even though the patient subjects of the main and subordinate clauses are different, the different-subject marker cannot be used, since the implicit agents of the two clauses are the same.

(5.10) [[ʔaːt   kiʔ   p-aːʔ-kaː   (*ta)-x] ʔeːpoɬ kiʔ   mos
         limberbush the   Irr-Pass-seek DS-Aux   ratany the   also
         si- aːʔ-kaː   ʔa=ʔa]
         Irr-Pass-seek Aux=Decl
         'If limberbush is looked for, white ratany should be looked for also.'

Under the analysis of the embedded passive clause shown in Figure 5.8,[16] the implicit agent, a null pronoun with an unspecified referent (pro$_{ARB}$), occupies the base specifier of *v*P position, just as any agent-referring NP would in an active clause.

What makes the passive construction different from the active construction is that the passive morphology on the verb causes the accusative case of *v* to be transformed (effectively) into a kind of ergative case, that is a case that must be checked with the base specifier of the *v*P. Although the agent NP moves to the specifier of IP position where it can check the EPP feature of I, it cannot check the nominative case feature of I. The patient NP moves to the higher specifier of IP position to check the nominative case feature (and the other nominal features of I). As in the case of reflexive control in Inuit (Section

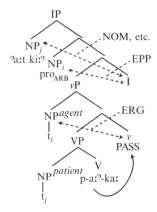

FIGURE 5.8. Passive clause in Seri

5.2.1), the controller of switch reference in Seri must be the NP in the lowest specifier position of IP (i.e. the first subject). This is a natural result insofar as switch reference seems to be incorporable into a more general theory of anaphora (Finer 1985, Enç 1989) and the same kind of condition apparently must be an available option for reflexive control in some languages.

The Jarawara reversal construction and inverse voice phenomena more generally (see Section 2.2.3) are also amenable to a kind of multiple-subject analysis, insofar as 'base specifier of *v*P' is a kind of subject. Following Ura's (2000) analysis of inverse voice in Kinyarwanda, the following clauses, which exemplify the direct and inverse constructions of Jarawara, can be analysed as shown.

(5.11) a. [$_{IP}$Mioto$_i$ [$_{vP}$Watati$_j$ t$_i$ [$_{VP}$ t$_j$ wa-ka] *v*] I]
           Mioto(Masc)   Watati(Fem)   see-DeclMasc
           'Mioto saw Watati.'
      b. [$_{IP}$Watati$_i$ [$_{vP}$ t$_i$ Mioto   [$_{VP}$ t$_i$ hi-wa] *v*]   hi-ke]
           Watati(Fem)   Mioto(Masc)   Inv-see   Inv-DeclFem
           'Mioto saw Watati.' (or, 'Watati was seen by Mioto.')

In the direct voice, the agent originates in the specifier of *v*P position but cannot check its case with the *v* and therefore moves to the specifier of IP position, where it checks the nominative feature of I, as well as any other nominal features of I (including the EPP feature and the gender feature that is manifested morphologically in the gender agreement suffix). The patient moves, presumably overtly, to the specifier position of *v*P to check the nominal features of *v*, including its accusative case feature. In the inverse voice, the accusative case of the *v* (which could be called 'ergative') is assigned to the base specifier of vP due to a voice feature on the v, which is sometimes morphologically manifested on the amalgamated verb (assumed to move to v overtly, in a way not shown here) as well as on the auxiliary (assumed to be overtly in the I position). Since the patient NP, which may still move to the higher specifier position of vP cannot check its case with the v, whose only case is assigned to the agent NP, it moves higher up to the specifier position of IP, where it checks all the nominal features of I, including the nominative case feature. Thus, the apparent syntactic-function reversal is due to the fact that in each voice one NP moves to the specifier position of IP and one stays in a specifier of vP position. The former has the subject properties and privileges, the latter has the O properties. However, the underlying subjecthood of the agent (= NP in the base specifier of vP) and the underlying objecthood of the patient (= highest base argument of the VP) can be used to account for the constraints on the pronominal forms that show up in cases where the features of the NPs in question are other than 3rd singular.

As indicated by the following examples (= (2.64)), preverbal pronouns indexing the agent and patient show up in a fixed order (patient < agent), independently of voice. Moreover, an accusative suffix can appear on the patient-referring pronoun only in the direct voice and a copy pronoun of the nominative NP shows up in a pre-auxiliary, or postverbal position.

(5.12) a.   *Direct voice; feminine suffixes because both pronominal slots are filled*
         aba   mee(-ra) otaa   kaba-haro otaa   ama-ke
         fish(Masc) 3Nsg(-O) 1NsgExcl eat-TnsFem 1NsgExcl extent-DeclFem
         'We were eating fish.'

       b.   *Inverse voice; feminine suffixes because both pronominal slots are filled*
         aba   mee(*-ra) otaa   kaba-haro mee ama-ke
         fish(Masc) 3Nsg(-O) 1NsgExcl eat-TnsFem 3Nsg extent-DeclFem
         'We were eating fish.' (or, 'Fish was being eaten by us.')

The proposed structures of the two clause types yield a natural account of both the positions and the form of the pronominal elements, if they are analysed as non-moving adjuncts that are coindexed with the first specifier of the verbal/auxiliary heads to which they attach, as illustrated in the analysis shown in Figure 5.9.

Dative subject phenomena in languages such as Icelandic as well as dative quasi-subject phenomena in other languages (see Section 2.3.1), also appear to be amenable to some version of a multiple-subject analysis (e.g. Belletti and Rizzi 1988, Ura 1999). Consider, for example, the following schematic analyses of Icelandic dative passive clauses (= (4.27)).

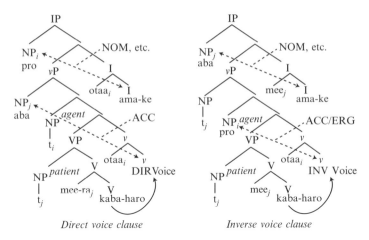

Direct voice clause   Inverse voice clause

FIGURE 5.9. Direct vs. inverse voice in Jarawara

(5.13) a. [IP Bilarnir_i   voru [_vP sýndir [VP t_i t_v   henni]]]
           cars.Nom   were   shown   3SgFemDat
           'The cars were shown to her.'

     b. [IP Henni_i   voru [_vP sýndir [VP   bílarnir t_v t_i]]]
           3SgFemDat   were   shown   cars.Nom
           'She was shown the cars.'

It is assumed here that the passive 'be' auxiliary is overtly in I and the main
verb moves to the *v* position overtly and that, due to the passive morphology,
the implicit agent is suppressed and the accusative case of the *v* is taken away,
although it is unclear how crucial these assumptions are. The recipient NP has
an inherent dative case by virtue of its semantic role and base position.
As such, it cannot check the nominative case feature of I. The patient NP
must check the nominative case feature and person/number (agreement)
features of I. Since this is possible without overt movement, as shown by
(5.13b), the case and person/number features of I must be able to be 'weak',
although the EPP feature must be strong, since some NP must move overtly
to the specifier of IP position. There are two possibilities, the dative NP moves
overtly to the specifier of IP position, as in (5.13b), in which case it has all
the typical 'subject' privileges associated with this position. The patient
NP covertly checks the case and person/number features of I, for which reason
it is the 'subject' only with respect to case and agreement morphology.
The other possibility is that the patient NP simply moves overtly to the
specifier of IP position and checks all the nominal features of I, as in
(5.13a), and has both the coding and behavioural properties of the 'subject'.

Although why the two possibilities should exist in Icelandic is not entirely clear, the grammatical properties of the two constructions are accounted for straightforwardly.

The psych verb alternation discussed in Sections 1.2, 3.3.5, and 4.3.3 can presumably be handled in essentially the same way (modulo whatever differences may be attributable to the base positions of the arguments of psych verbs and the lack of an agent role). Other languages may allow the dative NP in certain dative constructions to move overtly to IP, without, however, gaining all the subject privileges of the language by virtue of not checking the case and person/number features of I. For languages like French, which do not allow the 'dative' NP in psych verb constructions to move overtly to the specifier of IP position at all and restrict its subject properties to limited kinds of control of adverbial phrases and the like, it may be that the dative NP is subject-like only by virtue of covertly checking some feature of I (although why such should occur at all is not entirely clear).

An interesting question that arises is whether the passive construction in all languages might be analysed in a way similar to the proposed analyses of either the Seri passive or the Jarawara inverse, or whether such a possibility is at least more widely utilized. It is commonly assumed, following the influential analyses of Chomsky (1981), Jaeggli (1986), and Baker *et al.* (1989), that passive morphology has the effect of not only suppressing (or itself taking) the accusative case otherwise destined for the patient NP, but also causing the agent NP to not be introduced in its canonical position (i.e. a specifier of vP position in the Minimalist framework). If the agent semantic role is implicit, it is associated with the passive morphology rather than with an NP; if the agent is expressed as an oblique, it is an adjunct that shares the agent semantic role by virtue of being necessarily coindexed with the supposedly nominal passive morphology. This sort of analysis is problematic from the point of view of the Uniform Thematic Alignment Hypothesis (Baker 1988*a*, 1997), insofar as the agent semantic role is not uniformly associated with the base specifier of vP position. An associated problem is that it is not clear why passive agents have quasi-subject properties in many languages. Consider, for example, the fact that the pivot in the raising-to-object construction in Halkomelem is restricted to the S/A (subject) or the otherwise oblique agent of the embedded clause (see Section 2.2.1). What this means is that either the absolutive NP of a passive clause or the agent can show up as the (absolutive) O of the main clause, as illustrated by the following examples (= (2.42)):

S of embedded passive clause = O of x̌ec-

(5.14) a. ʔi   cən   x̌eʔx̌cí-t   kʷθə Bob
        Aux 1Subj wonder.Cont-Tr Det   Bob
          [ʔu   ʔi-ʔəs   ṡʔləm-ʔət-əm? ʔə-ƛ̓’   John   Ø]
          Lnk   Aux-3SgSubj look-Tr-Intr Obl-Det John
        'I'm wondering if Bob is being watched b John.'

Agent of embedded passive clause = O of x̌ec-

    b. ʔi   cən   x̌eʔx̌cí-t   kʷθə   John
        Aux 1Subj wonder.Cont-Tr Det   John
          [ʔu   ʔi-ʔəs   láʔləm-ʔət-əm?   Ø   kʷθə Bob]
          Lnk   Aux-3SgSubj look-Tr-Intr   Det Bob
        'I'm wondering if Bob is being watched by John.'

Given that raising from oblique does not otherwise occur in Halkomelem and seems to be unprecedented from a crosslinguistic perspective, it is worth wondering whether the agent NP in the passive construction has something structurally in common with absolutive subjects. For example, it might be that the agent NP is invariably introduced in the specifier of *v*P position and can perhaps move to a specifier of IP position, which may be a prerequisite for raising into a higher clause. Unfortunately, exactly how such an analysis could be made to work with respect to all details remains unclear. For example, it is not clear how it might be guaranteed that the passive agent is necessarily marked like an oblique when the patient raises to check the absolutive case of the higher I (in a simple main clause, for example) and yet nevertheless need not be oblique in principle, in that it too can check the absolutive case of the I in a higher clause. In a theory such as Relational Grammar in which the necessity of checking case features determines neither syntactic function nor position in a clause, the analysis is more straightforward. Agents are always initial subjects. In passive clauses they are simply necessarily demoted in some way. Although there may be a universal constraint on raising constructions limiting the pivot to subjects, neither position nor case is relevant to the precise condition in Halkomelem. Rather, the pivot must simply be a subject in *some* stratum.

5.3.2 *Applicative constructions and the indirect object notion*

There have been a number of different TG approaches to applicative and double-object constructions. If the traditional indirect object notion has a configurational characterization, it may only be manifested in these constructions. Consider, for example, the following examples from Halkomelem (= (2.70a–b)).

(5.15) a. ni   ʔám-əs-t-əs   kʷθə   sqʷəmə́yʔ   ʔə   kʷθə   sθ'ám?
           Aux   give-Recip-Tr-3A   Det   dog   Obl Det   bone
           'He gave the dog the bone.'

      b.   ni   qʷ'ə́l-əɬc-t-əs   ɬə   sɬéni   ʔə   kʷθə   səplíl
           Aux   bake-Ben-Tr-3A   Det   woman   Obl Det   bread
           'He baked the bread for the woman.'

These are transitive clauses, as there is a transitive suffix on the verb and there is an agreement marker for the 3Sg A (expressed as a null pronoun in these cases), which only occurs in transitive clauses. However, the patient is not an O, as evidenced by the fact that it occurs in a PP with the all-purpose oblique preposition and has none of the behavioural properties of an O. The recipient NP in (5.15a) and the beneficiary NP in (5.15b), on the other hand, behave like the O of an ordinary transitive clause, not only in lacking a preposition and controlling O agreement (when not third person), but also by their behaviour with respect to passivization, quantifier float, possessor extraction, and various A-/S-/O-restricted syntactic phenomena, as discussed in Section 2.2.4. Being an ergative language, the agent only needs to check its case with the v and need not move overtly. Since the preferred word order for the NPs, when overt, is A < O and the verb immediately follows the clause-initial auxiliary (which may be assumed to occupy an initial complementizer position), the simplest analysis is that the verb overtly raises (through all verbal head positions) to I and the NPs remain within the vP, which is the result of all the nominal features of I being weak. The higher grammatical prominence of the applicative O can be attributed to its being introduced in a slot between the v and the VP. In the case of (5.15b), for example, the benefactive applicative affix can be analysed as a verb with a beneficiary argument, as shown in Figure 5.10. Following Ura (2000), the intermediate verbal category is simply labelled V_{mid} here.[17]

The motivation for introducing the applicative O in a higher slot within the extended verb phrase is that it has primary O properties crosslinguistically, independently of whether the patient is treated like an oblique or not. The primary O properties are necessarily associated with the applicative O because, by virtue of its higher base position, it must necessarily be the NP that moves overtly or covertly to check the absolutive case feature of I (in an ergative language) or the accusative case feature of v (in an accusative language). In any case, the traditional indirect object grammatical relation can be defined as the NP which originates in the specifier position of the V_{mid}P, although 'primary object' would presumably be a better designation.

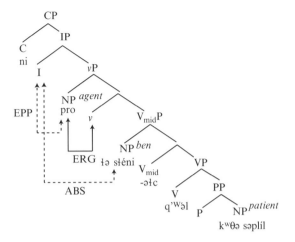

FIGURE 5.10. Benefactive applicative construction in Halkomelem

With respect to benefactive and recipient applicative constructions, English differs from Halkomelem (independently of ergativity) primarily in that the patient is (at least) a quasi-O (see Sections 1.3.2 and 2.3) and the V_{mid} is not associated with phonological content in the form of an applicative affix. The double-object construction might be analysed as shown in Figure 5.11 (based on Ura 2000). The applicative O is the primary O since it checks the accusative case of *v* and is in a higher position in the tree. The V_{mid} has a weak accusative case feature which the patient NP can check covertly, accounting for its quasi-O properties. Languages in which both the applicative O and the patient manifest primary O properties (i.e. symmetric applicative languages), including perhaps dialects of English that allow promotion of either the patient or the applicative O in the passive construction, might be characterized as allowing overt movement of the patient to a specifier position of the $V_{mid}P$, which would give it configurationally equivalent status with the applicative O.

One potential drawback of such an analysis is that it is unclear how the relationship between the double-object construction and the alternative construction that has the recipient in a PP with *to* might be accounted for. If it is assumed that the recipient PP originates in a lower position within the VP than the patient and the patient checks the accusative case feature of *v*, it is necessary to either abandon the default assumption that semantic roles are associated with initial positions in a uniform way (e.g. Baker 1988*a*, 1997, Hale and Keyser 1993) or to entertain the problematic hypothesis that *give the boy a bike* and *give a bike to the boy* have a sufficiently different meaning as to

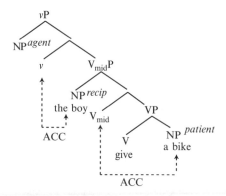

FIGURE 5.11. Double-object construction in English

warrant claiming that the semantic roles are different. On the other hand, if it is assumed that the recipient semantic role is always associated with the specifier position of the $V_{mid}P$ and what differs is only whether the preposition *to* is present (to case-license the recipient NP or perhaps as a manifestation of an inherent dative case), some ad hoc stipulation is required to guarantee overt movement of the patient NP to a higher position than the recipient just in case the latter is a PP.

Another alternative would be to have the recipient always originate in a PP in a lower position than the patient within the VP and have it move to a higher position in the tree, perhaps a higher specifier of VP position, just in case the preposition is null, essentially following the GB-style analysis shown in Figure 5.2, which is based on the analysis of applicative constructions proposed by Baker (1988*a*, 1988*b*). Particularly for constructions such as the goal applicative construction in Halkomelem, illustrated by the following examples (= (2.73c–d)), the P incorporation approach seems to be the most straightforward.

(5.16) a.   ni   ném   ʔə-ƛ̓   John
            Aux   go   Obl-Det   John
            'He went to John.'

      b.   ni   ném-n-əs-əs   kʷθə   John
            Aux   go-Goal-Tr-3A   Det   John
            'He went to John.'

Assuming that semantic roles have a uniform configurational instantiation crosslinguistically, the goal argument must be a PP complement of the V. One need only say that if the P that indicates the goal semantic role takes the form of a verbal affix, the NP must enter into an absolute case-checking relation with I (in an ergative language like Halkomelem) and therefore has the properties and privileges of an O.

Needless to say, the combination of different potential ways of characterizing PP/NP alternations, various potential base and target postions for NPs within an extended VP with uncertain limits, and the possibility of both overt and covert movement, leads to the possibility of numerous alternative analyses of applicative phenomena.

5.4 Related theories

The connections between TG and Relational Grammar and Lexical-Functional Grammar, both of which differ from TG in that they divorce syntactic functions from structural positions, are discussed in Section 3.4. One key idea of the Mimimalist approach is that the amalgamated verb (i.e. V plus v and possibly V_{mid}) combines with its dependents one at a time, starting with the most oblique and ending with the subject/agent, in such a way as to build a complex structure that reflects degrees of obliqueness. This idea has its roots in Categorial Grammar (e.g. Dowty 1982, Oehrle *et al.* 1988), which attempts to have syntactic phrase structure representations mirror Montague-style semantic composition (Dowty *et al.* 1981). The Minimalist device of feature checking as a way of accounting for case and agreement, among other things, is analogous to the device of unification in a family of formal theories of which Head-Driven Phrase Structure Grammar (Pollard and Sag 1994, Sag *et al.* 2003) is the most well known. In this theory, a verb, for example, has a bundle of semantic and grammatical features, including possibly features concerning the person, number, and case of the items with which it can combine. The features of all words are represented in tree structures. In a well-formed tree structure the grammatical features of the arguments of a verb must match the feature specifications of the verb, for example. Technically, the feature content of the constituents of phrases can 'unify' at the phrasal level only if there are no incompatibilities. In terms of grammatical relations, Head-Driven Phrase Structure Grammar, by and large, shares with TG the view that position in phrase structure trees determines (or correlates with) syntactic functions. Although verbs bear a specific 'subject' feature that licenses a constituent in the phrase structure with a special function (unlike in TG), there is also a special subject position that is superordinate to the phrase consisting of the verb and its other arguments (i.e. a position analogous to the clausal specifier position in TG).[18] Other syntactic functions are not, however, distinguished by specific positions in a hierarchically complex tree structure. Rather, it is assumed that the non-subject arguments of a verb are more oblique than the subject and are ranked according to degree of obliqueness *vis-à-vis* each other, which correlates simply with linear order (at least in English and many other languages).

Notes

1 Introduction

1 An analysis of roles according to which the subject of *steal*-type verbs is a recipient and the subject of *give*-type verbs is a source is presented in Jackendoff (1990) where these NP are considered to also have the roles agent and subject.

2 This is a tack that is sometimes taken. Most textbook characterizations of the agent role, such as Radford's (1997: 326) definition of *agent* as the 'instigator of some action' are based directly or indirectly on such influential definitions as Fillmore's (1968) 'typically animate perceived instigator of the action'. Other theorists have defined the concept in such a way as to encompass even participants about which it is difficult to say that they do anything—perhaps something as schematic and potentially all-encompassing as 'first cause' or 'autonomous cause' (Delancey 1991, Croft 1991) or even Pāṇini's 'independent participant' (Kiparsky 2002)—which do not entail the common conception of an agent as either typically animate or volitionally instigative.

3 More precisely, one might say that case relations in this theory are considered to be grammatical relations that can be roughly characterized semantically. In fact, the distinction between syntactic functions and semantic roles is simply not systematically drawn in Lexicase Grammar. Case relations are fundamentally conceived of as a set of basic roles around which the grammars of languages revolve.

4 In an active transitive sentence, the actor macrorole is borne by the (nominative) agent. In a passive sentence the actor macrorole is borne by the (nominative) patient.

5 It is perhaps worth noting that Old English *like* had a dative experiencer and a nominative stimulus, apparently with the possibility of alternating frames like those of Icelandic *henta* (Allen 1986, 1995). Over time the dative subject frame prevailed and the case marking pattern evolved into the nominative–accusative one of modern English (*She likes him*). See Section 4.4.2 for further discussion.

6 A key difference with the Role and Reference Grammar actor notion is that it is assigned in a uniform way across paraphrases of a proposition, such that the patient subject of a passive sentence, for example, is *not* the actor, and the actor role would also not vary across the two paraphrases of an Icelandic *henta* sentence (see Section 4.3.3).

7 This kind of statement, here and elsewhere, is of course subject to the qualification that what is meant by *subject* may possibly vary across languages and theories.

8 An even rarer type of language allows agreement with subject, direct object, indirect object, and beneficiary (e.g. Choctaw). An example from Kinyarwanda of four verbal indexes (for subject and three objects including beneficiary), which

could be considered to be a kind of agreement marking (example (2.78)) is discussed in Section 2.2.4. The idea that indirect object necessarily occupies a slot on a hierarchy of agreement possibilities is challenged by the Hokan language Seri, which distinguishes for purposes of agreement subjects, direct objects, and obliques in general (see example (2.43a) in Section 2.2.1).

9   For the sake of simplicity, I describe the situation as one in which pronominal clitics are proclitics (i.e. verb-initial). Actually, they can sometimes be enclitics, mainly with infinitival verb forms. In this case, the orthographic system represents them with hyphens (e.g. *amá-lo* 'love.Inf-3SgAcc'). One of the ways Brazilian and European Portuguese differ is with respect to the proclitic vs. enclitic distinction, the latter using the enclitic option much more. Being phonologically dependent on a verb, the dative and accusative pronominal forms are generally considered to be clitics, although they might actually be better analysed as pronominal affixes, as has been argued to be the case for the cognate elements in French (Miller and Sag 1997).

10 Although *lhe* and the accusative pronominal clitics are glossed '3Sg', they (especially *lhe*) can be given a 2nd person interpretation, by virtue of the fact that the category '2nd person' is routinely realized with pronominal forms that are grammatically 3rd person. For example, the 2nd person informal full pronoun *você* triggers 3rd person agreement on the verb when it is used as a subject. Although widely prescribed against, *lhe* is often used for direct objects, but only with the 2nd person interpretation, such that in addition to *Eu te amo* 'I love you' (with 2nd person dative/accusative clitic *te*) and *Eu amo você* 'I love you', both of the following are possible: *Eu lhe amo* 'I love you' and *Eu o amo* 'I love you/him'.

11 This kind of analysis is sketched in Napoli (1993: ch. 3), where the label 'first object' is used informally for O1s, although the possibility that these are really also indirect objects is left open.

12 A definition in terms of 'all P-marked NPs that have the same kind of semantic role as O1s' makes it possible to include, for example, the addressee of the *of*-marked NP in *I asked a question of the teacher*, which can alternatively be an O1 (*I asked the teacher a question*) or the beneficiary *for*-marked NP in *I baked a cake for my mother* (cf. *I baked my mother a cake*). For a sober discussion and unresolved analysis of this and other difficulties that arise in an attempt to identify an indirect object category in English, see Kaplan (1995: ch. 7).

13 See, for example, the strict adjacency principle of Government-Binding Theory (Chomsky 1981, Stowell 1981), according to which a verb can only assign its structural accusative case to an NP that is right-adjacent to it.

14 Some speakers (apparently mainly of British English) allow an O2 to be the subject of a passive clause (e.g. Czepluch 1982, Postal 1986: 58, Siewierska 1991: 97, Ura 2000: 244). Even for American speakers, it is also at least easier to get the O2 to be the subject of a passive clause if the O1 is a pronoun (Oehrle 1976: 177).

15 In some cases, intransitive verbs with an oblique complement allow their only non-subject dependent to be a subject in the passive construction (e.g. *This bed*

has not been slept in). There are various analyses of this latter phenomenon, sometimes called pseudopassive, including one according to which *slept in*, for example, is a compound verb whose direct object dependent is expressed as its subject (for a detailed overview see Postal 1986: ch. 6). By expressing the generalization concerning object preference in the passive construction with the qualification 'given a choice between two non-subject dependents', the pseudopassive case is taken out of the equation, whatever analysis is adopted.

16   *Tough* movement, for example, is not restricted to objects (*People like these are hard to talk to*).

17   Role and Reference Grammar (see Section 4.1.3) and Functional Grammar (see Section 4.4.1) also do not recognize the indirect object relation.

18   For example, at least in the version of the theory articulated in Falk (2001), the analysis of semantic roles is in terms of a hierarchy with agent at the top and a slot occupied by beneficiary or patient, followed by instrument, theme, and locational roles (see Section 3.4.1). Beneficiary, however is in fact used as the term for a generalized role that I am calling 'recipient' and 'theme' is used (with verbs such as *give*) for what I am calling 'patient.'

19   This is also the approach taken in Radford's (1997: 519) introduction to syntactic theory and English grammar. A blend of this kind of analysis and the standard Relational Grammar analysis is also proposed in Farrell (1994*a*). The NPs in *to*-phrases are analysed as obliques at all levels. All and only O1s are claimed to be initial indirect objects. As in such languages as Tzotzil (Aissen 1983) and Halkomelem (Gerdts 1988*a*) (see Section 2.2.4), however, indirect objects are assumed to be obligatorily promoted to direct object, such that the main idea of the Relational Grammar analysis is maintained. That is to say, O1s behave in key ways like prototypical direct objects because they are final direct objects.

20   The verb-adjacency constraint might in fact be attributed to a universal principle, given that the more specific roles encompassed by 'recipient' are inherently roles of animate participants and there appears to be a general preference in languages for NPs designating more animate NPs to precede NPs designating less animate NPs, as expressed in the animated-first principle of Tomlin (1986).

21   The term *oblique* has also been used to designate cases other than nominative, in languages with morphological case-marking systems of the kind found in Latin, Greek, and Sanskrit (see Blake 1994: 31).

22   There are other languages that collapse lots of semantic roles with prepositions or case markers but do make some distinctions. Austronesian languages, in particular, seem to operate with few dependent-marking categories. In Chamorro, for example, A/S/O are unmarked and other dependents of verbs are either marked with a generalized oblique preposition or a semantically specific preposition for locative dependents (Gibson 1980).

23   As Fillmore pointed out, one can analyse the subject of *This key opened the door* as having the semantic role of instrument. However, as has often been noted, the possibility of being a subject doesn't extend to most constituents with an

instrument role (e.g. *This funnel filled the glasses with wine*, *This bullhorn addressed the audience*). Thus, there is no reason to assume that so-called instrumental subjects are not simply conceived of as agents, by routine meta-phorical extension from the protoype (Delancey 1991). Constituents that behave like adjuncts in one paraphrase can routinely be the subject or the object in another, both in English (e.g. *Labor Day saw the Democrats on the brink of losing power* vs. *One saw the Democrats on the brink of Losing power on Labor Day*—see Perlmutter and Postal 1984) and in languages such as Kinyarwanda (Kimenyi 1980) with robust 'promotion to object' strategies that can affect adjuncts of various kinds. In Kinyarwanda, dependents interpreted as having the instrument role can clearly have the direct object syntactic function and are presumably, therefore, arguments rather than adjuncts (see the Kinyarwanda examples (2.78) in Section 2.2.4).

24 Although Kroeger (1993), for example, analyses the so-called nominative case as indicating the subject, which implies that sentences such as (1.39b–d), for example, are essentially passive clauses, this analysis is not uncontroversial (see Section 2.2.5).

25 Whaley claims that passive *by* phrases behave like adjuncts with respect to VP pseudoclefting based on examples such as *What was done by the man was to give Mary a book*. Not only is this sentence a rather odd paraphrase of *What the man did was give Mary a book*, it also is *not* a pseudocleft version of a passive clause, as the object is not promoted to subject, the verb is not in a past-participial form, and there is no *be* auxiliary.

26 See also Baker (1997) for a similar conception of how semantic roles can be reduced to three basic types.

2 Grammatical relations across languages

1 Although relatively rare, there are languages that utilize neither head marking nor dependent marking to indicate grammatical relations. It has been argued for one of the better known cases of this type of language, that is Chinese, that the grammar is organized around topic-comment structure and grammatical relations such as subject and direct object are not distinguished at all (La Polla 1993). Tripartite systems, in which A, S, and O are all morphologically distinguished, are also rare. There are languages that distinguish all three for certain grammatical phenomena, such as relative clause formation in Kamaiurá (discussed in Section 2.1.3). The complex case-marking systems of Australian languages often display tripartite properties with respect to classes of NP types, although only a few, such as Wangkumara and Galali, have been reported to consistently use a tripartite marking system across all NP constituents (Dixon 1994: 41).

2 A tacit assumption here is that a *se* clause with O pivot is transitive and therefore has an A, in spite of the absence of an overt O. In some Romance languages, such as Italian (e.g. Rosen 1988, La Fauci 1988), there are good reasons to claim that *se* clauses are intransitive. The same kind of evidence doesn't exist for Brazilian

Portuguese. In any case, there is a type of *se* clause that has an overt direct object and an indirect object pivot (see (1.15a)). Thus, the point that the controller can be either an S or an A is valid independently of the transitivity of sentences such as (2.2a).

3　It does not appear to be possible to reduce the postverbal placement of the S of intransitives to a neat class of verbs, such as telic verbs, for example, or inanimate Ss, although animacy and telicity are among the influencing factors. See Dutra (1987) for a detailed study of the phenomenon and Perlmutter (1976) for relevant discussion.

4　However, 'nominative' is sometimes used instead of 'absolutive', as in Bittner and Hale (1996*a*), in such a way as to highlight the similarity in terms of syntactic behaviour between S/O in certain ergative languages and S/A in accusative languages. There are also languages in which the absolutive marker in the ergative domain of the grammar counts as the nominative marker in the accusative domain.

5　Consistent with the choices made for other languages, here and throughout I substitute *A* and *O* in glosses for Gerdts' *Erg* and *Obj*, respectively. I use her *Subj*, with the understanding that this means S/A, as it does, in effect, for her.

6　Nouns in this language almost always end in an *-a* suffix that Seki analyses as a case marker, which she labels 'nuclear'. Since this is used for all NPs in the S, O, and A categories as well as objects of postpositions, possessors within NPs, and nominalized verbs in various functions, it does very little, if anything, to discriminate grammatical relations. In all the examples discussed here and elsewhere, this suffix is not indicated as such or glossed.

7　This is a bit of a simplification. More precisely, when the A is 1st person and the O is 2nd person, a number hierarchy also comes into play. In this situation, only if the A is also higher on the number hierarchy (plural > singular) does it take precedence with respect to the verbal morphology. If the two dependents are of equivalent rank with respect to number, both the A and the O are indexed with a portmanteau prefix (Seki 2000: 160), as in example (2.21b).

8　There are, however, languages in which the apparent semantic basis for unaccusativity is obscured by unexpected classifications of various kinds, as noted in Dixon (1994: 74).

9　Here and elsewhere, I use A and O in the glosses for Choctaw agreement morphology, whereas Davies uses Nom and Acc respectively. Although participant control appears to be the main factor determining the distinction between the S_a and S_o categories, as is often the case in split-intransitive systems (e.g. Dixon 1994: ch. 4), there are some verbs that seem not to follow the general pattern. In Choctaw, for example, 'die', numeral predicates, and verbs of existence take A marking, even though it seems difficult to conceive of them as ascribing control to a participant. Dixon considers Choctaw to fall into a special category of languages, because it also has semantically-sensitive dative agreement morphology that increases the complexity of the grammar. In essence, it is fundamentally a split-intransitive language with a dative quasi-subject and dative quasi-object overlay that is amenable to varying interpretations.

10   Note that a pormanteau prefix such as *oro-* in this example indexes both the A and O, just in case neither is 3rd person and they are equivalent in terms of number (see note 7 in Chapter 2).

11   What differs is only that I follow Durie (1985) in indicating clitics with the '=' notation, and don't explicitly indicate pronoun optionality in some of the examples.

12   The O can be unincorporated only if two of three conditions are met: (i) it is human-referring, (ii) it is animate singular, or (iii) it has a demonstrative or numeral modifier (Allen *et al.* 1984: 293–97, Rosen 1990: 683).

13   Glosses are changed from the original to conform to the general system employed in this book. Moreover, certain derivational affixes of no significance in the present context are not glossed.

14   See also Bittner (1987) on some of the precise semantic correlates of the anti-passive vs. active distinction.

15   Certain glosses are changed from the source to conform to the general system employed in this book or to avoid implicitly endorsing a particular analysis. Moreover, certain irrelevant details are not explicitly indicated. Tense morphemes, for example, can indicate several tense categories (recent past, immediate past, etc.) as well as evidentiality information and gender agreement. I only indicate the gender category that these encode, since that is what plays a relevant role in the discussion here.

16   There are a number of agreement and pronoun restrictions that make the grammar of Jarawara rather complicated. For example, the form of the pronominal element on or preceding a mood suffix in an inverse clause (i.e. the second *o-* in (2.63b)) is actually determined on the basis of person (1st/2nd > 3rd) rather than syntactic function.

17   This definition abstracts away from the effects of other derivational operations such as passivization or reciprocalization, which might detransitivize an applicative clause. It also implicitly excludes what would have to be analysed as an anti-applicative construction in Inuit, as described in Bittner and Hale (1996a). Either the recipient or the patient can be the O (with characteristic absolutive marking, i.e. zero case). However, the verb bears the so-called applicative affix when the patient is the O and the recipient is in the dative case form, rather than when the recipient is O and the patient is in the instrumental case form. One could include this construction in the applicative class by defining the applicative construction as one with a 'non-canonical' mapping of O with semantic roles. It would also be necessary, of course, to assume that the recipient is the canonical O in Inuit, that is that Inuit is a kind of primary-object language in the sense of Dryer 1986.

18   Gerdts glosses the applicative morphemes with *AdvA, AdvB*, etc., for type A/B 'advancements'. I use, instead, theory-neutral descriptive names for what I characterize as a phenomenon that closely parallels the so-called voice phenomenon in Philippine languages. What I am calling the recipient applicative morpheme—

following the idea, from Section 1.3.2, that recipient is the prototype for a family of more specific roles—is used at least for addressees as well as transfer-of-possession recipients.

19 It is not the case that oblique dependents can't be relativized or focused on in clefting or *wh*-question constructions. However, a different construction with a nominalized verb must be used.

20 Of course, as with passive and inverse voices, lines could be drawn in such a way as to exclude one or more construction types from an 'applicative' classification. For example, one might take overt morphological marking of the construction to be criterial, in which case the 'double-object' constructions of English and Korean, for example, would be excluded. As there are clear commonalities as well as differences across languages and constructions, various kinds of line drawing could be done for labelling purposes.

21 Although the applicative analysis of Philippine voices has been an integral part of the ergative approach, it could conceivably be incorporated into other approaches as well. For example, under the accusative approach, one might analyse locative, benefactive, and instrumental voices as involving promotion of obliques to O (= applicative) with obligatory promotion of applicative Os to S (= passive).

22 This terminological distinction roughly parallels that of *oblique/dative subject* vs. *I-nominal* adopted in Moore and Perlmutter (2000) and Sigurðsson (2002). *Quasi-subject* is more general than *I-nominal*, which is meant to cover only the dative dependents in what has been called an inversion construction in Relational Grammar. The dative dependent in an inversion construction is analysed as an initial subject and final indirect object. Its restricted subject-like properties are attributed to its initial subjecthood.

23 At least for many speakers the *a*-marked direct object does not appear to be truly dative-marked, insofar as the dative clitic that typically (often obligatorily) appears with the verb in a sentence with an indirect object, as in the case of (2.105a) does not occur with the *a*-marked O. For some speakers an accusative clitic could be used instead, especially if the O is pronominal (*Marta la vio a ella* 'Marta 3SgFemAcc-saw her'). There are, however, dialects/idiolects in which the dative clitic is routinely used for both Os and IOs.

24 As in other Romance languages, the *se* morpheme can be used to indicate an inchoative or accomplishment interpretation of a verb. Thus *se cansar* can mean 'to get tired'.

25 There are certain verbs, such as *lembrar* 'remember' and *esquecer* 'forget' whose stimulus dependent can either be *de*-marked or not. The stimulus is a straightforward O in one of the alternative constructions. The status of the *de*-marked NP is harder to establish because in most potential O-behaving situations, the construction would be indistinguishable from the alternant with the O. The *de*-marked NP with these verbs does, however, behave like a quasi-object in that it can be the pivot in the otherwise A/S/O-restricted *o que* pseudocleft construction

(*O que lembro é da alegria da minha mãe* 'What I remember is of-the my mother's joy').

26 In conversational discourse 3rd person accusative clitic forms are generally avoided in favour of what could be analysed as a null pronoun (e.g. Farrell 1990, Kato 1993). This null pronun interpretation is possible for *Minha mãe gosta* 'My mother likes Ø (= it/him/her).' However, it is not clear that this is an O-defining property of dependents, since the omission of obliques can sometimes yield a similar interpretation (e.g. *A gaveta não está cheia. Então vou colocar mais algumas coisas* 'The drawer isn't full. So, I'm going to put a few more things Ø (= in it).'). Athough there is a clear difference between the possible (albeit formal) use of a 3rd person pronominal clitic with a verb such as *amar* 'love' and the ungrammaticality of such a clitic with *gostar* 'like', the situation is more complex with 1st and 2nd person pronominal clitics, which are routinely used in all modes of discourse and for which there is no phonological dative vs. accusative contrast. Although some speakers consider it odd to use 1st and 2nd person clitic pronouns with *gostar*, it is not hard to find examples in actual discourse, such as *Me faz um bem … o jeito que ele me gosta* 'It does me good … the way he 1Sg-likes' (from a Brazilian internet blog) or *Eu te gosto, você me gosta desde tempos imemoriais* 'I 2Sg-like, you 1Sg-like since time immemorial' (from a poem by Carlos Drummond de Andrade).

3 Relational Grammar

1 The RG characterization of the defining property of passive clauses differs from the characterization given in (2.35). In RG, it is the promotion of a 2 to 1 from a transtitive stratum that is criterial. Nevertheless, essentially the same range of construction types are identified by the RG definition and (2.35), since any passive clause with the agent demoted from 1 would be analysed as having an advancement to 1, even if it is a null 'dummy' that advances. Thus, impersonal passive constructions of the form *Was danced by the children* (which do not occur in English but do in other languages) are analysed as having a null dummy subject that advances from 2 to 1. Whether passive advancements from 3 or oblique (rather than 2) to 1 need to be recognized is an unsettled issue (see Postal 1986).

2 There are various potential ways of looking at the so-called 'pro-drop' situation that one finds in Kamaiurá and many other languages. One could say, from an RG perspective, that the arguments of the verb are manifested as independent pronouns that bear the grammatical relations represented in the relational network and determine the morphology on the verb. By rule these pronouns are 'dropped' or deleted. One could also say that the inflectional morphemes themselves bear the grammatical relations or that abstract (phonologically null) entities with person-number features bear the grammatical relations and determine the forms of the morphology on the verb. Whichever analysis one adopts, the relational networks themselves would not differ substantially. For the sake of

simplicity, I just put the grammatical relations in the tabular stratal diagrams of the relational networks above the associated inflectional morphemes.

3   It is not actually necessary to make any assumptions that have not been appealed to elsewhere with good reasons. The idea that recipients, for example, can be initial obliques in langues is adopted in Rosen's (1990) analysis of Southern Tiwa. As for instruments, one could assume that they are necessarily initial obliques in all languages, following the usual RG assumption; but that they can and sometimes must advance to 3 in Tagalog.

4   This analysis, which allows the promotion of a dependent to 1 to induce demotion to 3 for the 'overrun' 1, also entails a version of RG without the Chômeur Law (also known as the Overrun Law), which requires demotion to chômeur in such cases. Independent reasons for abandoning this law are discussed in Perlmutter and Postal (1983). The RG 1–2 reversal analysis for inverse voice languages (Rhodes 1976, Perlmutter and Rhodes 1988, Section 3.3.3 below) would be banned by the Chômeur Law. The simpler of the two analyses of Icelandic psych verbs given in Section 3.3.5 also assumes that there is no Chômeur Law. The virtue of having the 1 demote to 3 in Tagalog is (i) that it allows a unified account of the case marking for final 2s, instrumental NPs, and demoted 1s (i.e. they are all final objects), and (ii) that it accounts for the term-like behaviour of demoted 1s with respect to adjunct-fronting. An alternative would be to have an overrun 1 always demote to 2, inducing demotion of the initial 2 to 3 in certain cases. It is difficult to see how this more complex alternative might be empirically distinguished from the 1–3 demotion analysis.

5   Also known as the 'ergative hypothesis', due to the terminological innovation introduced in Burzio's (1986) translation of the RG analysis of Italian unaccusativity phenomena into the Government-Binding framework of Transformational Grammar. The terms *unaccusative* and *unergative* are rather unfortunate to begin with, inasmuch as the subject of what would generally be considered unaccusative verbs is often treated like an accusative dependent. Calling this class of verbs 'ergative', while appropriately naming the class of verbs that contrasts with unergative verbs, is at least as confusing, inasmuch as the phenomenon of split-intransitivity is unrelated to the phenomenon of ergativity, in the sense of most descriptive and typological work.

6   Whether 'controller of action' is the right semantic notion here is immaterial. More nuanced accounts could presumably be given by appealing to the Role and Reference Grammar distinction 'actor' vs. 'undergorer' (see Section 4.1.3) or some kind of account in terms of the agent vs. patient semantic entailments (Dowty 1991, Ackerman and Moore 2001).

7   For the sake of brevity, I focus attention here on two of the potential diagnostics of unaccusativity in English. Others include possible construal with a resultative adjective (*the lake froze solid*) (see especially Levin and Rappaport Hovav 1995: ch. 2); the possibility of locative inversion (Coopmans 1989, Levin and Rappaport Hovav 1995: ch. 5), which is constrained much like expletive *there* insertion;

inability to be suffixed with 'agentive' *-er* (*freezer* = agent of transitive freeze; not patient of intransitive *freeze*) (Rappaport Hovav and Levin 1992, Farrell 1994*a*); and inabilitity to undergo 'pseudopassivization' (**This tree was fallen from* vs. *This bed was slept in*) (Perlmutter and Postal 1984). A purely semantic constraint in terms of the patient semantic role is proposed for resultatives in Goldberg (1991). That the constraint on agentive *-er* suffixation is semantically constrained in a different way than the other phenomena is made clear in Ryder (1999) and Farrell (2001), one kind of evidence being that the class of intransitive verbs that do undergo *-er* affixation (supposedly unergatives) overlaps partially with the class of verbs that form participial adjectives (supposedly unaccusatives) (e.g. *the escaped prisoners* vs. *the escapers*). Although pseudopassivization does, by and large, fail with the class of verbs that can form participial adjectives (*a fallen leaf* vs. **This tree was fallen from by a leaf*), it appears that a semantic constraint on pseudo-passivization is needed independently of the verb classes defined by participial adjective formation. The verb *jog*, for example, would be unergative rather than unaccusative by the participial adjective criterion (**the jogged person*); yet, this verb, like putative unaccusatives, does not allow pseudopassivization (**Central Park was jogged in this morning*). Again, there is a mismatch between the verb classes defined by these two phenomena and there is a semantic factor at play: the pseudopassive subject must have as a referent something that is construed as being clearly affected (hence, *This bed appears to have been slept in* vs. **This hotel appears to have been slept in*).

8   While acknowledging unaccusative mismatches and the relevance of lexical semantics in 'unaccusative' phenomena in English, Levin and Rappaport Hovav (1995) argue for the view that split intransitivity is both semantically motivated and syntactically manifested in the way that the unaccusative hypothesis suggests. This stance is also taken, for example, for Italian in Farrell (1994*b*) and for French in Legendre (1989*b*). That this stance can be taken is not being questioned here. Rather, it is being suggested that building a solid case for the necessity and explanatory utility of such a stance remains a clear challenge for RG or any other theory that adopts the unaccusative hypothesis. With this said, it must be acknowledged that Italian, taken on its own, presents a compelling case for the unaccusative hypothesis, inasmuch as the unaccusative diagnostics generally pick out a unified class of dependents in which (underlying) direct objects of transitive clauses are generally included (Rosen 1988, Perlmutter 1989).

9   It would be fruitless to try to engage the posited initial 1-hood of the experiencer in accounting for the 'subject' properties of the dative experiencer in the imper-sonal construction. One might say, for example, that the notion of 'subject' that most phenomena in Icelandic are sensitive to is 'working non-expletive 1', that is: a dependent that is a 1 in some stratum, a final term, and not an expletive. This would account for the subject properties of the experiencer in the impersonal construction (3.16b). The problem is that the personal construction, illustrated by

(3.16a), would have two working non-expletive 1s, that is both the stimulus final 1 and the experiencer, which is an initial 1 and final 3.

10 The null expletive pronoun is required, due to the Motivated Chômage Law (3.2d)—to get the stimulus 1 to retire to chômeur—and the Final 1 Law (3.2c), which requires that a clause have a final 1.

11 For dialects that allow the O2 to be a passive-clause subject (see note 14 in Chapter 1), either object can presumably be intrinsically [−r], as in symmetrical applicative languages (Bresnan and Moshi 1990).

12 An arc with no final stratum coordinate technically gets 'erased', for example, either by itself or, more commonly, by some other arc. An arc whose presence is entailed by some other arc A in a network is said to be sponsored by A. Thus, for example, in the case of, say, a 2–3 demotion construction, a 2-arc in stratum s sponors and is erased by a 3-arc in stratum $s+1$.

4 Role and Reference Grammar

1 Because the Natural Semantic Metalanguage of Wierzbicka dispenses with the predicate-calculus formalism and allows meanings of verbs to be stated in a form of ordinary English that is built out of semantic primitives (e.g. *put* = x does something to y; because of this y goes to someplace (z)), verb meanings elsewhere in this book are expressed using a simplified version of this metalanguage (see, for example, Figure 1.2).

2 Aktionsart (or 'aspectual') distinctions among verb classes are motivated empirically, in English and other languages, on distributional grounds (e.g. Vendler 1967, Dowty 1979, Foley and Van Valin 1984, Filip 1997). For example, stative verbs in English differ from all others in that they do not generally occur in the present progressive construction (*She is singing a song* [activity] vs. *She is liking the pizza* [state]) and can denote a present time state of affairs, rather than a habitual state of affairs, in their present tense form (*She likes the pizza*). Activity verbs do not occur with prepositional adjuncts that designate temporal endpoints (*She jogged for an hour/*in an hour*), unlike accomplishment verbs (*She learned the song in an hour/*for an hour*). The key point is that there is an evidentiary basis for the LSs posited for verbs in the RRG framework.

3 Since the variable x occurs in two places in the LS for *run*, the subject of *run* has two semantic roles: mover and theme. Although theme is the default choice for undergoer, the fact that such verbs have only one macrorole puts the principle in (4.4) in play. Since there is an activity predicate in the LS of *run* the single macrorole is necessarily actor. The least-marked actor assignment is to the mover.

4 Thus, the default for Brazilian Portuguese is that the most patient-like argument on the actor–undergoer hierarchy is the undergoer, whereas in Halkomelem, the second-most patient-like argument is the default undergoer.

5 RRG has formal mechanisms to distinguish robust head-marking languages, in which the verbal affixes themselves are characterized as the primary manifestation

of LS arguments, from languages with agreement, in which NPs, which are the primary manifestation of LS arguments, may simply 'control' agreement marking. For the sake of simplicity, no attempt is made here to systematically draw this distinction.

6   Since dative case-marked NP arguments are considered 'direct', the correspondence between 'direct non-macrorole core argument' and '2nd object' in the sense of Dryer (1985) or Bresnan (1982*a*) is also imperfect. A further distinction that can be drawn among PPs is argument-adjunct vs. argument (Van Valin and La Polla 1997: 160–3). The idea is that the goal argument of a verb such as *put*, for example *in the box* in *Sam put the rabbit in the box*, is an argument-adjunct since the LS of the verb is underspecified with respect to the specifics of the locative relation involved: *on the box, in the box*, and *under the box*, for example, are all possible. Thus, *the box* in such cases is an argument of a predicative P, in a way that *the boy* isn't in *give the book to the boy*.

7   In languages such as Icelandic, discussed in Section 4.3.3, the traditional indirect object category is overtly indicated by dative case marking on NPs. The category can be defined as 'direct core non-macrorole argument'. In Brazilian Portuguese, on the other hand, the traditional indirect object category consists of a subset of NPs that occur in a PP with the preposition *para* 'for' or *a* 'to' as head, that is those which can be realized as a dative pronominal clitic and can be a reflexive/ reciprocal *se* pivot (see Section 1.3.2). This class of NPs can be defined neither as direct core non-macrorole arguments (because they are not 'direct') nor as oblique non-macrorole arguments, because they constitute only a subset thereof. Although the semantic role 'recipient' may be the prototype, it is insufficient as a defining criterion, as non-recipient possessors can be dative clitics (*Aquilo não lhe-pertence* 'That doesn't 3SgDat-belong') as can perceivers (*Aquilo lhe parece doido* 'That 3SgDat-seems crazy'). The notion animate oblique argument comes close, but fails to exclude, for example, animate source oblique arguments (*Eu recibi uma carta de sua mãe* 'I reveiced a letter from your mother' vs. **Eu lhe recibi uma carta* 'I 3Sdat-received a letter'). Of course, the problem that RRG faces in specifying the category of arguments that can be dative clitics in Brazilian Portuguese is not solved in an interesting way in theories that simply claim that 'indirect object' is a primitive category.

8   In Van Valin and La Polla (1997) the term *grammatical relation* is used to signify essentially only 'syntactic function' in the sense used in this book, whence the claim that Acehnese has no grammatical relations. Another way of looking at the matter, of course, is that the boundary between syntactic functions and semantic roles is unclear and perhaps largely an analytical artefact. Clearly, actor and undergoer are at most quasi-semantic roles, given that such matters as whether a verb or verb class has one or two macroroles and whether the location-type or theme-type semantic role is chosen as undergoer with 3-argument verbs are *not* semantically determined. The fact that the actor ('semantic role') almost invariably corresponds to the initial subject ('syntactic function') of Relational Gram-

mar shows how much the terminological distinction between *semantic role* and *syntactic function* may be drawn in different ways for the same state of affairs.

9   The glosses for the inflectional morphology are changed somewhat from the original to conform to the general schema used here and to be consistent with the glossing schema used with other Inuit examples discussed elsewhere.

10   Note that argument-modulation passive clauses, unlike argument-modulation antipassive clauses, are characterized as M-transtitive. This brings out a difference between the RRG notion of M-transitivity and the common notion of syntactic transitivity which is appealed to in the description of passive voice in Section 2.2.1, where it is claimed that passive is, in effect, a detransitivization phenomenon (as in Dixon 1994, for example). In the RRG analysis of the English passive construction, a non-actor argument (typically the undergoer) is the PSA. The actor macrorole is not taken away, however, from the highest-ranking argument on the actor-preference hierarchy; it is simply associated with an unspecified argument position in the LS or with an adjunct PP. Thus, the passive construction is M-transitive (i.e. it has both actor and undergoer macroroles), although it is generally syntactically intransitive inasmuch as it has only one direct core argument. In antipassive constructions with argument modulation as in Dyirbal or Inuit, on the other hand, the undergoer macrorole is suppressed, yielding an M-intransitive clause. However, an antipassive clause may apparently be syntactically transitive, since it may have two direct core arguments, as in Dyirbal.

11   This kind of a PSA-modulation-only analysis is presented for the Nilo-Saharan language Lango (Noonan 1992) in Van Valin and La Polla (1997: ch. 7) and Van Valin (to appear: ch. 4). For inverse-voice languages of the Algonquian kind (see Section 2.2.3), RRG makes possible the traditional morphological inversion analysis, according to which the interpretation of the agreement morphology of the verb differs between active and inverse voices and there is no PSA modulation (Van Valin and La Polla 1997: ch. 7).

12   Antipassive has been claimed to occur, for example, in French (Postal 1977, Herslund 1997), although whether the constructions at issue would be analysed as antipassive in RRG is unclear.

13   In the Relational Grammar analysis of Marlett (1984) and Farrell *et al.* (1991), the constraint is stated in terms of the notion 'first subject'. In a passive clause, the initial subject is the agent/actor and the final subject is the patient/undergoer. The initial subject is the first subject (i.e. subject in the earliest stratum). In all other clauses in Seri, the final subject would be the first and only subject.

14   According to Barðdal, *henta* and most of the verbs in the same class are stative and the alternative syntactic frames are semantically equivalent in essentially the same way that active and passive paraphrases are. For this reason, it is assumed that the LS of *henta* contains only the state predicate **like′** and is the same whether the dative or the nominative NP is the PSA. The *be pleasing to* and *be pleased with* English glosses are used simply to give idiomatic English translations with the

PSA varying in the way that it does in Icelandic. Icelandic also has psych verbs that are more like English *please*; they do not alternate and have a nominative actor PSA and an accusative undergoer.

15   Another principle—not active, or barely active, in Icelandic and English—yields ergative phenomena, that is the lowest-ranking argument with respect to the actor end of the actor–undergoer hierarchy is the preferred PSA.

16   The category 'DCA' includes the actor in an M-transitive clause as well as the S of an M-intransitive clause. In fact, as a general rule, all members of this category can control a floated quantifier or be a relativization pivot.

17   An alternative analysis might be that *cansar* is a one-argument verb and the *de*-headed PP that can occur with it is an adjunct, similar to *por causa do sol* 'because of the sun' in *Ele cansou por causa do sol* 'he got tired because of the sun'. Although such an analysis is semantically reasonable, the *de*-headed PP with *cansar* does not display the syntactic properties of a typical adjunct, as illustrated by the following examples:

(i) a.   O que aconteceu nesse lugar foi que *eu conheci ela.*
          'What happened in this place was that I met her.'
    b.   O que aconteceu por causa do sol foi que *ele cansou.*
          'What happened because of the sun was that he got tired.'
    c.   O que aconteceu foi que *todo mundo gostou do filme.*
          'What happened was that everyone liked the movie.'
    d.   *O que aconteceu desse filme foi que *todo mundo gostou.*
          'What happened of this movie was that everyone liked (it).'
    e.   *O que aconteceu nesse lugar foi que *eu pensei.*
          'What happened about this place was that I thought.'
    f.   *O que aconteceu dessa música foi que *eu cansei.*
          'What happened of this song was that I got tired.'

As in English, it is possible in Brazilian Portuguese to focus on a verb phrase constituent in a pseudocleft construction only if all complements of the verb are included with it, as in the case of the italicized focused phrases in (ia–c). It is possible to leave out an adjunct, as shown by (ib–c). It is not, however, possible to leave out a complement, as shown by (id–e). The ungrammaticality of (if) suggests that the stimulus PP of psychological *cansar* is a complement. Most importantly, for present purposes, however, even if the *de*-marked stimulus PP of *cansar* were analysed as an adjunct, the problem of the quasi-object status of the stimulus of *gostar* would not be solved. One would presumably want to say that the stimulus of *gostar* is more object-like in its behaviour than the stimulus of *cansar* because it is a complement and it is nevertheless oblique-like due to its non-macrorole status. Its special properties would simply follow from its status as a non-macrorole complement. But the problem is that there are other non-macrorole complements of verbs of cognition and emotion, such as the PP complement of *pensar* 'think' (*Eu pensava em você* 'I was thinking about you,' literally 'in you'), which do not have any of the object-like properties of the stimulus of *gostar* (e.g. **Eles só se pensam* 'They only think about each other', **Essas pessoas são difíceis de não pensar* 'These people are hard not to think (about)').

18   This is the simplest version of the algorithm for assigning semantic functions to the A1, A2, and A3 categories and is one that works for English. In order to account for complications that arise in certain languages, the possibility of allowing the A2 to have variable semantic functions even in clauses with three arguments is entertained (Dik 1997: ch. 11).

5 Transformational Grammar

1   In addition to the syntactic transformations, Figure 5.1 shows in the surface structure representation the effects of the transformational rules of the phono-logical component of the grammar, which technically operate on the surface structure representations. These phonological rules, among other things, change the abstract representations of *may PST* (i.e. *may* plus a past tense morpheme) into *might* and *put-en* (i.e. *put* plus a past-participial suffix) into *put*. Certain other aspects of the derivation, such as placement of word boundaries, are also not made explicit.

2   In Figure 5.2, the PP and the direct object NP are shown as sisters of the verb, as they are in classical TG and in at least early versions of GB, including Chomsky (1986). By the end of the GB period, other representational systems for multiple complements had been developed (notably the so-called VP shell of Larson 1988), such that a binary-branching constraint on phrase structure, which would be-come *de rigueur*, could be maintained. The Minimalist approach to multiple-complement and double-object constructions, which respects the binary-branch-ing constraint, is discussed in Section 5.3.2.

3   In the *Aspects* model, as well as in early versions of GB, the clause was given the category label S (for sentence) and was assumed to have inflectional and gram-matical elements under a node usually labelled Aux (for auxiliary), as shown in Figure 5.1. Partly to allow a uniform template for all phrasal categories, the IP analysis of the clause was introduced in Chomsky (1986). Following Pollock (1989), the individual inflectional elements (tense, agreement, aspect, etc.) have been commonly analysed as heading individual phrases of their own category, which are embedded within each other in an elaborate way. These distinctions, which are largely orthogonal to grammatical relations and which have been implemented in numerous ways, are abstracted away from here.

4   The idea of LF is not new to the Minimalist programme, as it has its roots in GB accounts of the semantic scope properties of quantifiers and other similar elements (May 1985), and ultimately in the Generative Semantics tradition within TG (e.g. Lakoff 1971). What is new is its extended use to account for certain

grammatical-relation phenomena and other routine matters of word order variation.

5   The guiding principle is known as the Uniform Thematic Alignment Hypothesis (UTAH) (Baker 1988*a*), which is a TG analogue of the Uniform Alignment Hypothesis of RG.

6   Realizing the vision of reducing all semantic roles to structural positions is contingent, in part, on being able to pack much of the equivalent of lexical conceptual structure in the sense of, say, Jackendoff (1990) into the syntactic representation of phrase structure, as was attempted early in the history of TG in the movement that came to be known as Generative Semantics (e.g. Lakoff 1971, McCawley 1971, 1973). Some empirical difficulties with this vision as implemented in Hale and Keyser (1993) are noted in Farrell (1998). See Baker (1997) and Gruber (2001) for more comprehensive accounts of what might be required to fully implement the vision. Baker, for example, suggests an analysis in the Generative Semantics spirit wherein semantic primitives such as CAUSE and GO are placed under *v* and V, for example, and the verb *send* replaces the amalgam CAUSE-GO (created by incorporation of V into *v*) at some point in the derivation. As Baker correctly notes, such an endeavour leads inexorably to a variant of a theory such as Cognitive Grammar (see Section 4.4.2), in which no distinction is drawn between grammatical and conceptual structure.

7   I follow Baker (1997) in the assumption that the patient (or 'theme') originates in a specifier position of the VP. Hale and Keyser (1993) adopt the opposite analysis, with the patient in the lowest position. What I am calling NPs are generally analysed as determiner phrases (DPs) in this theory, that is as phrases headed by an article or other determiner (possibly null) that has an NP as its complement. Since the NP/DP distinction is not relevant to the issues of concern here, it is suppressed merely for the sake of consistency with terminology employed elsewhere.

8   It is also often assumed that heads can have a feature specifying the lexical category of the specifier it must have. This feature is systematically ignored here.

9   In one version of the theory (e.g. Chomsky 1993, Watanabe 1993, Radford 1997), an AgrO (object agreement) head that projects an AgrOP (either above *v*P or between *v*P and VP) is postulated. The direct object then moves (overtly or covertly) to the specifier position of AgrOP to check its nominal features with AgrO.

10   In a transitive VP, the patient, assumed to be in the specifier position, is higher than the other argument. In an intransitive VP, there is at most one NP.

11   The ergative vs. absolutive distinction has been a much-considered matter that has given rise to a number of different analyses, often correlated with different basic assumptions about the overall theory of movement, case, and grammatical relations, which vary somewhat from author to author and across time periods. The

account sketched here, based on Ura (2000), is chosen for its balance of relative simplicity, relative effectiveness, and up-to-dateness. For some alternatives, see Levin (1983), Marantz (1984), Murasugi (1992), and Bittner and Hale (1996*a*, 1996*b*). Although Bittner and Hale's account of ergativity vs. accusativity and related typological distinctions is probably the most comprehensive, it doesn't fit neatly into either the GB or the Minimalist paradigm and is too complex to be given justice here, although some of its ideas are incorporated in places in the analysis presented here.

12   Ura (2000: 190) notes that the controller of reflexivization in Dyirbal can be either the A of a transitive verb or the S of an intransitive verb, suggesting that the agent of a transitive construction has a subject property. However, as Dixon (1994: 138) makes clear, reflexivization involves adding a reflexive morpheme which indicates agent/patient coreference and involves absolutive marking of the single expressed NP. Thus, reflexive clauses are *intransitive*. In the Minimalist analysis the reflexive morpheme must be characterized as suppressing the ergative case of the *v* and one of the arguments (either agent or patient). The remaining argument is morphologically and syntactically an S that is indistinguishable from the S of any intransitive clause (i.e. the only NP in a specifier of IP position and the checker of absolutive case). Thus, whether there is compelling empirical motivation for the posited movement of the ergative case checker (agent of transitive) to a specifier of IP position in Dyirbal is unclear. In the analysis of Bittner and Hale (1996*a*), although the patient (absolutive NP) moves to the specifier of IP position, the agent (ergative NP) is subject-like by virtue of its base position as the specifier of *v*P, from which it does not move.

13   It is, of course, curious that the ergative NP, hypothesized to be the lower specifier of IP, actually precedes the absolutive NP in Inuit. Ura provides no explanation. Bittner and Hale (1996*a*), whose analysis differs primarily in that it assumes that the ergative NP remains in the specifier position of *v*P, merely suggest that the linear order is changed at the level of 'phonetic form'. In other words, they assume that there is some kind of exceptional linearization rule that fixes the order that the phrase structure specifies.

14   Taking into account the person/number features of the different- and same-subject morphemes, ignored here for the sake of simplicity, and analysing switch reference in terms of obviation, Bittner and Hale use the glosses 3Sg.Proximate and 3Sg.Obviative for SS and DS, respectively.

15   Alternatively, a null expletive pronoun could be posited as a nominative filler of the specifier of IP position, which is what Bittner and Hale propose.

16   Note that the basic phrase structure of Seri is different from that of English and the other languages considered above because as an SOV language the heads of phrases follow both specifiers and complements.

17   Other possibilities include calling the intermediate verb phrase an 'aspect phrase' (e.g. Baker 1997), or an indirect object agreement phrase or AgrIOP (e.g. Radford 1997). Larson (1988), whose analysis focuses specifically on English, simply places the 'indirect object' in the specifier position of the lower VP and the patient in a lower position.

18   See, for example, Pollard and Sag (1994: 362). In early versions of the theory, subjects were assumed to be simply the least oblique of the arguments of a verb.

References

ACKERMAN, F. and J. MOORE (1999) ' "Telic entity" as a proto-property of lexical predicates', in M. Butt and T. H. King (eds), *Proceedings of the LFG 99 Conference*. Stanford, CA: CSLI Publications.

—— —— (2001) *Proto-properties and Grammatical Encoding*. Stanford, CA: CSLI Publications.

AISSEN, J. (1983) 'Indirect object advancement in Tzotzil', in D. M. Perlmutter (ed.), *Studies in Relational Grammar 1*. Chicago: University of Chicago Press, pp. 272–302.

—— (1987) *Tzotzil Clause Structure*. Dordrecht: D. Reidel.

—— (1988) 'Extensions of brother-in-law agreement', in M. Barlow and C. A. Ferguson (eds), *Agreement in Natural Language: Approaches, theories, descriptions*. Stanford, CA: CSLI Publications, pp. 219–35.

—— (1997) 'On the syntax of obviation', *Language* 73: 705–50.

—— (1999*a*) 'Agent focus and inverse in Tzotzil', *Language* 75: 451–85.

—— (1999*b*) 'Markedness and subject choice in optimality theory', *Natural Language and Linguistic Theory* 17: 673–711.

—— (2003) 'Differential object marking: Iconicity vs. Economy', *Natural Language and Linguistic Theory* 21: 435–83.

ALLEN, B. J. and D. G. FRANTZ (1983) 'Advancements and verb agreement in Southern Tiwa', in D. M. Perlmutter (ed.), *Studies in Relational Grammar 1*. Chicago: University of Chicago Press.

——, —— and D. B. GARDINER (1984) 'Noun incorporation in Southern Tiwa', *International Journal of American Linguistics* 50: 292–311.

ALLEN, C. L. (1986) 'Reconsidering the history of *like*', *Journal of Linguistics* 22: 375–409.

—— (1995) *Case Marking and Reanalysis: Grammatical relations from Old to Early Modern English*. Oxford: Oxford University Press.

ALSINA, A. and S. A. MCHOMBO (1990) 'The syntax of applicatives in Chichewa—problems for a theta theoretic asymmetry', *Natural Language and Linguistic Theory* 8: 493–506.

ANDERSON, J. M. (1971) *The Grammar of Case: Towards a localist theory*. Cambridge: Cambridge University Press.

—— (1977) *On Case Grammar: Prolegomena to a theory of grammatical relations*. London: Croom Helm.

ANDERSON, S. (1976) 'On the notion of subject in ergative languages', in C. Li (ed.), *Subject and Topic*. New York: Academic Press, pp. 1–23.

ARANOVICH, R. (2000) 'Split intransitivity and reflexives in Spanish', *Probus* 12: 165–86.

ARNOLD, J. E. (1997) 'The inverse system in Mapudungun and other languages', *Revista de Lingüística Teórica y Aplicada* 34: 9–48.

—— (1998) *Reference form and discourse patterns*, Stanford: Ph.D. Dissertation.

BAKER, M. C. (1988*a*) *Incorporation: A theory of grammatical function changing.* Chicago: University of Chicago Press.

—— (1988*b*) 'Theta theory and the syntax of applicatives in Chichewa', *Natural Language and Linguistic Theory* 6: 353–89.

—— (1996) *The Polysynthesis Parameter.* Oxford: Oxford University Press.

—— (1997) 'Thematic roles and syntactic structure', in L. Haegeman (ed.), *Elements of Grammar: Handbook in generative syntax.* Dordrecht: Kluwer, pp. 73–137.

—— K. JOHNSON and I. ROBERTS (1989) 'Passive arguments raised', *Linguistic Inquiry* 20: 219–51.

BARRY, A. K. (1998) *English Grammar: Language as human behavior.* Englewood Cliffs, NJ: Prentice Hall.

BARÐDAL, J. (2001) 'The perplexity of dat-nom verbs in Icelandic', *Nordic Journal of Linguistics* 24: 47–70.

BELL, S. J. (1976) *Cebuano subjects in two frameworks*, MIT: Ph.D. Dissertation.

—— (1983) 'Advancements and ascensions in Cebuano', in D. M. Perlmutter (ed.), *Studies in Relational Grammar 1.* Chicago: University of Chicago Press, pp. 143–218.

BELLETTI, A. and L. RIZZI (1988) 'Psych-verbs and θ-theory', *Natural Language and Linguistic Theory* 6: 291–352.

BERINSTEIN, A. (1990) 'On distinguishing surface datives in K'ekchi', in P. M. Postal and B. D. Joseph (eds), *Studies in Relational Grammar 3.* Chicago: University of Chicago Press, pp. 3–48.

BICKEL, B. and Y. P. YĀDAVA (2000) 'A fresh look at grammatical relations in Indo-aryan', *Lingua* 110: 343–73.

BITTNER, M. (1987) 'On the semantics of the Greenlandic antipassive and related constructions', *International Journal of American Linguistics* 53: 194–231.

—— and K. Hale (1996*a*) 'The structural determination of case and agreement', *Linguistic Inquiry* 27: 1–68.

—— and —— (1996*b*) 'Ergativity: Towards a theory of a heterogeneous class', *Linguistic Inquiry* 27: 531–604.

BLAKE, B. J. (1990) *Relational Grammar.* London: Routledge.

—— (1994) *Case.* Cambridge: Cambridge University Press.

BLOOMELD, L. (1917) *Tagalog Texts with Grammatical Analysis.* Urbana-Champaign, IL: University of Illinois Studies in Langauge and Literature.

BOLINGER, D. L. (1971) *The Phrasal Verb in English.* Cambridge, MA: Harvard University Press.

BOSSONG, G. (1991) 'Differential object marking in Romance and beyond', in D. Wanner and D. A. Kibbee (eds), *New Analyses in Romance Linguistics: Selected papers from the 18th linguistic symposium on Romance languages.* Amsterdam: John Benjamins, pp. 143–70.

BRESNAN, J. (1982*a*) *The Mental Representation of Grammatical Relations*. Cambridge, MA: MIT Press.

—— (1982*b*) 'The passive in lexical theory', in J. Bresnan (ed.), *The Mental Representation of Grammatical Relations*. Cambridge, MA: MIT Press, pp. 3–86.

—— (1994) 'Locative inversion and the architecture of universal grammar', *Language* 70: 72–131.

—— (2000) *Lexical-functional Syntax*. Malden, MA: Blackwell Publishing.

—— and J. M. KANERVA (1989) 'Locative inversion in Chichewa: A case study of factorization in grammar', *Linguistic Inquiry* 20: 1–50.

—— and L. MOSHI (1990) 'Object asymmetries in comparative Bantu syntax', *Linguistic Inquiry* 21: 147–85.

BURZIO, L. (1986) *Italian Syntax: A government-binding approach*. Dordrecht: D. Reidel.

CARNIE, A. (2002) *Syntax: A generative introduction*. Malden, MA: Blackwell Publishing.

CENTINEO, G. (1986) 'A lexical theory of auxiliary selection in Italian', *Davis Working Papers in Linguistics* 1: 1–35.

CHOMSKY, N. (1957) *Syntactic Structures*. The Hague: Mouton.

—— (1965) *Aspects of the Theory of Syntax*. Cambridge, MA: MIT Press.

—— (1981) *Lectures on Government and Binding*. Dordrecht: Foris.

—— (1986) *Barriers*. Cambridge, MA: MIT Press.

—— (1993) 'A minimalist program for linguistic theory', in S. J. Keyser and K. Hale (eds), *The View from Building 20*. Cambridge, MA: MIT Press, pp. 1–52.

—— (1995) *The Minimalist Program*. Cambridge, MA: MIT Press.

COMRIE, B. (1978) 'Ergativity', in W. P. Lehman (ed.), *Syntactic Typology*. Austin, TX: University of Texas Press, pp. 329–94.

COOPMANS, P. (1989) 'Where stylistic and syntactic processes meet: Locative inversion in English', *Language* 65: 728–51.

COOREMAN, A., B. Fox and T. GIVÓN (1988) 'The discourse definition of ergativity: A study in Chamorro and Tagalog texts', in R. McGinn (ed.), *Studies in Austronesian Linguistics*. Athens, OH: Ohio University Press, pp. 387–425.

CROFT, W. (1991) *Syntactic Categories and Grammatical Relations: The cognitive organization of information*. Chicago: University of Chicago Press.

—— (1993) 'Case marking and the semantics of mental verbs', in J. Pustejovsky (ed.), *Semantics and the Lexicon*. Dordrecht: Kluwer, pp. 55–72.

—— (2001) *Radical Construction Grammar: Syntactic theory in typological perspective*. Oxford: Oxford University Press.

CZEPLUCH, H. (1982) 'Case theory and the dative construction', *The Linguistic Review* 2: 1–38.

DAHLSTROM, A. (1991) *Plains Cree Morphosyntax*. New York: Garland.

DAVIES, W. D. (1986) *Choctaw Verb Agreement and Universal Grammar*. Dordrecht: D. Reidel.

DE GUZMAN, V. P. (1988) 'Ergative analysis for Philippine languages: An analysis', in R. McGinn (ed.), *Studies in Austronesian Linguistics.* Athens, OH: Ohio University Press, pp. 323–45.

DELANCEY, S. (1981) 'An interpretation of split ergativity', *Language* 57: 626–57.

—— (1991) 'Event construals and case role assignment', in *Proceedings of the 17th Annual Meeting of the Berkeley Linguistics Society.* Berkeley: University of California, pp. 338–53.

DIK, S. C. (1978) *Functional Grammar.* Amsterdam: North-Holland Publishing Co.

—— (1980) *Studies in Functional Grammar.* New York: Academic Press.

—— (1997) *The Theory of Functional Grammar.* Berlin: Mouton de Gruyter.

DIXON, R. M. W. (1972) *The Dyirbal Language of North Queensland.* Cambridge: Cambridge University Press.

—— (1979) 'Ergativity', *Language* 55: 59–138.

—— (1994) *Ergativity.* Cambridge: Cambridge University Press.

—— (2000) 'A-constructions and o-constructions in Jarawara', *International Journal of American Linguistics* 66: 22–56.

—— and A. Y. AIKHENVALD (2000) 'Introduction', in R. M. W. Dixon and A. Y. Aikhenvald (eds), *Changing Valency: Case studies in transitivity.* Cambridge: Cambridge University Press, pp. 1–28.

DOAK, I. G. (1998) *Coeur d'Alene grammatical relations,* University of Texas, Austin: Ph.D. Dissertation.

DOBROVIE-SORIN, C. (1994) *The Syntax of Romanian.* Berlin: Mouton de Gruyter.

DOWTY, D. R. (1979) *Word Meaning in Montague Grammar: The semantics of verbs and times in generative semantics and in Montague's PTQ.* Dordrecht: D. Reidel.

—— (1982) 'Grammatical relations and Montague grammar', in P. Jacobson and G. K. Pullum (eds), *The Nature of Syntactic Representation.* Dordrecht: D. Reidel, pp. 79–130.

—— (1991) 'Thematic proto-roles and argument selection', *Language* 67: 547–619.

—— R. WALL and S. PETERS (1981) *Introduction to Montague Semantics.* Dordrecht: D. Reidel.

DRYER, M. S. (1978) 'Some theoretical implications of grammatical relations in Cebuano'. Paper presented at University of Michigan Papers in Linguistics 2, Ann Arbor, Michigan.

—— (1983) 'Indirect objects in Kinyarwanda revisited', in D. M. Perlmutter (ed.), *Studies in Relational Grammar 1.* Chicago: University of Chicago Press, pp. 129–40.

—— (1986) 'Primary objects, secondary objects, and antidative', *Language* 61: 808–45.

DURIE, M. (1985) *A Grammar of Acehnese.* Dordrecht: Foris.

—— (1988) 'Preferred argument structure in an active language: Arguments against the category "intransitive subject" ', *Lingua* 74: 1–25.

DUTRA, R. (1987) 'The hybrid S category in Brazilian Portuguese: Some implications for word order', *Studies in Language* 11: 163–80.

DZIWIREK, K. (1994) *Polish Subjects.* New York: Garland.

ENÇ, M. (1989) 'Pronouns, licensing, and binding', *Natural Language and Linguistic Theory* 7: 51–92.

—— (1991) 'The semantics of specificity', *Linguistic Inquiry* 1–26.

FALK, Y. (2001) *Lexical-functional Grammar*. Stanford, CA: CSLI Publications.

FARKAS, D. F. (1978) 'Direct and indirect object reduplication in Romanian', in *Papers from the Fourteenth Regional Meeting of the Chicago Linguistic Society*. Chicago: University of Chicago, pp. 88–97.

FARRELL, P. (1990) 'Null objects in Brazilian Portuguese', *Natural Language and Linguistic Theory* 8: 325–46.

—— (1994*a*) *Thematic Relations and Relational Grammar*. New York: Garland.

—— (1994*b*) 'The locative alternation and multistratalism', *Linguistics* 32: 5–42.

—— (1998) 'Comments on the paper by Lieber', in S. G. Lapointe, D. Brentari, and P. Farrell (eds), *Morphology and its Relation to Syntax and Morphology*. Stanford, CA: CSLI Publications, pp. 34–53.

—— (2001) 'Functional shift as category underspecification', *English Language and Linguistics* 5: 109–30.

—— (2004) 'Psych verbs with quasi-objects', in A. S. da Silva A. Torres, and M. Gonçalves (eds), *Linguagem, cultura, e cognição: Estudos de linguística cognitiva*. Coimbra: Almedina, pp. 367–84.

—— S. A. MARLETT, and D. M. PERLMUTTER (1991) 'Notions of subjecthood and switch reference: Evidence from Seri', *Linguistic Inquiry* 22: 431–55.

FILIP, H. (1997) *Aspect, Eventuality Types and Nominal Semantics*. New York: Garland.

FILLMORE, C. J. (1968) 'The case for case', in E. Bach and R. T. Harms (eds), *Universals in Linguistic Theory*. New York: Holt, Rinehart, and Winston, pp. 1–88.

FINER, D. L. (1985) 'The syntax of switch reference', *Linguistic Inquiry* 16: 35–55.

FOLEY, W. A. and R. D. VAN VALIN, JR. (1984) *Functional Syntax and Universal Grammar*. Cambridge: Cambridge University Press.

FRANKS, S. (1995) *Parameters of Slavic Morphosyntax*. Oxford: Oxford University Press.

GERDTS, D. B. (1988*a*) *Object and Absolutive in Halkomelem Salish*. New York: Garland.

—— (1988*b*) 'Antipassives and causatives in Ilokano: Evidence for an ergative analysis', in R. McGinn (ed.), *Studies in Austronesian Linguistics*. Athens, OH: Ohio University Press, pp. 295–321.

GIBSON, J. D. (1980) *Clause union in Chamorro and in universal grammar*, University of California, San Diego: Ph.D. Dissertation.

GIVÓN, T. (1978) 'Definiteness and referentiality', in J. Greenberg (ed.), *Universals of Human Language, Vol. 4*. Stanford, CA: Stanford University Press, pp. 291–330.

—— (ed.) (1984) *Syntax: A functional-typological introduction*. Amsterdam: John Benjamins.

—— (ed.) (1997) *Grammatical Relations: A functionalist perspective*. Amsterdam: John Benjamins.

GOLDBERG, A. E.(1991) 'A semantic account of resultatives', *Linguistic Analysis* 21: 66–96.

GOLDBERG, A. E. (1995) *Constructions: A construction grammar approach to argument structure.* Chicago: University of Chicago Press.

GREEN, G. M. (1974) *Semantic and Syntactic Regularity.* Bloomington: Indiana University Press.

GRIMSHAW, J. (1990) *Argument Structure.* Cambridge, MA: MIT Press.

GROPEN, J., S. PINKER, M. HOLLANDER, R. GOLDBERG, and R. WILSON (1989) 'The learnability and acquisition of the dative alternation', *Language* 65: 203–57.

GRUBER, J. S. (1965) *Studies in lexical relations,* MIT: Ph.D. dissertation.

—— (2001) 'Thematic relations in syntax', in M. Baltin and C. Collins (eds), *The Handbook of Contemporary Syntactic Theory.* Malden, MA: Blackwell, pp. 257–98.

HALE, K. and S. J. KEYSER (1993) 'On argument structure and the lexical expression of syntactic relations', in K. Hale and S. J. Keyser (eds), *The View from Building 20: Essays in honor of Sylvain Bromberger.* Cambridge, MA: MIT Press, pp. 53–109.

HALLIDAY, M. A. K. (1973) *Explorations in the Functions of Language.* New York: Elsevier North-Holland.

—— (1985) *An Introduction to Functional Grammar.* London: Arnold.

HARRIS, A. (1982) 'Georgian and the unaccusative hypothesis', *Language* 58: 290–306.

—— (1990) 'Georgian: A language with active case marking', *Lingua* 80: 35–53.

HENDERSON, T. S. T. (1971) 'Participant-reference in Algonkin', *Cahiers linguistiques d'Ottawa* 1: 27–49.

HERRIMAN, J. (1995) *The Indirect Object in Present-day English.* Göteborg: Acta Universitatis Gothoburgensis.

HERSLUND, M. (1997) 'Passive and antipassive in a functional description of French reflexive verbs', *Hermes, Journal of Lingusitics* 19: 75–92.

HOCKETT, C. (1958) *A Course in Modern Linguistics.* New York: Macmillan.

HOLISKY, D. A. (1987) 'The case of the intransitive subject in Tsova-Tush (Batsbi)', *Lingua* 71: 103–32.

JACKENDOFF, R. S. (1972) *Semantics in Generative Grammar.* Cambridge, MA: MIT Press.

—— (1977) *X-bar Syntax: A study of phrase structure.* Cambridge, MA: MIT Press.

—— (1987) 'The status of thematic relations in linguistic theory', *Linguistic Inquiry* 18: 369–411.

—— (1990) *Semantic Structures.* Cambridge, MA: MIT Press.

JAEGGLI, O. A. (1986) 'Passive', *Linguistic Inquiry* 17: 587–622.

JESPERSEN, O. (1927) *A Modern English Grammar on Historical Principles.* London: Allen & Unwin.

JOHNSON, D. E. and P. M. POSTAL (1980) *Arc Pair Grammar.* Princeton, NJ: Princeton University Press.

JOSHI, S. (1993) *Selection of grammatical and logical functions in Marathi,* Stanford: Ph.D. Dissertation.

KAPLAN, J. P. (1995) *English Grammar: Principles and Facts.* Englewood Cliffs, NJ: Prentice Hall.

KATO, M. A. (1993) 'The distribution of null pronouns and null elements in object position in Brazilian Portuguese', in W. J. Ashby, M. Mithun, G. Perissinotto, and E. Raposo (eds), *Linguistic Perspectives on the Romance Languages: Selected papers from the 21st symposium on Romance languages.* Amsterdam: John Benjamins, pp. 225–36.

KEENAN, E. L. and B. COMRIE (1977) 'Noun phrase accessibility and universal grammar', *Linguistic Inquiry* 8: 63–100.

KIMENYI, A. (1980) *A Relational Grammar of Kinyarwanda.* Berkeley: University of California Press.

KIPARSKY, P. (1998) 'Partitive case and aspect', in M. Butt and W. Geuder (eds), *The Projection of Arguments: Lexical and compositional factors.* Stanford, CA: CSLI Publications, pp. 265–307.

—— (2001) 'Structural case in Finnish', *Lingua* 111: 315–76.

—— (2002) 'On the architecture of Pāṇini's grammar'. MS, Stanford University. *http://www.stanford.edu/~kiparsky/.*

—— and F. STAAL (1969) 'Syntactic and semantic relations in Pāṇini', *Foundations of Language* 5: 83–117.

KISHIMOTO, H. (1996) 'Split intransitivity in Japanese and the unaccusative hypothesis', *Language* 72: 248–86.

KISSEBERTH, C. W. and M. I. ABASHEIKH (1977) 'The object relationship in Chimwi:ni, a bantu language', in P. Cole and J. Sadock (eds), *Syntax and Semantics 8: Grammatical relations.* New York: Academic Press, pp. 179–218.

KLAIMAN, M. H. (1990) *Grammatical Voice.* Cambridge: Cambridge University Press.

—— (1993) 'The relationship of inverse voice and head-marking in Arizona Tewa and other Tanoan languages', *Studies in Language* 17: 343–70.

KOOPMAN, H. and D. SPORTICHE (1991) 'The position of subjects', *Lingua* 85: 211–58.

KROEGER, P. (1993) *Phrase Structure and Grammatical Relations in Tagalog.* Stanford, CA: CSLI Publications.

KURODA, S.-Y. (1988) 'Whether we agree or not: A comparative syntax of English and Japanese', *Lingvisticae Investigationes* 12: 1–47.

LA FAUCI, N. (1988) *Oggetti e soggetti nella formazione della morfosintassi romanza.* Pisa: Giardini Editori e Stampatori.

LA POLLA, R. J. (1993) 'Arguments against "subject" and "direct object" as viable concepts in Chinese', *Bulletin of the Institute of History and Philology* 63: 759–813.

LAKOFF, G. (1971) 'On generative semantics', in D. D. Steinberg and L. A. Jakobovits (eds), *Semantics: An interdisciplinary reader.* Cambridge: Cambridge University Press, pp. 232–96.

LANGACKER, R. W. (1987) *Foundations of Cognitive Grammar, Volume 1: Theoretical prerequisites.* Stanford, CA: Stanford University Press.

—— (1991) *Foundations of Cognitive Grammar, Volume 2: Descriptive application.* Stanford, CA: Stanford University Press.

—— (1999) *Grammar and Conceptualization.* Berlin: Mouton de Gruyter.

LARSON, R. K. (1988) 'On the double object construction', *Linguistic Inquiry* 19: 335–91.

LEGENDRE, G. (1987) *Topics in French syntax*, University of California, San Diego: Ph.D. Dissertation.

—— (1989*a*) 'Inversion with certain French experiencer verbs', *Language* 65: 752–82.

—— (1989*b*) 'Unaccusativity in French', *Lingua* 79: 95–164.

—— (1990) 'French impersonal constructions', *Natural Language and Linguistic Theory* 8: 81–128.

LESOURD, P. (1976) 'Verb agreement in Fox', in J. Aissen and J. Hankamer (eds), *Harvard Studies in Syntax and Semantics 2*. Cambridge, MA: Harvard University Linguistics Department, pp. 445–528.

LEVIN, B. (1983) *On the nature of ergativity*, MIT: Ph.D. Dissertation.

—— and M. RAPPAPORT HOVAV (1995) *Unaccusativity: At the syntax–lexical semantics interface*. Cambridge, MA: MIT Press.

MARANTZ, A. (1984) *On the Nature of Grammatical Relations*. Cambridge, MA: MIT Press.

MARLETT, S. A. (1984) 'Switch reference and subject raising in Seri', in E.-D. Cook and D. B. Gerdts (eds), *Syntax and Semantics 16: The syntax of Native American languages*. New York: Academic Press, pp. 247–68.

MATTHEWS, P. (1997) *The Concise Oxford Dictionary of Linguistics*. Oxford: Oxford University Press.

MAY, R. (1985) *Logical Form: Its structure and derivation*. Cambridge, MA: MIT Press.

McCAWLEY, J. D. (1971) 'Prelexical syntax', in R. J. O'Brien (ed.), *22nd Annual Round Table on Languages and Linguistics*, 19–33. Washington, DC: Georgetown University.

—— (1973) 'Syntactic and logical arguments for semantic structures', in O. Fujimura (ed.), *Three Dimensions of Linguistic Theory*, 259–376. Tokyo: Tec Co.

McCLURE, W. (1990) 'A lexical semantic explanation for unaccusative mismatches', in K. Dziwirek, P. Farrell, and E. Mejías-Bikandi (eds), *Grammatical Relations: A cross-theoretical perspective*. Stanford, CA: CSLI Publications, pp. 305–18.

McGINNIS, M. (2002) 'Object asymmetries in a phase theory of syntax', in J. T. Jensen and G. v. Herk (eds), *Proceedings of the 2001 CLA Annual Conference*. Department of Linguistics: University of Ottawa, pp. 245–56.

MEGERDOOMIAN, K. (2000) 'Aspect and partitive objects in Finnish', in R. Billerey and B. D. Lillehaugen (eds), *Proceedings of the 19th West Coast Conference on Formal Linguistics*. Somerville, MA: Cascadilla Press, pp. 316–28.

MERLAN, F. (1985) 'Split intransitivity', in J. Nichols and A. Woodbury (eds), *Grammar Inside and Outside the Clause: Some perspectives from the field*. Cambridge: Cambridge University Press, pp. 324–62.

MILLER, P. H. and I. A. SAG (1997) 'French clitic movement without clitics or movement', *Natural Language and Linguistic Theory* 15: 573–639.

MINGER, D. L. (2002) *An analysis of grammatical relations and case marking in Icelandic*, University of California, Davis: M.A. Thesis.

MITHUN, M. (1991) 'Active/agentive case marking', *Language* 67: 510–46.

MOHANAN, T. (1994) *Argument Structure in Hindi*. Stanford, CA: CSLI Publications.

MOORE, J. and D. M. PERLMUTTER (2000) 'What does it take to be a dative subject?' *Natural Language and Linguistic Theory* 18: 373–416.

MORAVCSIK, E. A. (1974) 'Object–verb agreement', *Working Papers on Language Universals* 13: 25–140.

MORIMOTO, Y. (2002) 'Prominence mismatches and differential object marking in Bantu', in M. Butt and T. H. King (eds), *Proceedings of the LFG 02 Conference*. Stanford, CA: CSLI Publications.

MULDER, J. G. (1994) *Ergativity in Coast Tshimian*. Berkeley: University of California Press.

MURASUGI, K. (1992) *Crossing and nested paths: NP movement in accusative and ergative languages*, MIT: Ph.D. Dissertation.

MUSGRAVE, S. (2001) *Non-subject arguments in Indonesian*, University of Melbourne: Ph.D. Dissertation.

—— (To appear) 'The grammatical function OBJ in Indonesian', in S. Musgrave and P. K. Austin (eds), *Voice and Grammatical Functions in Austronesian*. CSLI Publications.

NAPOLI, D. J. (1993) *Syntax: Theory and problems*. Oxford: Oxford University Press.

NICHOLS, J. (1986) 'Head-marking and dependent-marking grammar', *Language* 62: 56–119.

NIKOLAEVA, I. (1999) 'Object agreement, grammatical relations, and information structure', *Studies in Language* 23: 377–407.

NOONAN, M. (1992) *A Grammar of Lango*. Berlin: Mouton de Gruyter.

OEHRLE, R. T. (1976) *The grammatical status of the English dative alternation*, MIT: Ph.D. Dissertation.

——, E. BACH, and D. WHEELER (eds) (1988) *Categorial Grammars and Natural Language Structures*. Dordrecht: D. Reidel.

ORTIZ DE URBINA, J. (1989) *Paramaters in the Grammar of Basque: A GB approach to Basque syntax*. Dordrecht: Foris.

PARK, H.-Y. (2002) 'Object asymmetries in Korean', in M. Butt and T. H. King (eds), *Proceedings of the LFG 02 Conference*. Stanford, CA: CSLI Publications.

PAYNE, T. E. (1982) 'Role and reference related subject properties and ergativity in Yup'ik and Tagalog', *Studies in Language* 6: 75–106.

PERLMUTTER, D. M. (1976) 'Subject downgrading in Portuguese', in J. Schmidt-Radefeldt (ed.), *Readings in Portuguese Linguistics*. Amsterdam: North-Holland, pp. 93–138.

—— (1978) 'Impersonal passives and the unaccusative hypothesis', in *Proceedings of the Fourth Annual Meeting of the Berkeley Linguistic Society*. University of California, Berkeley, pp. 157–89.

—— (1982) 'Syntactic representation, syntactic levels, and the notion of subject', in P. Jacobson and G. Pullum (eds), *The Nature of Syntactic Representation*. Dordrecht: D. Reidel, pp. 283–340.

—— (ed.) (1983) *Studies in Relational Grammar 1*. Chicago: University of Chicago Press.

PERLMUTTER, D. M. (1984) 'Working 1s and inversion in Italian, Japanese, and Quechua', in D. M. Perlmutter and C. Rosen (eds), *Studies in Relational Grammar 2*. Chicago: University of Chicago Press, pp. 292–330.

—— (1989) 'Multiattachment and the unaccusative hypothesis: The perfect auxiliary in italian', *Probus* 1: 63–119.

—— and P. M. POSTAL (1983) 'Some proposed laws of basic clause structure', in D. M. Perlmutter (ed.), *Studies in Relational Grammar 1*. Chicago: University of Chicago Press, pp. 81–128.

—— and P. M. POSTAL (1984) 'The 1-advancement exclusiveness law', in D. M. Perlmutter and C. Rosen (eds), *Studies in Relational Grammar 2*. Chicago: University of Chicago Press, pp. 81–125.

—— and C. ROSEN (eds) (1984) *Studies in Relational Grammar 2*. Chicago: University of Chicago Press.

—— and R. RHODES (1988) 'Thematic-sytactic alignments in Ojibwa: Evidence for subject–object reversal'. Paper presented at the Annual Meeting of the Linguistic Society of America.

PINKER, S. (1989) *Learnability and Cognition: The acquisition of argument structure*. Cambridge, MA: MIT Press.

POLLARD, C. and I. A. SAG (1994) *Head-driven Phrase Structure Grammar*. Chicago: CSLI & University of Chicago Press.

POLLOCK, J.-Y. (1989) 'Verb movement, universal grammar, and the structure of IP', *Linguistic Inquiry* 20: 365–424.

POSTAL, P. M. (1977) 'Antipassive in French', *Lingvisticae Investigationes* 1: 333–74.

—— (1986) *Studies of Passive Clauses*. Albany: State University of New York Press.

—— (1989) *Masked Inversion in French*. Chicago: University of Chicago Press.

—— (1990) 'French indirect object demotion', in P. M. Postal and B. D. Joseph (eds), *Studies in Relational Grammar 3*. Chicago: University of Chicago Press, pp. 104–200.

—— and B. D. JOSEPH (eds) (1990) *Studies in Relational Grammar 3*. Chicago: University of Chicago Press.

RADFORD, A. (1988) *Transformational Grammar: A first course*. Cambridge: Cambridge University Press.

—— (1997) *Syntactic Theory and the Structure of English: A minimalist approach*. Cambridge and New York: Cambridge University Press.

RAPPAPORT HOVAV, M. and B. LEVIN (1992) '-*Er* nominals: Implications for the theory of argument structure', in T. Stowell and E. Wehrli (eds), *Syntax and Semantics 26: Syntax and the lexicon*. San Diego: Academic Press, pp. 127–53.

RAPPAPORT, M. and B. LEVIN (1988) 'What to do with θ-roles', in W. Wilkins (ed.), *Syntax and Semantics 21: Thematic relations*. San Diego: Academic Press, pp. 7–36.

REX, S. M. (2001) *Unaccusativity in Spanish*, University of California, Davis: Ph.D. Dissertation.

RHODES, R. (1976) *The morphosyntax of the Central Ojibwa verb*, University of Michigan: Ph.D. Dissertation.

ROBERTS, I. G. (1987) *The Representation of Implicit and Dethematized Subjects*. Dordrecht: Foris Publications.

ROBERTS, L. (1995) 'Pivots, voice and macroroles: From Germanic to universal grammar', *Australian Journal of Linguistics* 15: 157–214.

ROEPER, T. (1987) 'Implicit arguments and the head-complement relation', *Linguistic Inquiry* 18: 267–310.

ROSEN, C. (1984) 'The interface between semantic roles and initial grammatical relations'. D. M. Perlmutter and C. Rosen (eds) *Studies in Relational Grammar 2*. Chicago: University of Chicago Press, pp. 38–77.

—— (1988) *The Relational Structure of Reflexive Clauses: Evidence from Italian*. New York: Garland.

—— (1990) 'Rethinking Southern Tiwa: The geometry of a triple agreement language', *Language* 66: 669–713.

—— and K. WALI (1989) 'Twin passives, inversion, and multistratalism in Marathi', *Natural Language and Linguistic Theory* 7: 1–50.

ROUNDS, C. (2001) *Hungarian: An essential grammar*. London: Routledge.

RUWET, N. (1972) *Théorie syntaxique et syntaxe du français*. Paris: Editions du Seuil.

RYDER, M. E. (1999) 'Bankers and blue-chippers: An account of -*er* formations in present-day English', *English Language and Linguistics* 3: 269–97.

SAG, I., T. WASOW, and E. M. BENDER (2003) *Syntactic Theory: A formal introduction*. Stanford, CA: CSLI Publications.

SAPIR, E. (1917) 'Review of Uhlenbeck, C. C., 'Het passieve Karakter van het Verbum transitivum of van het Verbum actionis in Talen van Noord America' ('The passive character of the transitive verb or of the active verb in languages of North America')', *International Journal of American Linguistics* 1: 82–86.

SCHACHTER, P. (1976) 'The subject in Philippine languages: Topic, actor, actor–topic, or none of the above', in C. Li (ed.), *Subject and Topic*. New York: Academic Press, pp. 491–518.

—— and F. T. OTANES (1972) *Tagalog Reference Grammar*. Berkeley: University of California Press.

SEKI, L. (2000) *Gramática do Kamaiurá, língua Tupí-Guaraní do Alto Xingu*. Campinas: Editora da Unicamp.

SIEWIERSKA, A. (1991) *Functional Grammar*. London: Routledge.

SIGURðSSON, H. Á. (2002) 'To be an oblique subject: Russian vs. Icelandic', *Natural Language and Linguistic Theory* 20: 691–724.

SILVERSTEIN, M. (1976) 'Hierarchy of features and ergativity', in R. M. W. Dixon (ed.), *Grammatical Categories in Australian Languages*. Canberra: Australian Institute of Aboriginal Studies, pp. 112–71.

SINGH, J. D. (2001) *Kārake*. Westerville, OH: Pāṇini Foundation.

STAROSTA, S. (1988) *The Case for Lexicase: An outline of lexicase grammatical theory*. London: Pinter Publishers.

STOWELL, T. (1981) *Origins of phrase structure*, MIT: Ph.D. Dissertation.

TALMY, L. (1996) 'Fictive motion in language and "ception"', in P. Bloom, M. A. Peterson, L. Nadel, and M. F. Garrett (eds), *Language and Space*. Cambridge, MA: MIT Press, pp. 211–76.

—— (2000) *Toward a Cognitive Semantics: Concept structuring systems (vol. 1); typology and process in concept structuring (vol. 2)*. Cambridge, MA: MIT Press.

TESNIÉRE, L. (1959) *Éléments de syntaxe structurale*. Paris: Klincksieck.

TOMLIN, R. S. (1986) *Basic Word Order: Functional principles*. London: Croom Helm.

URA, H. (1999) 'Checking theory and dative subject constructions in Japanese and Korean', *Journal of East Asian Linguistics* 8: 223–54.

—— (2000) *Checking Theory and Grammatical Functions in Universal Grammar*. Oxford: Oxford University Press.

—— (2001) 'Case', in M. Baltin and C. Collins (eds), *The Handbook of Contemporary Syntactic Theory*. Malden, MA: Blackwell, pp. 334–73.

VAN VALIN, R. D., Jr. (1990) 'Semantic parameters of split intransitivity', *Language* 66: 221–60.

—— (1991) 'Another look at Icelandic case marking and grammatical relations', *Natural Language and Linguistic Theory* 9: 145–94.

—— (1993) 'A synopsis of role and reference grammar', in R. D. Van Valin Jr. (ed.), *Advances in role and Reference Grammar*. Amsterdam and Philadelphia: John Benjamins, pp. 1–164.

—— (To appear) *Exploring the Syntax–Semantics Interface*. Cambridge: Cambridge University Press.

—— and R. J. LA POLLA (1997) *Syntax: Structure, meaning, and function*. Cambridge: Cambridge University Press.

VENDLER, Z. (1967) *Linguistics in Philosophy*. Ithaca, NY: Cornell University Press.

VESTERGAARD, T. (1977) *Prepositional Phrases and Prepositional Verbs*. The Hague: Mouton.

WATANABE, A. (1993) *Agr-based case theory and its interaction with the a-bar system*, MIT: Ph.D. Dissertation.

WHALEY, L. J. (1993) *The status of obliques in linguistic theory*, State University of New York, Buffalo: Ph.D. Dissertation.

—— (1997) *Introduction to Typology: The unity and diversity of language*. New York: Sage Publications.

WIERZBICKA, A. (1996) *Semantics: Primes and universals*. Oxford: Oxford University Press.

WOLFART, C. H. and J. F. CARROLL (1981) *Meet Cree: A guide to the language*. Lincoln: University of Nebraska Press.

WOODBURY, A. (1977) 'Greenlandic eskimo, ergativity, and relational grammar', in P. Cole and J. M. Sadock (eds), *Syntax and Semantics 8: Grammatical relations*. New York: Academic Press, pp. 307–36.

YANG, B.-S. (1996) 'A role and reference grammar account of unaccusativity: Split intransitivity', *Linguistics* 4: 77–93.

ZAENEN, A. (1993) 'Unaccusativity in Dutch: Integrating syntax and lexical semantics', in J. Pustejovsky (ed.), *Semantics and the Lexicon.* Dordrecht: Kluwer, pp. 129–61.

—— J. MALING, and H. THRÁINSSON (1985) 'Case and grammatical functions: The Icelandic passive', *Natural Language and Linguistic Theory* 3: 441–83.

ZAGONA, K. (2002) *The Syntax of Spanish.* Cambridge: Cambridge University Press.

ZUBIZARRETA, M. L. (1987) *Levels of Representation in the Lexicon and in the Syntax.* Dordrecht: Foris Publications.

Index